An Awakening:
The Emergence of
Indigo Consciousness

JARI A. MIKKOLA

"An Awakening," is a brilliant piece of work that attempts to piece together the complexities of how the human brain functions and how it is responsible for an "emergence of consciousness," regarding many generations of Indigo Children all around the world.

First Edition
First Printing, 2015

ISBN-10: 0692516816
ISBN-13: 978-0-692-51681-2

Printed in the United States of America

DEDICATION

I would dedicate this book to two of my dearest and oldest friends for all their patience and encouragement while keeping me focused long enough to complete this book; Mr. Bob Cracknell and Ms. Diana Caprio.

Robert inspired me to believe and trust my inherent faculties, or as he so eloquently put it, "Be willing to risk ridicule for what you feel, sense, and believe to be the truth. It's when you question yourself that you yourself will become confused, and consequently lose focus of the task you have undertaken. "

Without Diana's encouragement to keep on writing, this book may not be in your hands now. There were many times I found myself frustrated with everything that flooded my head at once, and Diana's guidance helped me stay focused; otherwise, 'The Awakening' may have never been completed.

Without Diana's words of encouragement is what gave me the strength and fortitude to finish what seemed to be a massive undertaking. "You have a very important message to share with everyone who is, or has been, going through what you have had to endure your whole life. They too need to know and understand what it means to grow up different and often confused as they seek an answer to the question 'why am different;' especially the new generations of today."

Thank you Robert, thank you Diana, I love you both.

TABLE OF CONTENTS

The Awakening: an Emergence of Indigo Consciousness

ACKNOWLEDGMENTS

There are many to whom I would like to convey a deep sense of gratitude. For it had they not been there to guide me through the process of becoming an author, this book may have never have come to fruition. They all know who they are, and how they provided me valuable support by talking things over with me, or holding my hand through the arduous processes of reading many of my drafts. For they have offered me valuable constructive criticism and comments (some of which they have allowed me to quote), that included editing, proofreading, and the design layout of this book.

I would like to offer a special thanks to my dear friend and author Micah Hanks, of the "Gralien Report," for his continued support to get this book published. For without it, I would have had no idea where to begin.

Also special thanks goes out to Diana Caprio and Jeff Mudgett for all their help editing and proofreading multiple sections of this book, for they have provided me very valuable criticism, suggestions, and well-needed encouragement every step of the way.

Last but not least: I beg forgiveness from all those who have been there for me helping me stay the course over many years of frustration and writers block, and whose names I have failed to mention herein.

INTRODUCTION

"It's my proud pleasure to introduce you to the author. Although we have known each other for a relatively short part of our lives, I am proud to say he has become a close friend in my life. Having stated this, I would also wish to make it quite clear that our friendship has nothing to do with my commending his work."

Robert Cracknell

The book, "An Awakening: the Next Generation of Intuitive Consciousness," by Jari Mikkola has in fact taken me quite by surprise. Over the short period of time we have known each other, we have discussed many topics of joint interest regarding many and all things paranormal; producing many lively discussions, and at times a healthy disagreement or two.

In truth, I believe there are others who are far more suited to introduce Jari and this excellent book than I am, however, before I proceed, allow me express what an honor it is that I have been asked me to write a short introduction for him. As he enters into the public's attention with a totally new and refreshing approach to a subject which, over the last four decades, I have personally been involved with; one that has even garnered me media attention worldwide in my field, that of a private investigator.

Due to the rapacious appetite of the film and television industry with regard to anything paranormal, the psychic faculties, UFOs, or other strange phenomena we don't yet comprehend, I must commend them for raising awareness and interest regarding these genres. Although it seems to have raised interest, it has unfortunately tarnished the truth for the sake of creating excellent films and television programs such as "The X Files, Taken," and "Dark Skies."

I personally became involved in this fascinating field in the mid 1950's when I first began to experience extremely odd and inexplicable stirrings about myself and the world in which I lived, although not entirely secular, or even humanistic. I instinctively knew in some strange way that 'shadows' I believed had been plaguing me were indeed a reality I could not explain. It was through the many panic attacks and nightly bouts of sleep paralysis I became compelled to analyze the cause of the frequent trauma and discomfort I had regarding these occurrences, and at times even found myself wondering, perhaps my affliction had been caused by a brain tumor.

I began to read books avidly concerning mysticism, the occult and obscure eastern philosophies in a quest to discover why I knew things I could not have possibly known. Like a sponge, I absorbed these works, which were in truth, beyond the basic education I had had to that point in my young life.

Eventually I was led to a book entitled "Projection of the Astral Body," written By Dr. Hereward Carrington and Sylvan Muldoon. My fears and anxieties concerning brain tumors disappeared over night.

I soon realized that I was at that time the alien term, 'psychic,' for which I could not possibly believe, yet my shadows were very real indeed. Carrington and Muldoon suggested in their book that what I required was light.

It wasn't long after reading their book, I discovered a Spiritualist Church in London. A 'medium' I met there soon became responsible for my receiving a message that to my amazement was a very accurate character assessment of myself followed by a revelation when she went on to tell me, "You have a spiritual gift; you are 'psychic' and will use your faculties throughout your life in a remarkable manner."

Imagine the impact that had on me! I had immersed myself totally for many years of time my life, with all the 'new' possibilities that this had suddenly opened up for me. It was in front of my eyes all the time.

Within a short period, I had discovered myself strutting around and quite arrogantly at that, on the many platforms of Spiritualism. I wallowed within a shallow dish of 'pseudo' fame, to the point where I was giving addresses on basic bias platitudes, and then by using this previously 'unknown psychic ability' I was able to amaze a ready pliant congregation with skills I had not adequately assessed. I was in fact "preaching to the choir."

I know now, and state categorically, I was wrong in so doing, for I had allowed myself to be enticed into that ever-cancerous ego that still prevails amongst the present 'wannabe' psychic celebrities, and still present in today's media culture; often with self-promoting theatrical presentations of their 'psychic medium' prowess. When in fact all they are doing is extending their somewhat 'limited' talents, if they even possess them at all, to include exorcism, ghost hunting, and past life regression, as a lame attempt to portray events that occurred in the distant past, when in reality, they haven't got a clue.

This brings me back to the book you now hold in your hand.

I only wish I had discovered a book early in my life like the one Jari Mikkola has written. His book should be considered a 'must read' for every serious proponent or student of anything paranormal when it comes to not only the 'precognitive faculties' but the science behind it of how knowledge, intuition, and evolution of human intelligence seems to be awakening in all of us. This book deserves, in my opinion, a rightful place within all the libraries and university around the world.

Yes, his concepts, ideas, and explanations will provoke reactions across the board, and on occasion controversy and disagreement among the many students of this complex subject.

When I examine my early views of Spiritualism, and its insistence that all mediums were simply a channel acting as a conduit to relay messages from 'the world of the dead' to 'the world of the living,' I could not easily accept the concept, however I did accept the fact that I was being played.

If I had only known then what I know now, that all the 'psychic faculties' lay dormant within each and every one of us, and is not dependent upon some quasi-religious cult, and is as natural as breathing, it would have saved me a lot of time, mistakes, and grief.

Jari introduces far more lucidly than I ever could have, theories that not only totally impressed me, but also allowed me to experience an epiphany to answers I had long searched for throughout my life. However, many years ago, as an empath, I would not possibly come close to explaining the mechanics, or the science behind of how or why I seemed to have the profound ability of 'precognition.'

Granted, in those days gone past, scientists and mathematicians that dared to utter the word, much less hover around the periphery of 'the Paranormal,' had a tendency to confine themselves in a laboratory where experiments could be repeated over and over again that attained the same results time after time; which is not necessarily the case today.

I am firmly of the opinion that any investigation into the mechanics of any or all of the 'psychic faculties' had to attract a scientist that was willing, with the cooperation of individual psychics (and not necessary those with a proven record of ability) to lay their career and reputation on the line. To think outside the box and formulate their own revolutionary theory from research they own. PSI is not a course taught at major universities around the world as a bonafide science simply because several scientists took a giant leap of faith. In fact, and in my opinion one of the finest examples of a scientific experiment, is that Jari includes at length in this book the science of psychometry (a science that allows scientific observers to analyze the facts provided by 'psychics').

"An Awakening: the Emergence of Indigo Consciousness," offers many points that only verifies what I have thought all along. And that is that there is no question in having 'precognitive faculties,' as they are inherent within every living person and creature on this planet, yet they are only now beginning to emerge as another innate and natural 'sense' that has been dormant for so long in nearly all humanity.

As you read this book and its wonderful content, I believe you will discover a truly incredible experience with every page. I myself have embraced this book, and my hope is that it will not only enlighten you as you search for answers, but that it will assist your journey to discover what of the 'precognitive faculties' are inherent and budding within you, or someone you know and love.

Take from it what you will.

Kind Regards,
ROBERT CRACKNELL

The Awakening: an Emergence of Indigo Consciousness

PREFACE

" The intuitive mind is a sacred gift and the rational mind is a faithful servant. We have created a society that honors the servant and is forgetting the gift."

Albert Einstein

Is it possible that the universe around us is nothing more than a reflection of ourselves?

Astronomers and neurologists have both taken notice that the neurons of the human brain amazingly appear to mirror a mapping recently completed of the entire universe as seen from Earth. Physicist have suggested that the universe may in fact have a consciousness of its own; a possibility that has both fascinated and confounded scientists and become the subject of countless science-fiction novels. So much so that many astrophysicists and theoretical physicists now believe, there exists much more evidence to support this theory than originally had been given little credence.

In an article that appeared in the journal, "Nature's Scientific Report," it stated that the universe is been expanding at such an accelerated rate since 'big bang,' the pattern of mapping eerily resembled the neuron distribution of a human brain. Is this observation merely a coincidence?

Our brain's neurons fire electrical impulses in a manner that when imaged digitally on a 'CAT Scan (Computed Axial Tomographic Scan),' were able to produce a digital 3D tomographic image of the brain that when rotated and examined side-by-side neurologists noticed an interesting pattern emerge. It wasn't long before they realized that by comparing the 3D images of the brain, to those rendered by astronomers of distant galaxies and galaxy clusters distributed throughout the entire universe appeared astounding similar, if not eerily identical to the neural patterns of the human brain.

Is it impossible? Perhaps maybe even ironic, that a 3D model of a global computer network infrastructure – like that of the Internet – would be far more familiar in appearance and no more a consciousness than the universe itself ever could be . . . right?

Well, not really. Although it may first appear to be nothing more than a strangely weird coincidence, there is evidence mounting that the universe does indeed have a 'consciousness,' and is only now coming to light (no pun intended). When I think of a 'consciousness' association to the universe, it appears to me there does seem to be an underlying fabric of distribution across the entire universe. A 'synchronized fabric' so compelling it garnered attention of Albert Einstein, only to culminate with his 'theory of relativity;.' a theory from which countless others have emerged; the M-theory, the string theory, the unified field theory, and many more.

All of which got me to wonder since I was but a young boy, "What exactly is this 'awareness' I seemed to be tuned into?" Was it a 'consciousness' greater than the sum of all humankind?

For many years, the answer eluded me, but was always in the back of my mind. Is it 'universal?' Does everyone have it? Is it our brain? Perhaps it even functions as a human brain. If so, did it co-exist with 'God,' the divine deity I had always been told to believe was a super intelligent, omnipotent, and conscious being who knew everyone's thoughts and actions, for which 'everyone' else was very ignorant to; but then again, perhaps not.

THE ANCIENT ANCESTORS

"Apart from relative existence there can be no such thing as consciousness, consciousness being the perception of relations. In order to be conscious there must be something of which we are conscious, and this something must differ from that which it is not – in other words, it must form a contrast or an apparent opposite."

Jacob Böehme (1575 – 1624)

'Consciousness' has often been described as a direct perception of truth (or fact) that supersedes the independent reasoning processes in which the human mind normally engages. It is an immediate 'cognition' not inferred or gained by any previous knowledge regarding a 'cognitive' event – a psychic moment if you will – of pure insight and non-inferential knowledge[1], simply put, "we just know that we know,"

22

as a profound 'instantaneous awareness' does not involve the rational process of logic.

Some will even tell you it is our own subconscious mind, tapping into an outside-unknown source referred to by many as a 'universal consciousness,' an 'intuitive consciousness,' or 'soul force.' I liken it to the simple concept first coined by movie legend George Lucas,' when he coined it as "the force" in his hit movie "Star Wars."

From the onset of time, mankind has engaged in deep philosophical thought for which the origin of 'consciousness' was first perceived as 'intuition' or 'precognition,' fodder for more interesting philosophical subjects. Individuals possessing the ability of 'precognition,' were quickly labelled oracles, heretics, witches, prophets, saints, or demons, because superstition dictated them as possessed. Fear powered destiny as well as humankind's evolution, in that by striking fear in people through religious belief and superstition, they could control them; in all four corners of the known world, throughout the ages.

Among them, the most passionate on the subject was the philosopher Socrates. He described 'precognition' as a voice that compelled man to action, calling this faculty a 'daemon,' which later became 'demon,' a muse for many writers, poets and composers throughout the 'dark ages,' and well into modern times that can best be and identified as an 'evil influence' on humanity. [1]

Parapsychologists – self-proclaimed scientists – study what is called PSI phenomena as an 'intuitive' cognitive process in which an 'unconscious' pattern is suddenly made 'conscious,' they believe our mind can perceive 'unconscious patterns' and quickly map them into 'conscious patterns' to draw us into an awareness. They believe these patterns may actually take on many different forms (for which I have found nothing that specifically defines them), other than men of science believed (and many still do) consciousness is in our brain, and our mind sorted memories through some hierarchical ordering process that eventually evolved human consciousness to a level much higher than ever thought possible. [2]

Our Ancestor's Realization of Consciousness

"In order to have 'consciousness' there must first be something of which 'to be conscious of." A contrast must first exist as two apparent opposites; differing from 'what is,' and 'what is not;' a yin and a yang. [3]

Many believed that Böehme had discovered a process from which to create order of chaos throughout the universe thus creating order of the many convoluted patterns of a 'universal chaos,' as described by the 'chaos theory' of today. Regarded as a revolutionary, Böehme also considered an 'occultist,' and much of what he had written was discovered in many the ancient Mayan and Egyptian cultures long before any of Böehme's writings.

P. D. Ouspensky, a Russian esotericist who revealed his doctrines only to a small select group of trusted people, claimed to have discovered the true knowledge behind humanity's relationship within this vast universe. In his book, "In Search of the Miraculous", Ouspensky calls the 'universal consciousness' a practical cosmic teaching of an Ancient Eastern approach referred to as the 'Fourth Way;' a conduct of life that addresses the existence mankind's rightful place within the universe. He believed that each and every human possesses an inner ability that continues to develop and transcends that of the physical human body – an abstract level to human consciousness he referred to as a 'waking sleep;' one that eclipses the natural state of human consciousness, that takes it to a much higher state within the 'universe.' [4]

In the book, "The Mayan Calendar and the Transformation of Consciousness." by Carl Calleman PhD, he attempted to explain the process by which human consciousness had evolved over the centuries using the ancient Mayan calendar as an example to extrapolate and define his theory. The Mayan calendar is based on 26,000 year cycles, divided into an 'intuitive chronology' of nine cosmic transits (steps) the Mayan's labelled as 'underworlds,' each one constructed to represent steps – not unlike those on any Mayan pyramid – where each exemplified 'a level of consciousness toward humanity's age of total enlightenment;' the ninth and final period ended on January 21, 2012. [5]

The Mayans once believed that man would eventually enter into a state they called 'an awakening;' as a new awareness to 'consciousness.' This awakening would expand our feeble understanding of our own 'consciousness' twenty-fold as well as redefine concept of linear 'time' and 'space' because humanity would not only be able to access a consciousness that spanned the entire universe, it would do faster than ever before while transcending what we call today, 'space-time. [5]

For seven millennia, Egypt has always been regarded as a universe within itself; one that had been dominated by sorcery, magic, and gods. When in all likelihood they were likely able to transform 'human consciousness' from a 'physical material universe,' limited by 'time' and 'space,' into a comprehensible science. Think about this for a moment; for centuries anything that could not be explained by our limited understanding or comprehension of science – in this case 'consciousness' – just had to be 'magic,' and we already know that anyone dealing with magic had to be a sorcerer, and therefore a 'demonic conjurer.'

Ancient teachings only became secret because many believed them to have been too esoteric, occult, or symbolic and went against Egypt's popular religious beliefs. However, those that chose to continue following the ancient ways also believed them to be the 'secrets to the universe' they labelled the 'magical keys of wisdom.' Ancient Egyptians accepted these beliefs as the gateway into an 'intuitive consciousness' that expanded not only 'human consciousness' and 'comprehension,' it transcended time, space, and dimension instantaneously.
Through the passing of time, these sacred ancient Egyptian principles became a unified source of information derived from the mystic, occult, and esoteric

disciplines, including astrology and magic, into a diverse number of contemporary sciences; chemistry, physics, philosophy, medicine, astronomy, geometry, architecture, music and mathematics.

Sadly, any knowledge and understanding of these sacred disciplines – once revered throughout the ancient world – were lost through the ages. Although the ancient priests and priestesses who practiced these sacred primal beliefs attempted to safeguard them, went into hiding and along with them the sacred principles they safeguarded, and eventually were lost, destroyed, or forgotten as mainstream science gained more and more acceptance throughout time.

It is therefore imperative that when these ancient secrets, once shrouded by allegory and mysterious symbology, are discovered they are researched and studied further. For now, all we have is the symbolism left behind by the Ancients as vague clues scattered all over the world on crumbling monuments and tombs.

For us to unravel these ancient mysteries, we must first gain a better perspective to the mind-set behind the Ancients, their cryptic teachings, vague messages, and similar symbology. It is only from the scant hints and clues that we may someday rediscover what was lost and reclaim what is now invisible. We must believe in what is unimaginable to span the many 'realms of consciousness' once taught by many ancient societies to learn their diversified disciplines. Perhaps then, we will learn how to make sense of it all and what the ancient priests and priestesses actually knew. "How far they were able to transcend consciousness? How were they were able to connect 'intuitively' to an unseen and unfamiliar 'consciousness' that spans the entire 'universe,' and are we capable ourselves to connect to it as well?"

From an Ancient Perspective

When dealing within the spiritual realms, the Ancients believed 'precognition' offered only limited access into other realities that could not go beyond a 'normal human state of consciousness.' It was their belief that they could only observe things as they were and only within their own limited understanding of the 'linear time and space' they occupied.

Do we truly know who we are and where we came from today? Is it possible to break free of the Ancient's limited perspective of 'time' or 'space?' What knowledge could we possibly gain about what we know about vast universe and reality we perceive ourselves in today? 'Knowing' is what many ancient Native American cultures describe it as an 'earth-mind,' knowledge that everything is connected to everything else and to everyone else within the universe.

Many of the Ancient cultures that have existed in the Americas have long understood that a 'universal consciousness' exists within our universe and that 'consciousness' can be accessed intuitively; a form of spirituality that manifests itself through symbols. As scientist study ancient symbols around the globe, a story of how the Ancients saw our creation is beginning to unfold one puzzle piece at a time; how everything is connects within this vast universe. It is through these ancient symbols scientists have been able to reveal the ancient beliefs of a pending 'conscious awakening' to the 'natural world' around them, allowing them to see who they were and where they came from, their relationship to others, the world, and the universe, as well as their place in it.

For thousands of years we have come to know the constellation 'Orion,' as a group of stars worshiped by many of the ancient cultures around the world. The Ancient Egyptians believed Sirius, the brightest star in the night sky and visually near Orion to be the goddess Isis; the goddess responsible for the Rebirth of Consciousness throughout the universe. With its color, blue light linked to a much higher reality of consciousness, an awareness of a future frequency that will eventually spiral its consciousness through all the patterns of Sacred Geometry on Mother Earth, to eventually unify humankind into single higher consciousness with the heavens.

The Ancient Anasazi in the four corners region of the United States believed that its intense blue color referred to Sirius as a 'Kachina Blue Blood' – the star-people who seeded our reality here on earth; possibly an alien race that came to earth.

The ancient Anasazi civilization was once comprised of an indigenous people dating as far back as the first millennium that mysteriously disappeared around 1300 AD. Centered in the desert region of the south-western in the United States, they are believed to been the ancient ancestors of many of the present-day Native American tribes–including the Hopi, Zuni, and Apache, including many of the smaller Pueblos (smaller tribes referred to as 'the ancient Puebloans' of the Anasazi) scattered throughout the region today. The Navajo phrase 'ãh nä sæ ze,' calls them 'the ancient enemies' and the word adopted today to describe this ancient civilization as the 'Anasazi.' Making it very clear the Navajo nation is definitely unrelated to the ancient Anasazi. [21]

The Hopi consider themselves to be among one of the oldest living cultures in the world (if not the oldest) that can trace their ancestral history back for millennia. A diverse ancestral people, the Hopi believe themselves to be living descendants of the ancient 'Anasazi' people, whose villages are among the oldest continuously occupied settlements on the North American continent. Hopi lands are isolated, remote, and barren and believed by the Hopi to have offered them the protection necessary to preserve their ancient culture from the outside world.

Hopi prophecy is rooted in antiquity and they believe that anyone who is genuinely seeking a spiritual path is spiritually one of them. Yet, anyone ruled by greed, anger and lies is a 'false Hopi,' regardless if they are born Hopi. The essence of the Hopi prophecy is that our collective future is in what they call 'the Emergence,' that has already begun, which will transition humankind into the Fifth World; one of the nine most important prophecies of the Ancient Hopi ancestors had established for all of humanity.

This ancient Native American Hopi prophecy states, "When the Blue Star Kachina (deity) makes its appearance in the heavens, the 'Fifth World' will emerge into view and the 'Day of Purification' will have arrived."

Blue Star Kachina prophecy predicts, "It will come when the Saquasohuh (Blue Star) Kachina finally dances in the plaza, after which the Blue Star Kachina will remove its mask to reveal enlightenment to the great consciousness of our forefathers." Some people speculate that the Blue Kachina is actually an off-world alien brother returning to earth, for which the 'day of purification' will herald in a consciousness to take humanity into another dimensional world the call, "the Fifth World." Which the Hopi believe process has already begun.

Could this ancient Hopi prophecy be thought to reveal an alternate reality, depicted through a metaphor by which our quest to unveil the long sought after answers to who we are, where we come from, and why we're here, or perhaps a search for a greater truth regarding a 'universal consciousness?' Many people all around the planet, are today beginning to believe something is changing and has been for some time that will affect thousands of souls at a global scale . . . calling it 'an awakening' of an unknown consciousness? Others believe they can even hear the pulse of the planet as a gentle low frequency hum emanating from deep within the earth, and go on to claim they can even feel the 'frequency' surging through them like the blue electrical discharge of static electrical discharge that is passing not only through them, but throughout the entire universe.

Is it an awakening to a 'universal consciousness' occurring as a 'spiritual epiphany' or just 'creative expression and imagination' or does it act like all of them; much like a tuning fork striking a specific frequency emitting a key into the 'higher levels of consciousness?'

Personally, I believe our soul itself does not just accesses a 'universal consciousness' but is part of it. We are all born with certain inherent faculties, and it is through these faculties we 'consciously sense' our connection to a 'higher consciousness.' The Ancients did, for they believed they knew the universe was all around us, and even though as humankind we may not necessarily understand the reality for which we live, I believe we have created the reality in which we live.

The Prophecy of a Modern Realization

In 1968, the musical "Hair" had become a huge hit on Broadway. Its opening song, "The Age of Aquarius," became a hit song popularized by "The 5th Dimension," winning two Grammy Awards (for Best Contemporary Song, and Album of the Year of the same title) in 1969, a cultural phenomenon best known as the 'Woodstock Generation.'

Was it irony, coincidence, or prophecy that this song, is associated to one of the twelve constellations in the Zodiac that became to represent an astrological 'shift of consciousness,' during the astronomical transition of our passing through the galactic plane of our Milky Way galaxy that occurred at the beginning of the new millennium and the Mayan calendar? The Ancient Egyptians recognized this group of stars in their hieroglyphs not only as representative of a 'water bearer,' but as a prophecy foretelling of the 'new age of consciousness' that would turn the world upside-down (figuratively speaking of course). The ancients considered Aquarius as a celestial representation of the River Nile, the 'giver of life' to the Ancient Egyptians, in the virtue that without the Nile no life can exist in the vastness of the desert, much less their 'great' Egyptian civilization.

The Ancients predicted a new 'Age of Aquarius' would dawn as the Earth entered a 'Galactic Winter Equinox' during the planet's progression through our Milky Way's galactic center; taking mankind into what the Ancients referred to as the 'Precession of the Age;' that happened to also coincide with the Mayan calendar and the Hopi people. The 'Process of Purification' began shortly after sunrise on the Gregorian date of 21 December 2012; heralding in a process known as the 'Great Conjunction;' would occur as a series of four major celestial events occurring in unison, a convergence and synchronization that would complete the purification process and thereby herald in the Seventh Age; 'the Age of Aquarius.'

Although the four celestial events have already converged and marked the dawning into the 'Age of Aquarius' it should also be noted that these events were so precise, they could only have been witnessed from latitude 30^0 north. The event began with the 'Rising of the Earth's Winter Solstice Sun,' that put the Earth half above and half below the horizon of the Galactic Plain. By drawing an 'Imaginary Line that Bisects the Milky Way' along the galactic horizon, with the celestial dome, the hemisphere above the horizon became visible at the precise moment of the 'Great Conjunction,' and the celestial hemisphere below the horizon was no longer visible.

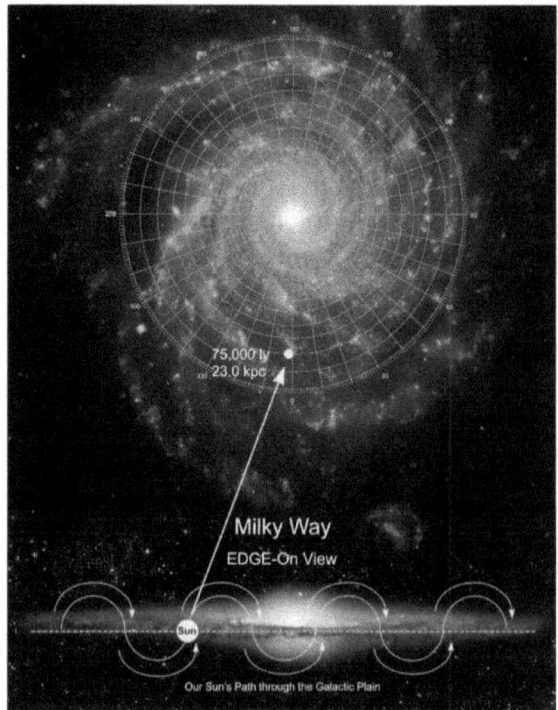

75,000 ly
23.0 kpc

Milky Way
EDGE-On View

Our Sun's Path through the Galactic Plain

Because the Milky Way is representative of the 'Waters of Life,' for which the 'Tree of Life' to the Ancient Egyptians that sprang from the roots, a 'Great Conjunction' it became a representation of how the Egyptian Ancient civilization evolved to create order. The myth further explained through their understanding of the origins of the universe as being a primordial ocean the Ancients called 'Nun.' This included their observation of the Sun's elliptical course as it traveled across the sky for a one-year period, to create the optical illusion by which the Egyptian's were able to gauge the four seasons. All of which were in prefect alignment of the Constellation Sagittarius, another important aspect of the Great Conjunction that defined the celestial gateway that pointed to the center of the Milky Way Galaxy and representative of a 'Stellar Womb' from which it conceived an estimated 200 billion suns all representing galactic ova.

To the Ancient Egyptians, Sagittarius heralded humanity the entrance of a galactic birth canal as a means for our Sun (an integral part of the Great Conjunction), as the father of the new 'New Great Age.'

A New Great Age

"...our ancestors devised every method imaginable to alert us to a single fact; now is the time of the most extraordinary conditions and opportunities that accompany the rarest of events, the shift from one world age to the next." Gregg Braden. [59]

It is therefore no coincidence that several great Ancient peoples, all opposite sides of the world that include the Mayans, the Aztecs, the Incas, the Anasazi, and Egyptians, (all of which had had no known physical contact with each other) were able to calculate the exact moment in time, the direction of mankind would take in its evolution. A genesis that would herald in a 'higher consciousness' for all of humanity; the Ancients all called it the 'New Great Age.'

However, with this prediction, the Ancients also issued a dire warning to those who will be experiencing the prophecy of the 'Great Age,' for it will not be an easy transition. Instead, it will cause great pain and turmoil for all those who do not embrace change easily and refuse to relinquish their 'old way' of thinking. Instead, they will instead witness all the greatness of their generation and that of their ancestors, begin to crumble and burn all around them. Corruption of governments, corporations, family dynasties, and powerful individuals will then become exposed for all to see and their world will crumble as a series catastrophic and disastrous events, and witnessed by all who embraced this 'new age' of 'evolutionary consciousness.'

Yet, are they really disasters or just part of an evolutionary transition? After all, it is only human nature to cling to the familiar and reject with fear the unknown.

The Ancient's believed the 'Great Age' would in fact become an era of enlightenment, tolerance, understanding, education and an era of personal responsibility. Those who used tactics designed to deceive by means of superstition, corruption, terror, lies, fear to control the masses, and no longer believed. Once exposed for what 'their' tactics truly are, the masses will no longer accept, nor tolerate them; ushering in an era where science will begin to excel over religion and even the mightiest will falter. Technology will advance quickly and humanity will progress faster than it ever has before throughout history.

During this period knowledge, truth, and trust will govern all of humanity. All the old ways will lay discarded and abandoned as the 'New Great Age' opens up a world of peace, cooperation, and prosperity.

Humankind has never before experienced a period in recorded human history when war has torn the world apart. Nor has there ever been such significant changes in any of the world's major religions or political systems; only turmoil, mass genocide, corrupt regimes, wars and rumors of war. Corporations and governments have become so symbiotic in a greed and corruption that it's difficult to distinguish who is working for whom. Today the younger generations have grown exhausted of masked lies, pompous clichés and decaying promises handed down by the previous generations. Nor do these younger generations feel they need any of the sanctions and hegemonies they've inherited from their ancestors. Instead, they will put their faith into an open set of values that demonstrates truth; and which their elders will consider revolutionary.

The 'Great Age' of Aquarius began revealing itself as the 'new age consciousness' by several rebellious generations over the last 50 plus years; including the golden 50's, the psychedelic 60's, the Woodstock 70's, that very possibly go as far back as the roaring 20's. The fact remains, as we look around us, it is obvious have already progressed so far past what our Ancient Ancestors heralded as the beginning of the 'Age of Aquarius, the Great Age' and the 'Age of Enlightenment,' we can no longer see, nor ever fathom going back to a world once ruled by ignorance.

SCIENCE, LOGIC, AND REASON

"A human being is a part of the whole called by us a 'universe,' a part limited in time and space. He experiences himself, his thoughts and feelings as something separated from the rest – a kind of optical delusion of his own consciousness."

Albert Einstein

Most astronomers concur that the Milky Way, in which our sun resides, is an average-sized spiral galaxy that measures approximately 120,000 light-years across as an elliptical spiral. Within the Milky Way it is estimated there are roughly about 400 billion stars of various sizes and brightness, to which our sun is only average. However, our Milky Way is a rare titan galaxy when compared to most galaxies that are about one fourth the mass with less than 100 billion stars on average, and therefore not a very good representation of an 'average' galaxy in general.

An average human brain is composed of a network containing billions of neurons (about 100 billion neurons give or take a few million), or nerve cells, or about the size of average galaxies in this great vast universe. There are approximately the same numbers of neuroglia (often called 'glial cells') that support and protect the brain's delicate balance of neurons. Each neuron can also be connect up to 10,000 other neurons at any one time, each one passing signals back-and-forth to each other through as many as 1,000 trillion synaptic connections. Some scientist's estimate that our brain could be considered equivalent to a computer processor capable of processing a trillion bits per second, with a memory capacity that would wildly vary from 1 to 1,000 terabytes – the entire contents within the Library of Congress contains 19 million volumes representative of approximately only 10 terabytes of data.

A Scientific Deduction

The very complex process of information transmissions within the human brain involves a variety of steps that would provide much more detail than I could ever possibly represent within the pages of this book. Our brain can only be accomplished the complex processes involving memory encoding and our retrieval mechanism through a combination of chemicals, each and every one designed to spark a series of electrical impulses generated from these neurons.

Humankind's nervous system in general – our brain in particular – acts as the main component for neurons and nerve cells controlling the entire human body – by a number of electrical impulses designed to communicate an infinite number of instructions to and from our body, including our vital organs, our senses, and our mind. The debate however, rages on as to whether our brain, specifically our 'brain cells' also house our very essence of existence; our 'consciousness,' we have come to call our 'soul.'

During our early development through childhood, specifically adolescence, physical changes in our body known as 'puberty' occurs by a process known as 'pruning' begins to occur within as a young person's brain matures. During this period of growth, our brain under goes a growth spurt of where the overall number of neurons and synapses are reduced as much as 50%. Eliminated during this period are all the unnecessary neuronal structures as much more complex and far more efficient ones created that are better suited for the demands of adulthood. What is most interesting here is that in both 'Indigo' and 'highly intelligent children' the growth spurt seems to occur at a much earlier age; for which science has not yet been able to determine the reason why or how.

Consciousness

We are but a single planet spinning around a single average star in a galaxy we call the Milky Way. A small blue planet that happens to have been lucky enough to be in what astrophysicists call the 'Goldilocks' Zone,' not too far or not too close to the sun, that has been endowed with countless forms of life. However, we are nothing more than another planet no different from a grain of sand on beach on the edge of a dark sea we call a galaxy. We float through space at hundreds of thousands of miles an hour, in yet another gigantic ocean of blackness among billions of other galaxies, some small, some large, and many still forming and scattered throughout a universe that seems to have no beginning, no end, and no dimension.

Homo–sapiens are life forms that happen to possess the necessary ingredients to be classified as a 'living' entities in that we are all 'consciously aware' of our own existence, endowed with a mind in a body we call human, in that mankind demonstrates sufficient intelligence to ask the questions; "Where did we come from and why are we here?"

This miniscule sapphire we call Earth is but a 'grain of sand' that rests on a spinning sea of stars at the very edge of the Milky Way galaxy. Our galaxy is composed of over 300 billion stars, some very much like our own sun, others so tiny they're not worth mentioning or are near death, and many so large that the simplicity of our feeble human minds cannot possibly fathom their grandeur. Although the Milky Way is but a single galaxy with in a pool of over 250 billion scattered throughout the universe, we can only see our galaxy from our own vantage point on its outer edge. From this location, and with the help of the most powerful telescopes built to date – from Hubble to ALMA (Atacama Large Millimeter/Sub Millimeter Array in Chile) –it is estimated that there may be as many as 3,000 other solar systems within our vicinity.

Then multiply that number by how many stars may have discernible planets that are capable of supporting life within the 'Goldilocks Zone' swimming around in space within those billions of other galaxies and you can begin to deduce the possibilities that exist. Surrounded by an endless cloud of dark matter throughout the entire universe – all kept apart by dark energy – there is mostly likely so much more than we could possibly see, much less ever comprehend. All proving, we know virtually nothing at all about the universe in which we live.

This rhetorical exercise will most likely never be realized, especially with what still remains of my lifetime, but I do believe – perhaps in the not so distant future – mankind will be able to traverse much this galaxy, and with great ease discover strange new worlds. However, I do understand humanity can be extremely ignorant and often very arrogant to believe 'we are alone' in this great vast universe!

Is Life Itself Consciousness

This question, not adequately answered in any of my research documents, left with only more questions. Nor do I wish to convolute it by giving it an answer, because regardless of what I think, it would surely spark ire by both theologians and scientists alike. I will however, share with you my thoughts for what "I personally believe" is the moment at which life becomes a conscious entity.

We all know that both the sperm and the ova are single individual cells that carry genetic sequencing of DNA (yDNA: paternal and mtDNA: mitochondrial or maternal) and although cells do demonstrate signs of life at the cellular level, they themselves are neither 'intelligent' nor 'self-aware.' Neither can a cell demonstrate 'self-awareness,' much less a 'consciousness' of their existence.

We also know that when the sperm meets the ova, a miraculous event occurs, when the sperm from a male, penetrates a female ova (egg) and both cells merge to form a 'different single' cell that combines the DNA the sequencing from both parents. In essence, another life form with similar, yet different genetic sequencing. At the cellular level, a new cell will evolve on its own the DNA of both parents mingled to form a distinct combination that representative of both parents that will continue to grow larger and take on human form.

Is this then where life begins? Again, another resounding NO, for these cells still do not qualify as being neither 'intelligent, self-aware' or 'conscious' of their existence.

Then something intriguing and extraordinary begins to happen, these two cells begin by quickly multiply by factors of two; one becomes two, two becomes four, four becomes eight, and so on. However, it is not until these multiple cells become millions of cells before it becomes an embryo, and slowly begins to create its own circulatory system, blood cells, and identifiable organs – including a brain. It is only when this mass of cells has divided to a point that begins to take on the shape of a human fetus that 'consciousness' and 'self-awareness' can begin. However, at this point, the fetus cannot yet demonstrate an 'intelligence' or 'self-awareness,' as a conscious human being.

Yet, when a fetal heart begins to pump, and blood begins to circulate throughout a very tiny body no bigger than your thumb still connected by an umbilical cord to its mother, its newly formed brain will eventually begin to spark its first electrical impulse to signal the beginning of life. Then and only then, the fetus truly be considered to be 'human,' but at what point does it become 'conscious' and 'aware' of itself?

I believe it is when the chemical activity within its very small brain begins to spark enough neural impulses to regulate its own vital organs along a delicate neural network within its own body and back again, the fetus becomes an unborn infant and life can actually begin.

However, at this stage of fetal development the unborn infant will still not show any visible signs of 'intelligence, self-awareness', or a 'consciousness' for yet some time. Perhaps the BIGGER question is, "When does the fetus' brain actually begin to think?"

Mind or Soul

Although the fetus can qualify as a living human life form, has it met all the criteria demonstrating 'life' and 'conscious thought' within the confines of its womb? Perhaps, but does it not make more sense to believe the unborn fetus is 'conscious' when it begins to learn the soothing sound of its mother's voice, by reacting to stimulus such as speaking, humming, or singing to the unborn child. Scientists believe stress experienced by an expectant mother will often agitate the fetus within its inner sanctum, possibly demonstrating an 'intelligent awareness' within the womb. Thus, learning to suck their thumb calms the fetus, and it may even kick violently at loud noises such as screaming or yelling, or quiet down when hearing soft music to help it cope with displeasures, all constituting a 'conscious awareness.' So, when during fetal development does life occur?

We should instead be asking ourselves, "At what point does the fetus actually have a mind and soul?" Bringing to mind another philosophical question that defies a definitive answer, "What's the difference between a mind . . . and a soul?

The Mind and Soul Connection

I understand the 'mind' to be that part of us that controls our brain's 'conscious, subconscious' and even 'unconscious' connection to our soul, allowing us to become instinctively 'self-aware.' That part of our genetic program that defines who we are by allowing us to make split-second choices instantaneously. Be they right or wrong. It is what defines 'who we are,' what drives all of us to survive or perish, fail or succeed. As well as control all body's functions and basic survival instincts, controlled by the grey matter between our ears, as the delicate folds that make up our brain. It allows us to make choices, reproduce, make important decisions, experience life and question our own existence.

Our 'soul' on the other hand, is 'who we are.' The part of us that develops which morals we will end up accepting or rejecting, what character we will choose display or hide, and what is or is not appropriate for the 'self.' It is the very essence of what memories are important enough to remember or forget what is trivial, including which of life's experiences are most memorable, valuable or even worthy of remembering throughout our lives. Our 'soul' is our individuality, that part of us that uses our 'mind,' to allow us to think for ourselves, gather knowledge, remember morals, understand right from wrong, fair or unfair, and govern all we perceive to be ethical or spiritual within ourselves. Many believe the 'mind' and 'soul' is one in the same, but as you can see by my definition, I do not believe that at all.

Our physical body is simply a host − a temple that houses our 'soul,' an eternal 'consciousness,' that has existed long before we were ever united with a physical body and will continue on, <u>long after</u> our physical bodies have died.

Our 'mind' is very much part of a huge collective of souls directly linked our brain; very much like a 'computer (our brain)' connects through an 'Internet provider (the mind)' to the 'iCloud (our soul).' When the body dies, our mind will no longer function and the connection to the soul will be broken simply because our brain died; just as the computer will no longer be able to communicate to the iCloud when the connection is broken when the power is shuts down.

Our 'souls' has existed long before we were born into this physical world and it will continue on long after our deaths. Yet everything we ever learned and loved in our lifetime – love, knowledge, experiences, and memories – by those who have touched our souls, will remain. Our 'souls' are all part of a great, vast 'universal consciousness' comprised of a countless number souls scattered throughout the universe, a universe that has existed since time as we know it, began.

When our host body dies, so will the chemically induced neural impulses the brain once produced to control all the neural thought patterns used by our 'mind.' Everything we have learned and experienced becomes part of who we are. The human brain controls our 'physical body' and 'mind.' It is however through our 'mind' we 'think, analyze and decide,' our actions; what is important and all that is not. And although our 'minds' and 'physical bodies' will someday get separated upon our death, our 'souls' continue to exist, long after our bodies turn back to the earth from which we came.

When that occurs, everyone's 'soul' will be reunited with the countless other 'souls' to become once again part of what some have deemed to be a 'soul force,' others and I simply call it the 'universal consciousness.' Thus, for the lack of an outstanding definition I shall turn to a definition used by George Lucas his hit film "Star Wars," he simply called "the force."

Do I have empirical evidence this is the case, and everything I share with you is "the truth, the whole truth and nothing but the truth?" No, of course not, it is an educated 'gut feeling' from what my mind has been questioning, studying and learning since I was a child who has been searching for answers his entire life.

I questioned everything I was told was fact; by parents, teachers, journalists, and even theologians. I researched a countless number of books in a countless number of libraries for a countless number of hours. I desperately wanted answers. It may have been easier had I searched for the elusive 'Holy Grail' instead.

By the time I entered university, I began to conclude there simply <u>were no</u> answers to be had other than countless rhetorical references by 'religious zealots' claiming that since science can't explain it, it must surely be 'Devine Inspiration;' God must have will it through 'Intelligent Design;' n answer I never found cceptable.

You may or may not agree with what I have written within these pages, but the fact that you have read this far assures me you also seek knowledge and answers. What you about to read herein, has all become the very foundation of who I am; morals, opinions, and values; an integral part of my 'soul.'

Defining Precognitive Consciousness

What did our Ancient Ancestors believe regarding 'precognition' and 'consciousness?' To answer this I must first attempt to illustrate how 'precognitive consciousness' may work when compared to the successful methodology designed by Google for their Search Engine: a metaphor if you will. For those of you who have difficulty comprehending computer-mumbo-jumbo, please bear with me as I will try to make the point as simply as possible for all the non-geeks reading this book.

Nearly everyone on the planet at one time or another has used Google's Search Engine. It has after all, the most powerful search tool on the Internet, capable of bringing you a 'data search' nearly instantaneously classifying it as one of the most innovative power tools on the World Wide Web today. Facts are facts, and without search engines such as Google's, it would be nearly impossible to locate any of the information you requested quickly and accurately. Otherwise, it would not take seconds to complete a search, but hours or days at best, and perhaps months, or years to search the entire Internet adequately yourself. Google makes it all effortless and nearly instantaneous. In 2012 for example, Google processed over 3,565,277 search requests every minute of every day.

Traditional searches in the good-ole-days used to require days to process as the search transcend the World-Wide-Web locating new documents and web sites, digesting their content, and cataloging them. Once completed, it put the results into a searchable database (like a spreadsheet with billions of rows and columns populated with the search information), A LOT of data. To give you a good example of how much data we are speaking of here, it could easily fill over 30 volumes of Encyclopedia Britannica.

The search engine required what is referred to as a 'Metasystem;' composing many disassociated computer systems into a single unit by the use of 'Spiders,' and 'robots' (small programs that go out and do nothing but search the Internet for the requested data; referred to as 'bots'). These small programs require a lot of memory, and a lot of processing power, not to mention storage space for cataloging each-and-every search request. However, that in itself is simple and very time consuming when compared to the processes required to update each search request when accessing the 'stored' data, it must also sort and update it as it happen.

All databases have a simple search function built into their code, as do the facilities that require them; universities, governments, libraries, businesses, etc. Yet unlike other search engines, Google uses a special algorithm to generate the result results using a 'slave' process. Even though Google only shares certain facts about their algorithm, the specifics have been simplified as to how it actually works and how it is actually used is a proprietary 'top secret' and for obvious reasons. In doing so, it helps Google maintain their competitive edge over all the other popular search engines.

What makes Google's search engine unlike all the others is that it not only searches very large indices (indexes) of keywords, it stores and catalogs them within their databases located in hundreds of databases around the world. Giving the end-user (you) what seems to be an instantaneous response.

These Google 'spiders' function only is to locate billions of other database search engines from countless computer databases all around the world by putting them to work from the user's keyword search and instruct them where to put the end results of each individual search on screen. Only in this manner, Google is able to harness the power of thousands every search engine it finds, and virtually at the same time, in order have them work in unison, and essentially, how 'metasystem modelling' works.

The Mnemonic Hypothesis to Consciousness

Kenneth S. Bowers is one of the world's preeminent hypnosis researchers and an important contributor to personality, cognitive psychology, human memory, language comprehension, emotion, and behavior modification during the 1960s. He conducted a study contending that 'intuitive insight' is an 'instantaneous cognitive process' that involves the activation of an intuitive pattern consistent with the empirical scientific conception of what 'intuitive precognition' of the mind represents. Bowers believed that 'subconscious intuition' reaches across into a vast unknown 'consciousness' that often reveals itself as a 'hunch' or otherwise an 'instantaneous insight' to another person's thoughts.

'Mnemonic consciousness' involves a process that would identify specific patterns of the human thinking process in what Bowers termed the 'mnemonic network.' In other words, in very much the way that the Google Search Engine processes use a series of algorithms and short code(s) as a 'metasystem' intended to assist searching the Web, our memory makes similar associations between what we know and what we do not know or understand.[6]

This brings with it many more questions than answers; specifically what involves what and how much. Is memory is actually stored and available throughout the brain's cellular neural network? Where and how does a person actually access and the processes of 'mnemonic network' code? What would be the critical source information for a 'conscious, subconscious, unconscious' or an 'intuitive' search and retrieval of data; much less where it originated from?

Is 'intuition' and 'precognition' an elimination algorithm that performs an analysis as a series of steps necessary to solve a specific problem or even possibly answer a problem? Since Algorithms are used in the mathematical calculations of data processing and are the foundation for computer science today, could this process of elimination be described as an 'intuitive process' to lead us to conclude and recognize knowledge as an insight?

Think of your neural processes working on an Excel spreadsheet that would allow you to sort through an infinite number of possible combinations. Could the mind be a series of 'interactive intelligences' made up of algorithms in your mnemonic network sorting this data into recognizable combinations? This system of 'intuitive intelligence' would have to be a massive amount of data, not only large enough to allow us for the combining of infinite amounts of memory stored in nerve cells, but to access and process this data instantaneously. Would it then possible that when this data is combined and analyzed to form meaning it could be transferred to form an associated pattern instead of multiple data streams and algorithms in the brain?

Perhaps as data stored (say as a hologram) and recalled instantly as holographic or symbolic to represent memories, experiences, or events over an entire an entire lifetime. This might even offer an explanation as to what Böehme believed when it came to seeing patterns within an 'intuitive universe.'

Highly influential human emotions may in fact be a weakness to this process. Because our own perception of the 'intuitive, precognitive' and 'cognitive' results could logically make the wrong associations, and thus store the wrong conclusions based on the algorithm our consciousness used, and thus distorting truth. When it comes to human emotion, the intuitive processes based on experience, not logic; therefore, it could be entirely possible that one event pattern, linked to another, could open a door to not only can discover wisdom, but identify stupidity as well. [7]

Self–Awareness

What the in the name of hell does it all mean and does it have anything to do with 'precognition' and 'consciousness?' Well to be frank it would be like asking what does mean to be 'blond haired, blue eyed and left handed?' It just IS and NOT a choice anyone makes; they just are and learn to accept it.

I hope that everything to this point is beginning to come together and make a little bit more sense. For the 'Indigo Generations,' it is more a matter of 'how' and 'what' an 'Indigo' senses of the world around them.

I had to ask myself over-and-over again, based on the information I have researched and will be presenting to you herein; "Am I Indigo myself?" Now keep in mind, I often argue with myself and STILL manage to loose. So in order to answer myself I had to reflect and ponder this question. Yet, more importantly I had to accept the fact that I have always known I was a little bit it 'different,' some would say 'off,' from everyone else I grew up with. Okay, perhaps I was a little. Maybe even a lot! Yes, I seemed to possess an uncanny and inherent sense of knowing things I should not have known, nor could have possibly known since I was a very young child. 'I just seemed to know that I knew!'

Was it an innate sense of 'intuition' or 'precognition?' Perhaps even a faculty I just happened to be born with. After all, the tag 'Indigo Child' was not yet conceived to describe kid like me. Back around the 1950's I was set apart from the 'normal' kids as a really weird 'psychic kid;' who happened to scare the hell out of a lot of people, especially adults.

In reality, an 'Indigo Child' is a whole lot of things, but keep in mind being 'psychic' would be a big misnomer when trying to describe this unique group of people! For it is how an Indigo senses people, their surrounds, and events that sets them apart, and to varying degrees, even though what they is part of their a natural part of who we are, who we have always been, and what we are able to comprehend. What's interesting here is that the Indigo Child honestly believes everyone else can as well!

Everyone human on this vast planet throughout time has been able to display some form of 'precognitive intuition.' Each with different abilities or intensities; yet for a select few it had been their keen sense of an 'instantaneous awareness,' that set them apart, because their sense of 'precognitive intuition' went far behind what defines 'normal.' For many Indigo's this trait has been active since birth and what has set them apart from everyone else. Yet for everyone else it had laid 'dormant.' In fact, we are just now beginning to experience the 'Great Awakening' our Ancestors had predicted would occur when the 'New Great Age' was to be ushered in.

Many people have experienced 'déjà vu' at one time or another and can grasp and understand there exists a possibility that a greater 'consciousness' is what made it happen; although they may have been able to explain it. Then there are those who have no clue what so ever, as what had just happened and quickly forget it or brush it off. For them it never happened, because they chose to ignore it.

From the deserts of Egypt to the jungles of the Yucatan, our Ancestors predicted long ago that when the 'Age of Enlightenment' began, the numbers of those 'enlightened' would grow exponentially for two distinct reasons. The first being that although there are no definitive numbers of how many or at what age a 'Child' would be 'enlightened.'

Today, science has confirmed that there has been a dramatic increase of the intelligence measured in children around the world through IQ testing.

Secondly, many people have reported that although they themselves had been struggling to make-the-grade all their lives; from kindergarten to retirement, and many report they seem to have been awakened to a sudden 'enlightenment' of what they believe are 'psychic' moments of 'intuition' and it scares the hell out them. Perhaps some sort of 'trigger' has 'awakened' something with their 'genetic DNA coding' that has been inherent to the last few 'older generations' that is only now being 'turned on' through some sort of random modification or dormant DNA genes within their genome; and some again have no clue what-so-ever it's even happening, or choose not to acknowledge 'the change.'

Regardless of what you may or may not believe, the number is increasing as to the number of people who are reporting they are experiencing a new sense of 'enlightenment' for which they have suddenly realized their psyche is even being affected by another person's 'emotions, thoughts' and 'fears' before they had been vocalized. Is it the 'shift of consciousness,' foretold by our Ancient Ancestors?

Alternatively, it could instead be an evolution process that has begun to enable humans with an 'instantaneous awareness' to everyone's 'consciousness;' including a transcendence of, and to 'precognition'?

THE HUMAN BRAIN

"My brain is only a receiver, in the Universe there is a core from which we obtain knowledge, strength, and inspiration. I have not penetrated into the secrets of this core, but I do know that it exists."

Nikola Tesla

Indigo Children can inherently tune into the harmonics of a 'universal consciousness,' naturally, while others do so infrequently.

It didn't take me long as a boy to realize from a very early age that everybody demonstrated various degrees of intelligence. Nor was intelligence by any means associated, or responsible with 'common sense;' a quality many seemingly intelligent people seemed to lack.

Although, I never believed myself to be a 'specially gifted kid;' I must admit, then and now I have distained the label; although I knew everyone considered me a bit 'strange' and 'different,' but never really understood the reason why? Thus began my search to investigate the most complex and most understood organ of the human body – our brain.

Back in the early 70's, there really wasn't much information that could be considered a reasonable explanation. In fact, most of it was nothing more than theories that went substantiated by nothing more 'subjective evidence.' It wasn't until recently however, that more 'objective evidence' began to materialize, from which to base a reasonable conclusion.

The work of Luigi Galvani, an Italian physician from the 18th century, demonstrated promise when he applied an electric shock to certain muscles of the human body to make them twitch. Fascinated by the role electricity played on the human body, these very same scientists later determined electric currents seemed to flow through every single cell of the human body; more specifically certain impulses seemed to apparently mediate and initiate specific functions throughout our bodies.

The Hidden Potential of Our Brain

During this pubescent growth spurt, what is known is that our neurons become electrically excitable cells designed to process and transmit information through what scientists call 'electro-chemical signaling;' a process that many scientists are only now beginning to understand and even speculate that it may actually be the process of how memories are stored; but not where they are stored.

What most people do not know, understand, or even care, is that unlike all the other cells throughout the human body, the neurons of our brain can 'never' divide to replicate themselves as every other cell in our physical body does on a regular basis. Thus these cells are not continuously replenished with new ones, but only decay and die off as we get older, and whatever function(s) or memory(s) these dead cells had once controlled will never be replaced, making it much more difficult, if at all 'stored memories' (although there have been known to be a few exceptions).

Every neuron maintains an 'electrical voltage gradient' across its membrane; metabolically controlling the differences in the ions of chloride, potassium, sodium, and calcium within that brain cell, all of which have a different charge. If there is a significant change in that voltage generated, an electrochemical pulse (referred to as an 'action potential' or 'nerve impulse') and its activity measured and displayed by as 'brain waves' or 'brain rhythms.' The pulse generated, then travels rapidly along the cell's axons (appendages of the neuron that transmit impulses away from the cell's body) and transfers them to another neuron through specialized connections known as a 'synapse' to another neighboring neuron. They are then received by feathery extensions called 'dendrites (appendages looking like a feather bush protruding from a neuron)' that transmits the impulses away from the cell's body. [8]

Understand though, our human central nervous system is quite a complex mechanism that consists of two distinctive parts; a 'central nervous system' and the 'peripheral nervous system.' The 'central nervous system' encompasses the brain and spinal cord, while the 'peripheral nervous system' consists of an encapsulated collection of neural pathways with well over 100 billion inter-connecting neurons located throughout our entire body **outside** the cranium (skull) that extends down the spinal cord and all the associated spinal nerves pathways associated with it (or ganglia).

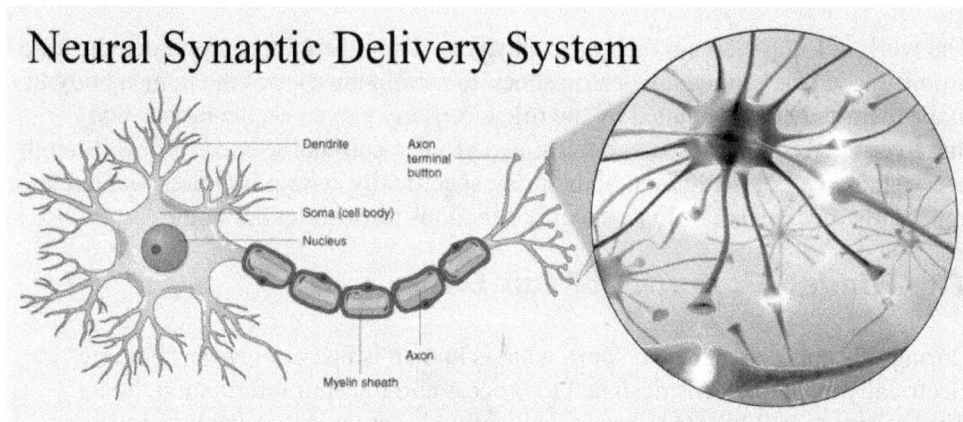

Neural Synaptic Delivery System

It should be clear that the most dramatic difference between these two systems is that, unlike the peripheral nerves, once the human brain or spinal cord damaged by accident or birth, diseased or injured, or simply by age. The central nervous system is NOT at all capable of either recovering or repairing the damage itself. These cells are essentially incapable of any significant regeneration and modern medicine simply does not yet have sufficient knowledge to assist . . . the damage for the most part, is permanent.

Let it be clear that while the peripheral nervous system has an intrinsic ability to repair and regenerate cells, as does the rest of our body, our brain and spinal cells don't. Although scientists around the world continue to study ways on how to assist repair of this natural boundary, in hopes to coax or stimulate the brain and spinal cord someday to do so, inroads have been small at best.

The Complexities of Memory

We have all heard many experts attempt to explain memory, often using the same metaphor used for files stored on a computer hard drive; a tiny filing cabinet filled with thousands of individual memory folders in which our personal experiences and important memories – filed, cataloged, and neatly stored away.

Some have even associated memory as a huge neural supercomputer housed within our brain. Today however, many experts now believe that our memory is far more elusive than that and certainly much more complex than we can even imagine. They have ascertained that memory is in fact NOT located in just one particular area of the human brain, or even within individual cells, but instead is a much broader and far more complex process than had been previously speculated.

Take for example, if I ask you the question "What did you have for breakfast this morning?" Would you be able to conjure up an image of meal? Perhaps you could visual a plate with bacon and eggs, a side of toast and glass of orange juice; or the process by which it was prepared.

Whatever popped into your mind did not just materialize in your head from an out-of-the-way neural highway that conjured it up by accessing it from different cells in your brain. Derived instead from what many scientists believe to have been such an incredibly complex process of constructive power using our brain. Everyone possesses what resembles disparate memory impressions from a complex web of brain cells (neurons) scattered throughout the brain; acting as 'our mind.' It is how and what we 'think,' how or why we able to 'reason,' as well as how and what we 'learn;' right from wrong and construct morals.

'Memory recall' is composed of a group of systems that function with different roles. That not only creates memories, it decides the many different processes to classify what is important, and what is not, then stores them and recalls them. Each disparate system functions cohesively (in a normally functioning human brain) together in unison, to thereby provide us with 'cohesive conscious thought;' what first appeared to be a simple 'recall' of memory turned out to be a much more complex process than scientists had previously understood. Neurologists are only now beginning to unravel the complexity of the brain and how each part of a specific memory is dissected, reassembled and presented to back to our conscious mind as a 'whole coherent thought.'

Please bear with me as I expand on all this scientific mumbo-jumbo, it is important on how it also relates the difference of how an Indigo Child's memory recall functions in correlation to everyone else's. Although scientists continue to work on the conundrum of this process, they still do not fully understand exactly what happens during the recall process, much less, where these memories are stored and accessed. Thus, until they can, we have absolutely no defined concept as to how or what happens to create or acquire memories; much less how quickly and how accurate those memories are in relation to time.

It has been a never-ending quest among researchers that has gone on for hundreds, if not thousands of years. However, there is sufficient information from which to extrapolate several theories and from which to draw several well-educated assumptions regarding the processes involved, encoding, storing, or retrieving human memories. [9]

In a study conducted on a cadaver in the 1950s, by Brenda Milner, PhD and pioneering neuroscientist, she implicated the 'hippocampus;' as an area of the brain with two small curved formations located near the center of the brain she believed were involved with the formation of 'new memories;' and crucial in the formation of memory storage and recall. Newer concepts also implicate the frontal cortex is also being involved in that long-term memories are eventually transferred to this frontal region of the brain. [10]

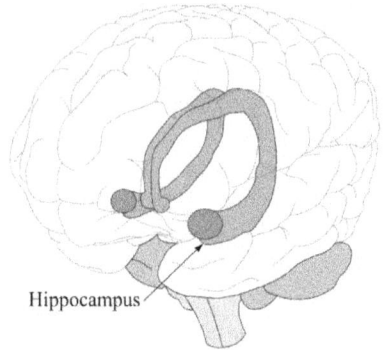

Hippocampus

Even though a lot of controversy still exists, there remains no consensus or viable theories by scientists of where, much less how, long-term memories are actually stored and recalled. Two scientists at the University of California in San Diego, Christine Smith, and Larry Squire, both PhDs, both believe that long-term memory is more dependent on the frontal cortex of the brain than it is on the hippocampus; even though both work synchronously.

When the frontal cortex was subject to a severe head trauma, they discovered that damage to the frontal cortex would not only 'impair long-term memories' (such as Alzheimer's), it could also cause short-term and even permanent amnesia. In other words, the location and recollection of memory (in the case of long-term memory loss) within the brain is dependent on two factors: "The age of the memory being recalled and which part of the brain was used to make the recall."

Their study concluded that recent memories were much more likely than long-term memories to be richer and much more vivid; determined by using functional Magnetic Resonance Imaging (fMRI Magnetic Resonance Imaging) of the brain to registers the blood flow to the functioning areas of the brain involved. Over their 30-years of their study with several subjects (patients), they determined the recalled event from memory was unrelated to the time at which the memory occurred, but to the richness of the event recalled. Their discovery allowed them to also deduce that most of the more detailed recalled memories were actually associated with 'important personal events' within each of the 'participants' lives, making the memory not only easier to remember, but remembered with much more detail and with a higher level of clarity.

Although this study does not answer the provocative question of where our memory is stored, or how it accessed, the Smith and Squire study does identify many of the processes the brain engages in to recall both short and long-term memories. "What we're trying to is create a fundamental understanding of how the brain works and then you can understand what happens when something goes wrong," Smith said. "It will further the basic understanding of neuroanatomy that supports learning and memory." [11]

Therefore, the next time you attempt to recall any given memory, whether long-term or short, it may very well be possibly that your hippocampus will be responsible for having encoded and stored the memory; and will be now accessing and recalling it via a chemically induced processes that will actually begin in the frontal cortex of your brain. If this is the case, then what is actually responsible for producing these chemical changes required to do so, the hippocampus or the frontal lobe?

THE MECHANICS

"The intricate inner workings of our DNA are changing . . . Brain-wave relationships are spontaneously moving into higher vibrational patterning as the electromagnetic fields within our DNA. Because of this, our brains are working together as cohesive units of consciousness. That means humanity is becoming more aware and moving toward becoming sentient beings - aware of everything all at once, all of the time."

Meg Blackburn Losey

What exactly did 'the Ancients' know regarding the significance of the tiny structure called the 'pineal gland?

Herophilis, a Greek anatomist of the 4th century B.C. believed the 'pineal gland' was a sphincter that regulated our flow of thought; thus suggesting the ancient Greeks may have had some insight to the 'pineal gland's function;' whereas the Ancient Egyptians referred to it as the 'Eye of Horus.' Both civilizations realizing it acted as a transducer to received signals from a metaphysical energy source which it converted to thought; another form of energy that manifested directly in our minds as a method of 'knowledge transfer' between the mental and physical realms.

Early Latin anatomists dubbed the pineal gland 'glandula superior,' or the 'master gland' to order to distinguish its specific function differently from the 'pituitary gland,' which Herophilis demoted by calling it the 'glandula inferior (the 'inferior gland).' This not only distinguished the 'pineal' as a 'gland,' they exalted its status over that of the 'pituitary gland;' a very small gland that residing at the very center of the brain.

The Ancients revered it as our 'third eye.' French philosopher René Descartes believed the 'pineal gland' to be a solution to a mystery that had puzzled scientists for centuries; how the human brain connects our mind to our conscious soul in a vast consciousness of other souls; a puzzle that had baffled scientists for centuries. Descartes believed the 'pineal gland,' was nothing more than a quiescent remnant of our prehistoric human physiology, and served very little function to 'modern man,' if any at all. [12]

However, this very small gland, located at the very center of our brain, now thought to be an integral part of the central nervous and endocrine systems, producing endocrine secretions to control the metabolic activity necessary to regulate the hormones within our body. We now know these secretions originate from the 'pineal gland' to coordinate the internal human circadian rhythms of our internal 'biological master clock.'

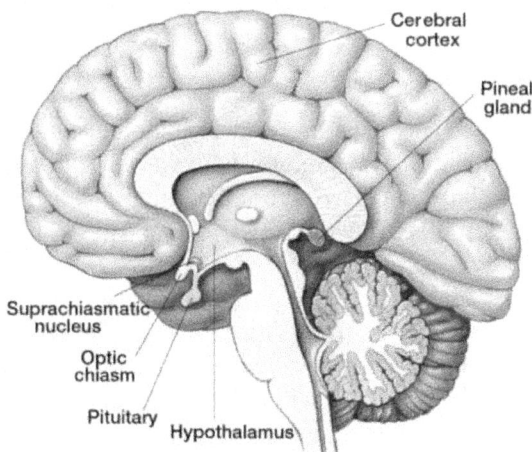

Being the smallest organ in our body, the 'pineal gland' has been surrounded by controversy and mystery for eons, so much so that it had easily become a subject of curiosity, speculation, and perhaps even pandemonium within scientific, theological, and philosophical circles that included physicians, biologists, anatomists, biochemists, physiologists, philosophers, religions and theologians over many centuries.

Positioned on the superior surface, at the foremost section of our brain, the 'pineal gland' sets between the two cerebral hemispheres of the brain and attached to the third ventricle. It resembles a very small grey white pine cone (thus its name), located directly at the top of the spinal cord and at the same level where our neck attaches our head, and between our eyebrows, is approximately ¼" long and weighs in at a mere 100 milligrams.

The ventricles of the pineal are filled with a clear cerebrospinal fluid that acts very much like saliva in our mouth that surrounds both the brain and the spinal cord; acting as a cushion, it distributes nutrients to the brain and down spinal cord while it simultaneously removes any of the waste by products from the cerebral system. In fact, the pineal gland is the only structure in the center of our brain – other than the 'pituitary gland' – that is bilaterally symmetrical in that when either of these two glands are sliced in half down the center from front to back they can be seen as exact mirror images to each other.

Scientists used to believe that since the pineal gland secreted more melatonin in children than in adults, thus deducing it was responsible for inhibiting puberty and may even contribute to slow down a child's sexual development and maturation in concert with the 'pituitary gland.' This assessment presumed simply because the 'pineal gland' has a tendency to shrink after puberty and thereby release less and less melatonin as the child develops through adulthood.

Herein is where it really begins to get interesting. The rekindled interest in the science behind our 'pineal gland' begins to unfold to define 'Indigo consciousness.' Many parents have discovered that the production of the 'melatonin hormone' affects the 'circadian rhythm' of our body, by onset by the 'darkness of night,' and by the serotonin hormone with the onset of the morning 'dawn (light).' Bringing to mind another question, "How does it affect the connection to our higher consciousness, much less maintained, long after an Indigo Child has gone through the process of puberty?"

A Modern Realization

It wasn't until modern researcher Aaron B. Leaner, an American dermatologist at Yale Medical School in the United States, in 1958, isolated melatonin as a hormone solely created by the 'pineal gland,' to provide conclusive proof that the 'pineal' was indeed a 'gland' and that it served a definitive function.

Then in the 1960's, a second hormone was identified that is produced by the 'pineal' and isolated by Dr. Daniel X. Freeman, a psychiatrist from Yale University he called 'serotonin.' His discovery and research of this strange substance never before noticed with brain tissue, led him to conclude serotonin' within brain tissue that had never been noticed, let him to conclude that the greatest concentration of this unique hormone was indeed being produced by 'pineal gland' and other nearby elongated cells called 'raphe cells' by the nuclei in the midbrain. Both of which played extreme role in the development of super-intelligent and consciously aware children with the onset of puberty and what makes them uniquely so.

The 'pineal gland' appeared to be the primary source of 'serotonin' that also acts as reservoir to not only store the hormone, but is responsible for the its distribution throughout brain, via the 'axon extensions;' tiny cell extensions between the brain's neurons that fire electrical impulses to particular areas of the brain where it's needed.

However, it was H.W. De Graff and E. Baldwin Spencer, two micro anatomists in 1866 that independently identified that the 'pineal gland' seemed to act very much like a rudimentary eye. In that, it possessed the same identical essential features of our two external eyes; including pigmentation and the retinal cells that surround an inner chamber filled with what appeared to be a globular mass. Surprisingly, it resembled the lenses within our eyes, and later proved the 'pineal gland' was actually able to respond to any direct environmental light by transmitting those signals along the very same nerve pathways used to carry images from our external eyes to our brain.

Was this discovery merely a coincidence or did the Ancients know this? Perhaps this is why the Ancients referred to the 'pineal gland' as our 'third eye,' or an 'eye of intuition.' Or perhaps, nothing more than a whimsical thought that derived from many other disassociated mystical beliefs…But then again, maybe not. [13]

The National Institute of Health, in Bethesda, Maryland, made another startling discovery regarding this ever-growing puzzle. Two other scientists, Julius Axelrod and Arthur Weissbach, discovered that 'serotonin' to be a necessary precursor for the production of 'melatonin,' because it is in fact produced from the very same 'serotonin' produced within the 'pineal gland' via a simple chemical pathway that transforms it into 'melatonin.' [33]

In all their research, these two scientists discovered that certain levels of 'serotonin' are actually responsible for human rational thought. When they alternated the concentration of 'serotonin' within the brain with a very minute quantity of a hallucinogen such as Lysergic Acid Diethylamide (commonly known as LSD); they were able to prove our perception of a 'normal reality' would be unhinged.

For those unfamiliar (not that I've used it) with LSD, it was said to be an illegal drug (created by the pharmaceutical company, Novartis. Ironically a client in my career) that was discovered to cause 'wild hallucinations' (a 'trip' if you will) in certain people and at varying degrees, and thought to destroy brain cells when used. What they discovered actually astounded them, for LSD was really 'depriving' serotonin production from ever reaching the brain cells by blocking all the production sites from producing any 'serotonin' at all. Thus, it wasn't the LSD at all that creating the effect of 'hallucinations' within the brain – as previously thought – it was the absence of 'serotonin' in the test subject's brain that caused them to 'hallucinate' and 'trip out.' What it surprisingly meant, was that the brain's level of 'serotonin' actually does have a much more profound effect on the human brain than was originally believed.

Understand too, that the 'pineal gland' acts as the physical medium that regulates the brain's chemistry; therefore, capable of altering our 'state of consciousness' as well as our perception of 'reality.' It also appears that our 'sexual identity' and our 'state of conscious awareness' are intimately relating to the laws of attraction set forth by our state of 'conscious, subconscious and unconscious awareness.'

This in-depth study provided very valuable information in that man can be imprisoned to the mundane – an everyday state of consciousness because of 'serotonin;' only to be held a prisoner, locked up by far more effectively than being incarcerated behind bars and bound by chains. Only this prisoner is unaware of their predicament only to experience imprisonment of the entire their entire body throughout their life.

What could be better than depriving the brain of 'serotonin' to hold any individual prisoners in their body? By far, it is much easier and far much more effective to hold a person's 'consciousness' and ultimately their 'soul' incarcerated without the use of a single iron bar or link of chain. The captive prisoner would not ever be capable or harnessing, perceiving, or experiencing, any higher state of 'conscious awareness' simply because their altered levels of 'serotonin' would bind their brain tissue better than iron chains or cell bars ever could. [14]

If an adult were able to experience the 'reality layers' a Indigo Child can see – or any child for that matter – they may think the sugar cube they dropped into their tea had been laced with LSD; all because 'serotonin production' in an adult brain is either very minute or non-existent in their brain. Because when the 'pineal gland' begins the production of serotonin, its effect subsides and subsequently the onset of puberty begins. Not also, that as the child grows older, they would soon be unable to enter into any of their previous diverse ranges of 'consciousness' or recall any of their 'conscious experiences' or 'alternate realities,' and forget ever having been able to do so after puberty.

How often have you watched a young child talk to an 'imaginary' friend? For a child, it is entirely normal to play within a multidimensional world of imaginary friends and places in which they are capable of traveling down a 'rabbit hole,' thereby go places normally inaccessible to 'adults.'

Ever had a child beg to have the light next to their bed left on? Of course, every parent has. When you think about it now, you may understand that it was very possible your child had been experiencing an 'alternate reality' could not explain, and it frightened them; both scenarios of which are due to the manner which their 'pineal gland' was functioning as a child; creating and converting 'serotonin' and 'melatonin' in their young developing bodies.

However, Indigo Children going into puberty will soon discover they will be able to realize it's an 'inherent' ability. One that will allow them enter into a much higher state of 'consciousness' than ever before; a state even capable of even spanning time, space and dimension; for them it will easy 'intuitive' and 'instinctive.'

They know where their soul has been in a any past lives they may have experienced, what they sensed, and how they communicate with countless other souls within an unseen 'universal consciousness.' So much so, it often surprises and shocks parents, friends, and teachers. For the most part, they seem to be not only wiser, but know more than their young lives should or even possibly could. Not only in what they say or do, but in how they are able to perceive number of other 'alternate realities;' that unless their parents are also Indigo, they could not possibly begin to even imagine; much less understand.

Establishing Connectivity

We all have a basic understanding of how radio waves are responsible for transmitting music, Wi-Fi, mobile and data communications, through the earth's atmosphere and into the farthest reaches of space. We also know we these radio waves are invisible to our consciousness, so that they are completely undetectable to nearly all life forms on the planet. What's even more fascinating about radio waves is they produced by an incredibly simple technology; one that has become the core of man's modern existence; so much so, nearly anyone can build a simple radio transmitter or simple receivers.

Face it, nearly everyone on the planet has listened to 'AM (Amplitude Modulation – carrier waves that remain constant)' or 'FM (Frequency Modulation – encoded carrier waves that vary instantaneously),' radio at one time or another. Add to that 'VHF (Very High Frequency, between 30-300 MHz; 10-1m)' and 'UHF (Ultra-High Frequency, between 300 megahertz and 3 gigahertz),' and you have television, citizens band radio, and short wave radio.

Most of us are also familiar that all radio waves operate at specific electromagnetic frequencies (radio waves) propagated, and transmitted via different types of antennas. What many people don't realize is that there are literally thousands of radio wave frequencies in use today; all of which can are designed to be transmitted and received through specifically designed electronic device to transmit or receive each and individual signal specifically, or a group of signals within a specific range.[17]

Are our brains capable of doing the exact same thing? We sure are, but not very easily as most signals are minute and nearly undetectable; perhaps even multiple frequencies. The problem is our brains have the tendency to them all simultaneously and subconsciously, but tunes them out because they appear to be either nothing but gibberish or nearly undetectable. This being case, understand however, it is **'not'** broadcasting like a citizens band radio; our brains send and receive 'information' to and from the 'universal consciousness' at unfathomable speeds.

Our brains are constantly oscillating many types of specific frequencies that 'transmit' and 'receive' information to and from our 'conscious, sub-conscious' and 'unconscious minds;' however, for the Indigo Child, it goes much deeper than that; it's an 'instantaneous intuitive awareness!'

Generating an Electro-magnetic Force

"All cells in a human body and for the most part all organisms on earth; from the simplest bacteria to the trees in the giant redwood forests of California, generate an electrical current." stated Professor Frances Ashcroft in her study entitled, "The Spark of Life." [24]

Once I got to thinking about it, without the electrical impulse traveling from my eyes to my brain, I wouldn't be able to write this book and you wouldn't be able to read it.

Since the 18th century, we have learned that electrical impulses control everything our body does. Minute electrical signals running through our bodies enable us to function as we do, and nearly every carbon entity on the planet. In Science 101, we learned all carbon life forms on the Earth are comprised of atoms. In turn, those atoms have protons (with a positive charge), each with a certain number neutrons (with a negative charge) and electrons (a neutral charge) within their makeup.

Therefore, when these electrical charges are out of balance, the positive atoms will become negative, and the negative atoms will become positive; a process called 'switching.' By 'switching the charge' from positive to negative, electrons are allowed to flow from one atom to the next and thereby create a steady flow of electrons known as an 'electrical current.' Since our bodies are a huge mass of atoms, we are in fact constantly generating an electrical current that in turn creates an 'electro-magnetic field (referred to often as EMF).'

Our central nervous system is transmitting a constant flow 'signals' to and from our brain; referred to as 'synaptic firing.' For example, when our brain tells our hand how to contract a specific finger, it sends a particular pattern of signals that tells our hands how to pick up a glass, point an index finger, or make a fist. These thousands of signals all carry an electrical message from point A (the brain) to point B (the hand); very much like those of a digital cable connecting your computer to the Internet delivering nothing more than a series of 1's and 0's to create 'law and order' within our own bodies. These signals however are not being transmitting data along an electrical wire, but by jumping an electrical charge from one nerve cell to another, until it reaches its final destination; the brain to the hand and back to the brain.

These processes travel nearly instantaneous and are the very key to our survival; much like picking up a hot skillet off the stove without thinking of using a potholder. The pain from that injury is instantaneously sends an electrical signal from your hand to your brain; instantly registering that your hand has just been seriously damaged.

In response you brain signals back another signal to drop the skillet to avoid further injury; again, nearly instantaneously. If our body were incapable of relating these messages at such a high rate of speed, humanity would have most likely died out a very long time ago. [24]

Although the electro-magnetic field that encompasses our entire body is barely detectable, a simple scientific instrument can still identify these weak frequencies; including those generated by the human heart, from only few feet away.

Since we now know our body generates electrical impulses through the neural network, understand too that it's not restricted to only 'life-critical' functions; it also includes those generated by thought, memory and recall, and emotion, regardless of our 'state of consciousness (conscious, subconscious, or unconscious).' Our brain executes billions upon billions of electrical impulses that in turn signals thousands upon thousands of chemical instructions during the migration process–both critical and non-critical information–along our central nervous expressway; each generating and transmitting specific frequency wave as it does.

Brain Waves

Scientists in 2011, at Washington University School of Medicine in St. Louis, Missouri, were able to identify the precise frequencies the human brain is capable of generating. This neural activity is believed to have provided neuroscientists with what they believe is sufficient concrete evidence to would grant them new and important insight to the phenomenon of 'precognition.'

"Analysis of brain function normally focuses on where and when the brain activity happens to occur," said Eric C. Leuthardt, MD. (who at the time served as an associate professor with the Department of Neurological Surgery and the Department of Biomedical Engineering at Washington University in St. Louis), "…what we've found is that the wavelength of the activity provided a third major branch of understanding to our brain's physiology."

Electrocorticography is the technique used to survey the cerebral cortices' electrical activity by creating an electro-encephalograph from electrodes attached to a test subject's brain, and later used to map out the specific regions to identifying when and where the identified activity had occurred. In the past, scientists were limited to measuring brainwaves by using only an 'electro-encephalograph (EEG).' Today, scientists can monitor brainwaves while being produced by simply observing the electrical impulses as the neurons simultaneously fire. The frequency generated by a specific wavelength can best be determined by this methodology, and down to the cycles per second (hertz -Hz). [17]

To the amazement of the scientists involved on this project, they were able to discover they able to not only verify the precise signals transmitted, they were able to map out from which region the brain the signals had originated within a single centimeter, for a better understanding. Professor Leuthardt, an assistant professor of neurosurgery at the university, stated, "An EEG can only monitor frequencies up to 40 hertz, but with electrocorticography we can actually monitor activity up to 500 hertz. That really gives us a unique opportunity to study the complete physiology of brain activity."

"Certain networks of brain activity at very slow frequencies did not change at all regardless of how deep under anesthesia the patient was," Leuthardt went on says. "…as certain relationships between high and low frequencies of brain activity did not change, which we also speculate may relate to some of the memory circuits."

Interestingly enough, these scientists were also able to identify that a series of frequency changes occurred during the loss of consciousness that 'reversed in precise order' when consciousness was regaining. They identified this activity has a frequency region known as the 'gamma band,' and believed to occur as the neurons transmits as specific set of instructions to other neurons nearby, as the test subject dropped off into an 'unconscious state' and later regained 'consciousness.' [17]

Their conclusion; the human brain regulates activity via means of electronic waves emitted at different frequencies (as documented by the EEG) that were associated with the various brain waves that also corresponded to both the 'conscious' and 'unconscious' states of activity, for which they documented the frequencies groups identified within the brain into five basic classifications.

I believe what they had actually discovered, to be quite profound. For I have always contended–and this may very well explain–that Indigo Children are able to connect to a 'universal consciousness' that will not only make them 'intuitively aware,' it actually provides them with an 'instantaneous knowledge' that is often confused as 'precognition;' effortlessly and without forethought, regardless of what state they may be in; 'conscious, subconscious' or 'unconscious.'

The activity that occurs within the brain would best be compared to igniting a virtual storm in our brain as electrical impulses fire off neurons, which in turn, generates 'distinct' and 'measurable' magnetic signatures. To everyone's surprise, these scientists and doctors alike soon discovered that the activity detected was actually composed by many different 'frequency harmonics,' both 'rhythmic' and 'non-rhythmic' waves and pulses that ranged from anywhere between 0.2 hertz to several hundred hertz.

It is these pulsations the scientists had categorized as identifiable signatures by segregating their particular properties and later associate them to the various 'states of consciousness.'

Frequencies & Consciousness

GAMMA WAVES are by far the most intense, easily agitated frequencies generated by the human brain. They occur during a state of excitability that often consciousness on alert. They are waves measured between the frequencies of 30 and 44 (Hz) and have the distinction of being the only frequency wave generated within every lobe of the human brain. These frequencies provide the brain the ability to multi-process information from a various areas of the brain when necessary and simultaneously if necessary according to many leading scientists who have hypothesized that at 40Hz of activity, our brain become quite capable of consolidating all the areas required to initiate simultaneous processing functions.

Individuals with higher IQ's, especially those that display Indigo traits, demonstrate an 'excellent' and 'efficient' memory capacity; whereas those deficient or incapable of running at more than 30Hz would be considered 'mentally deficient' to the point that they will most likely display some type of a learning disability.

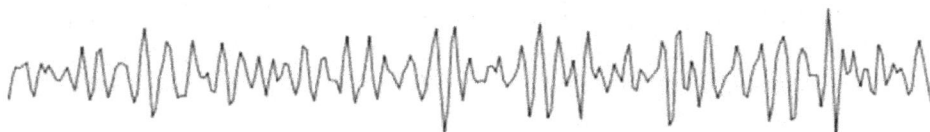

BETA WAVES occur during 'waking hours' and are responsible for generating 'normal' brain activity; between 18 to 38 hertz (pulses per second). The mental activity normally associated with Beta Waves are considered to be our 'normal state of consciousness' and for which, we are most aware. It is within this range we experience our normal dose of day-to-day mental stimuli; be it work or play.

External chemicals processes can also artificially induce or enhance the brain's Beta state, with such chemicals as alcohol, nicotine, caffeine, or amphetamines (in small quantities) can all induce or stimulate our minds into a 'normal state of consciousness.'

ALPHA WAVES transports the mind into a relaxed peaceful and meditative relaxation; occurring with a frequency between 8 to 13 hertz, and during a normal 'conscious state.' The 'Alpha Wave' demonstrates a higher awareness while relaxing; allowing the brain to focus as it concentrates brain activities to learning or performing a specific task or a number tasks.

The Alpha frequency equates to phenomenon that enhances a myriad of inherent human faculties; be they 'precognitive, out-of-body (O.B.E.), remote viewing,' or any other meditative trance-like states considered to be an 'intuitive faculty.' The Alpha Wave could in fact account for over half of an Indigo's 'precognitive' skills; most evident and quite prominent during long periods of relaxation when put in a 'subconscious state.' When an Indigo's eyes seem distant, as if they are 'caught up' in a daydream like state of 'deep concentration, thought' or 'introspect,' understand, it is most like the Alpha Wave that took them there.

THETA WAVES have a deep reflective quality that allows the mind to go into 'meditative state' with a frequency between 4 to 7 hertz. These are most responsible for 'memory consolidation, cognition, focused attention, learning, mental imagery, meditation,' and extended periods of 'deep relaxation.' The Theta frequencies are the least known type of harmonics examined outside the confines of the laboratory 'dream studies.'

Theta Waves, was easily identified when the test subject experienced a 'deep sleep' that involved 'rapid eye movement (REM) dream,' or while 'hallucinating.' Indigo Children however, seem to be able use the Theta frequencies during a 'state of consciousness.'

For the Indigo, it's an entirely simple exercise in which their 'intuitive awareness' actually becomes a normal way of strengthening of how their mind exercises their brain and how it connects to a much 'higher state of consciousness;' not unlike how aerobic exercises strengthen a person's heart.

It is only by studying Theta brain waves, that scientists have been able to unlock the mystery behind of how, why, and when the creation of 'serotonin' is blocked by our brain's chemical processes. In fact, it turned out be very same way 'normal thought functions' get impaired while under the influence of a 'hallucinogenic' drugs like LSD.

DELTA WAVES, are attributed to long periods of 'unconsciousness' after the subject was in a 'deep subconscious' sleep, that occurs within a frequency of between 0.5 to 3.4 hertz, which can also go as low as a single cycle per month, sometimes to the point it becomes pure 'Direct Current (DC).'

The Delta state of the brain is a 'deep state of unconsciousness' that displays NO Rapid Eye Movement (NREM). This phase of sleep usually occurs during the first half a normal long sleep period; at night, and is transitioned from the 'conscious' state of mind, to the 'subconscious' state of mind, and finally to the 'unconscious' state of mind. Outwardly, it can best be described as being, 'dead to the world;' a comatose 'state of unconsciousness' yielding not one single dream.

It can be induced by an over indulgence of alcohol, when the subject reaches that irresistible urge to sleep, or simply pass out right where they stand; perhaps the same natural triggers the body uses to repair itself to filter out excessive toxins, poisons, or an over-indulgence of alcohol; especially when the brain itself becomes damaged.

Other chemicals can inadvertently induce 'Delta frequencies;' medications such as sleeping pills, aspirin, muscle relaxants, narcotics, and barbiturates for example, all of which need to be used with extreme care. However, these substances may also cause some very dangerous affects–especially if taken excessively–and thus force the brain to inadvertently shut itself down by putting itself into comatose state; or worse, relax the body to the point of death. [27]

Harmonic Control

Is it possible that the brain activity can be influence through the power of suggestion? Very much so, in fact, Buddhist masters can place themselves into such a meditative state that it quells their own brain activity to the point they put themselves into such a tranquil state, they can even palliate or regulate pain.
The basic assumption made from this study, is that the human brain fluctuates its harmonics dependent on the stimuli experienced in a 'conscious' (fully awake and aware), 'sub-conscious' (asleep with REM sleep) state, or 'unconscious' (asleep with NREM sleep), based on the very same principles the brain electrochemically communicates data through our body's neurons, and the frequencies generated by them. [36]

This concept brings to mind two of very important questions:

1. Would it be possible to exploit the brain's full potential if we knew exactly

how the chemical and electro-magnetic frequencies affected memory, knowledge, experiences, and other the faculties of our mind?

2. Do certain electrochemical combinations generate specific electro-magnetic fields within the brain that would allow our minds to engage in processes that go far beyond our current scientific comprehension of a 'conscious, subconscious,' or 'subconscious' state?

The late Physicist Evan Harris Walker, a PhD. from the University of Maryland and member of the Parapsychology Association, believed our minds do not have any empirical qualities at all that can actually measure our 'conscious' state; nor that it is induced by specific chemical processes. However, it can instead be attributed to a process called 'quantum mechanical tunneling;' – a theory now consistent with the views of many other quantum physicists and brain scientists. He stated, "…to accept the conventional view in physics denies the paradoxes of quantum mechanics and the implications that go far beyond the mathematical formalisms."

Walker went on to state, "The measurement problem in Quantum Mechanics (QM) has existed virtually from the inception of quantum theory itself. It has engendered a thousand scientific papers in fruitless efforts to resolve the problem. One of the central features of the controversy has been the argument that characteristics of QM imply that an observer's thoughts can affect an objective apparatus directly, which in turn implies the reality not only of consciousness, but also PSI phenomena. I have written several papers saying that such a feature of QM is not a fault, but rather represents a solution to problems that go beyond the usual per-view of physics. Thus, I have developed a theory of consciousness and PSI phenomena that arises directly from these bizarre findings in QM, findings now supported by specific tests of the principles of objective reality and/or Einstein locality." [36]

Walker also persuasively demonstrated how his model of the human brain synapses exhibited QM phenomenon, while yet, two other scientists revealed still another model. David Bohm, an American theoretical physicist who corroborated ideas regarding quantum theory with other physicists and Basil Hilely, a British quantum physicist and professor emeritus of the University of London, made an assumption in their work that offered some very astounding similarities between 'quantum potential' and 'neurological connections' that occur within the human brain.[29] David Samuels, a neurologist on the Faculty of Chemistry (and founding father) at the Weizmann Institute, stated, "The brain's basic range of activities is driven by between 100,000 and 1 billion different chemical reactions every minute." The average human brain contains a minimum of 10 billion individual neurons or nerve cells - a figure that is even more astounding, when one stops to ask, "What frequencies do they all generate as they interact with thousands of other neurons." [28]

Mutation vs. Evolution

In 2003, scientists completed an important milestone in understand human evolution when geneticists were able to successfully map the entire sequencing of the human genome. Their hope is that this genetic blueprint will someday give up many of its secrets regarding diseases and maladies plaguing humanity for thousands upon thousands of generations; Parkinson's, cancer, Alzheimer's, diabetes, and many, many others.

This three-year project began in the year 2000 and concluded April 14, 2003, after all the partners of the International Human Genome Sequencing Consortium announced its successful completion. This group of global scientists and geneticists were finally able to identify well over three billion four-letter combinations that make up our human DNA genetic code; their hope and drive being that science may someday be able to reveal its many secrets to provide many valuable answers and clues on our evolution and overall function.

As Dr. Jane Rogers, head of sequencing at the Wellcome Trust Sanger Institute in Cambridgeshire, United Kingdom, put it, "It (our genome) will give scientists a reference from which to work from for many years to come." Yet despite our ever-expanding knowledge, geneticists continued to sequence many other mammalian genomes to provide us with clues that could perhaps provide answers as to how the human brain developed over thousands of years, by comparing it to the DNA of similar species (primates mostly), in hopes it to reveal how unique the human brain actually is by comparison.

As scientists continued to explore our genetic makeup, they soon discovered they faced an enigma that provided more questions than it did answer. For new startling clues continue to emerge that demonstrated as homo sapiens our brain has been undergoing an extremely rapid DNA evolutionary process since our genome was first completed in 2003; and because there's really nothing to compare it to prior, we have no idea when this evolutionary process began before its mapping. [34]

Considering this information, we must ask ourselves, "Is it possible that Indigo Children are the direct result of an evolutionary process, or even perhaps a natural mutation of humanity?"

In order to understand the question, we must first understand the make-up of specific DNA sequencing, comprised by specific genes that may have been permanently altered in order classify a specific genome modification as 'evolutionary.' Especially since mutations can range from a single DNA building blocks within a DNA base, to a much larger segments within the specifically targeted chromosome – or a larger number of multiple chromosomes – that was changed; either sequentially or simultaneously.

Natural Mutations

Established by a specific set of rules, the genetic code is that governs our individual makeup is encoded within that coding as a specific set of instructions; not unlike the operating system code of your personal computer. Whether it's our DNA or mRNA sequencing, the distinct protein patterns within your cells is already predetermined since birth.

Although every living organism on the planet contains an extraordinarily similar code, all living organisms express their sequencing differently, yet from the very same table of 64 simple entries. Each sequence, referred to scientifically as a 'codon,' is a nucleotide triplet of amino acid combinations. Just how these 'codons' are added or modified during a process called 'protein synthesis' from that genetic code (specifically those received from your mother's 'Mitochondria DNA' genetic code, operates under a distinct set of rules to convert 'codons' to 'amino acids;' a paradigm that underlies all of mankind's basic genetic coding.

These genetic mutations occur in one of two ways: either inherited 'as is' from our parental DNA or they are 'acquired' during your lifetime. These mutations are inherited from your parental DNA and either called 'germ line mutation' or a 'hereditary mutation,' and will remain present throughout your entire life and be present within virtually every cell of your body and get passed down to your offspring as well.

A mutation that occurs only within an ova or sperm cell, just after fertilization is called a 'de novo (new) mutations;' best explained as a mutated inherent disorder within your genome that gets passed down from generation to generation. Offspring who may also get these 'passed down mutated cells' within their genome, may not even be present in 'no one else' within their family or family's history; including siblings, be they 'positive mutations' (immunity from contracting specific diseases or infections) or 'negative mutations' (a propensity to acquire diseases such as cancer or Alzheimer's).

Until recently, Scientists had a misconception that our DNA code instructed our cells on how to produce the proteins required within our own cells. However, a new discovery, first published in mid-December 2013, has divulged quite startling information in that our DNA instructs our cells how to manufacture the 'proteins required' for replication, and in what specific order.

Another startling discovery was that there exists within our DNA coding, a second set of instructions within our DNA revealing that our body is, in a sense, 'bilingual.' The findings, first defined in the journal, "Science," states that this may in fact have some very significant implications on the manner by which medical geneticists interpret a patient's genome when interpreting it for diagnosis. What is most fascinating about this discovery is that the 'new code,' is actually a second layer of code layered on top of the existing DNA code; a code that scientists had barely finished mapping out, in what seems to be designed to enhance the existing coding. Coding that controls not only the makeup of 'what proteins get created,' but another set of code that issues a specific set of instructions on 'how' and in 'what order' those proteins get created; as an important control measure to prevent error.

In other words, any changes or mutations within our DNA (such as those normally been associated with the process of aging or viral attacks), will be prevented by doing more than what scientists had previously believed.

"For over 40 years we have assumed that DNA changes affected the genetic code solely impacted on how the proteins are made," said lead author John Stamatoyannopoulos, University of Washington associate professor of genome sciences and of medicine, "…now we know that this basic assumption about how the human genome was read, was missing the other half of the picture. Many DNA changes that appear to alter protein sequences may cause disease by disrupting these genetic control programs or even both mechanisms simultaneously."

By knowing how our genetic coding is actually issuing a specific set of genetic instructions, the University of Washington created a new descriptor to best describe the previously hidden code; a 'duon.' Each protein of the 64 possible combinations called 'codons,' researchers at have been able to determine codons that have a double meanings; for which a new a duality in that one is related to protein sequencing while the other is related to genetic control, both of which seem to have evolved in concert one to the other. Think of it a set of control instructions that help stabilize the DNA code within each of our genes; a beneficial feature as to how our cells produce the necessary proteins without the possibilities of errors. [63]

By now, I'm sure you're asking yourself, "WHAT THE HELL does Indigo consciousness have to do with all this?" Please hang in there with me, as we will soon get there, but the science is important.

Somatic Mutations

This new information has provided new insight on just how 'somatic mutations (acquired mutations)' can occur at some point during an individual's life that occurs only within their own genome. Scientists and researchers at this point in genetic study can only speculate the reason why. The number one consensus is that environmental factors are the most likely culprit.

For example, over exposure to 'ultraviolet radiation' from the sun by people who worship the sun or avid golfers, puts them in a 'high-risk' category that is capable of triggering certain cancer mutations with a genetically prone individual. Errors can also occur during the cell replication process of an individual after the division process is complete, and the replicated cells die off. The good news is, 'somatic mutations' of cells cannot be passed from one generation to the next, unless of course, the 'somatic mutation' occurred within the individual's sperm or ova cell.

'Somatic mutations' have also been known to occur during normal cell division during the early stages of embryonic development within the mother's womb. This is when most of the cells of the dividing paired cells (ova and sperm) can occur during the embryonic growth, and develops without the event of a single genetic change. Individual cells do however have the potential to mutate during the pregnancy; a situation called 'mosaicism;' when a faulty distribution of genetic material during 'mitosis (cell division)' occurs. Although these types of mutations are quite rare, they can.

When the genetic changes effect either a 'specific group' or an 'entire population,' a 'polymorphism,' is said to have occurred; a normal variation in DNA responsible for many of the normal differences between 'like' people; such as eye color, hair color, and blood type. Although most polymorphisms have no negative effects, some may contain a variation of codons that may influence specific generations of people, or put them at risk; a propensity of either developing certain disorders or be entirely immune them (the disorders).

Currently molecular biologists only know a very small fraction of what the 70,000-90,000 different combinations of nucleic acids in the human genome do, and many believe that what remains unidentified within the human DNA code is nothing more than a completely useless array of 'garbage code;' commonly referred to as 'junk DNA.'

If we 'don't' translate 'junk' to mean the 'garbage' or 'rubbish' we normally put on the curb side for disposal because it is no longer useful, to instead think of 'junk' as 'currently unused;' such as those stored in an attic for use another day. It actually makes much more sense in how we can begin to understand ALL the mounting evidence that indicates 'junk DNA' is NOT at all 'garbage!'

Scientists are only now beginning to understand that these pieces of dormant code may actually serve a very important regulatory role in the way 'DNA' actively 'enhances' or 'modifies existing code when needed, and triggered like an 'on' or 'off' switch. Thus, influencing the function and behavior of the other nearby 'DNA' code, thereby amending specific genes with a set of existing instructions that is simply need to be turned 'on' or turned 'off;' much the same way an electrical switch can controls the lights in a room. Scientists refer to these very important sets of instructions as 'codons.'

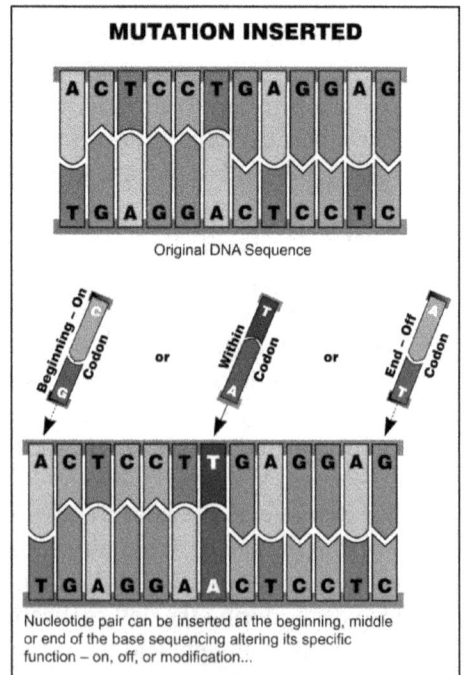

MUTATION INSERTED

Original DNA Sequence

Nucleotide pair can be inserted at the beginning, middle or end of the base sequencing altering its specific function – on, off, or modification...

MUTATION DELETED

A C T C C T G A G G A G

T G A G G A C T C C T C

Original DNA Sequence

A C T C C G A G G

T G A G G C T C C

Or nucleotide pairs can be deleted to
remove specific sequencing from
anywhere within the sequence...

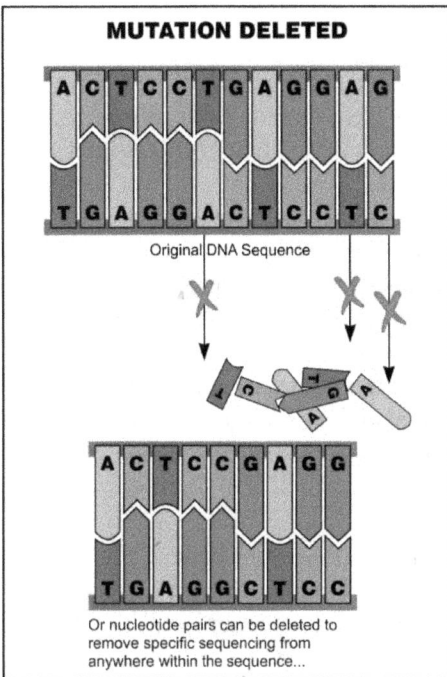

The ability to crack the human genetic code has existed for well over a half-century when scientists first learned how our DNA's four nucleic acid proteins (using letters to represent them: **A**–adenine, **C**–cytosine, **T**–thymine, and **G**–guanine) to actually encode them within our genomes. The Mammalian Regulatory Sequencing Project, is a team of molecular biologist at the University of California San Francisco who published an article in the journal, "Nature Genetics" that suggested a targeted gene therapy can utilized to fight off disease. This is accomplished by using dormant code (previously thought to be 'junk') by activating the code within certain cells to create the proteins necessary to improve that cell group's overall physiology.

Dr. Nadav Ahituv, a PhD in molecular biology and lead researcher or the project determined from the study that there appeared to be key bits of DNA coding the group called 'enhancers' (codons) that delivered a type of genetic regulator that doesn't operate as an 'all-or-nothing' component that controls whether or not the genes are active. What they discovered was that by changing the arrangement to a specific DNA sequence, within these 'enhancers' (codons) resulted in changes taking place within all levels of gene's activity. Changes that would be very much like changing the syntax of a sentence to have a different affect regarding its meaning.

This mechanism would be comprised of a specific set of instructions that would determine how our cell's 'read through' a distinctive set of sequences within our genetic codes (the three-letter combinations that compose nucleic acids), comprised within the codons, as well as the particular combinations of amino acids that get linked together, consequently creating a gene-encoded protein.

Although molecular biologists have been moving at a snail's pace to decipher the mysteries behind DNA, the process is only now beginning to reveal secrets never thought possible, as we begin to gain a better understanding behind the processes of cell division, maturation of genetic activation through observation, and the many patterns taking place during activation. All the while, trying to make sense of the many important roles our genome actually plays outside our own specific genetic makeup.

Scientists have recognized for some time now that damage to the human genome over time, many caused by mutations of DNA coding, had occurred before; only to be rectified by 'codons.'

"In 98% of DNA within the human genome, enhancers lie outside the genes referred to as 'non-coding.' Mutations within the enhancers have already been implicated in human limb malformations, deafness, skeletal abnormalities, other birth defects, including cancer." Ahituv said. [29]

These mutations occur as the result of errors during the replication process as the old cell gets replaced with a newly divided cell that has become corrupt the DNA code. Made evident by the damage scientists have witnessed as external stimuli or triggers. Like that of ultraviolet light of the sun on skin, cigarette smoke to lung tissue, or the normal cellular decay of cells all over the body we call aging. Codon switches activated during a mutation process can also domino into all types of ruthless forms of diseases, such as skin or lung cancer cells that can easily destroy healthy tissue and take it over. [35]

While our genes generally tend to resist change, a mutation can also lead the activation of very desirable traits; even across the entire populations or limited to within certain groups. A process is referred to as 'positive selection' in which a non-protein coding DNA regulates the processes that determine when and where specific genes will be 'activated (on)' or 'deactivated (off).'

"This has important implications for how we think about human evolution and disease." Said Dr. Adam Siepel, a Cornell associate professor of biological statistics and computational biology, in an article written by John Carberry, also of Cornell in 2006. [36]

The Extra-terrestrial Argument

"Look deep into nature, and then you will understand everything better."

Albert Einstein

Many people I have spoken with have theorized that 'Indigo Consciousness' can only be explained by an 'extra-terrestrial' explanation. Although I'm not entirely convinced, I cannot in good conscious rule this out. Especially when I asked myself, "Could an advanced or extra-terrestrial civilization been responsible for manipulating human DNA; or, perhaps helped it to become what we humans have become today?" A very intriguing question indeed, but despite much of the academic ridicule that has been bestowed on those claiming this to be so (like Erich von Däniken's or Zacharia Sitchin's theories on E.T. intervention), these ideas have indeed captured the world's imagination. Be it science fiction writers, Hollywood producers, or the myriad of genetic scientists who jumped the bandwagon by conducting independent extensive research today to answer the question.

When faced with understanding the magnitude of this question, the answers derived must satisfy three simple qualifiers to even consider as viable; is it POSSIBLE; is it PLAUSIBLE; and is it PROBABLE; but only in that order.

In an interview I conducted several years ago on this very subject with an up-and-coming geneticist and research scientist by the name of William Brown, who dedicated his entire field-of-study on the Science of Applied and Theoretical Resonance in biophysics at the 'Resonance Project Institute' in Hawaii under the guidance of director Nassim Haramein, his mentor. William explores every angle of the many scientific studies at his disposal; from physics, biology, advanced mathematical theories, and the nature of consciousness, he described his comprehensive synthesis on what he calls "The Science of Universal Life (SOUL)."

I should also mention that William is also an ardent practitioner of multiple spiritual modalities including meditation and yoga; he quickly discovered the process of combining his professional background in cellular and molecular biology, his explorations, and understanding of consciousness, were a natural process of combining to make his theories on consciousness and genetics, all-inclusive.

His work spans numerous laboratory facilities across the United States where has gained extensive experience in the field of molecular biology research. After 10 years of studying the biochemical processes of molecular biology, William began to investigate the biophysics behind living organisms, specifically the quantum electrodynamics and spin resonance of biological systems, which led him to a revolutionary way of viewing these systems as therapeutics and regenerative applications. William is currently working to bring forth many of the new technologies and ideas that may assist our civilization through the transformation of this critical nexus point of our physiology.

It was the early experiments during the 1940's that revealed to William that our genetic code (genes) are composed of simple chemical combinations-DNA (deoxyribonucleic acid) as mentioned earlier–the self-replicating material present in nearly all living organisms and the main constituent of 'chromosomes.' His fascination of how such a simple chemical could act as the molecule of inheritance, and had been a mystery until biophysicists discovered the DNA double helix in 1953.

Its structure turned out to be a great watershed of information that demonstrated how simple variations of just one single chemical could generate into a very 'unique' individual, or even perpetuate an entirely different species. Biophysics is the science that reveals how DNA serves as a 'keystone' to the 'book of life.' Inside cells chromosomes, our genes may be opened, closed, read, translated, and copied, very much like zipper, and thus allow scientists to realize that DNA proteins are very much like an open book to be read and to reveal the molecular machinery of life.

Over the last 13 years of the 21st century, biophysical inventions have decoded all the genes that make us 'uniquely human;' as well as the genes of from nearly 200 different species; genes inherent in more than 100,000 other species have also been identified and cataloged. Biophysicists the analyzed these genes to learn just why and how so many organisms seem to be related, and yet how so different individuals within the same species can be so different from one another.

William came to the understanding that even some of the most technologically advanced equipment available today cannot detect, nor fully harness, the incredible information and energy density of this quantum vacuum. Yet there is an amazingly coherent and superbly efficient system that accesses this infinitely deep reservoir of information, energy that on a routine basis those scientists believe to be a normal biological function, science calls an 'inherited living biological system.'

This, in-and-of-itself, makes the biological system one the most technologically advanced forms of matter that science has been able to establish, but more importantly it provides a model in which this sublime living technology can, and could have been reverse engineered and hybridized; yielding unimagined advances in our own externalized genetic technologies.

Although many of the technologies that can be produced by this level of 'genetic engineering' (any process by which genetic material-the building blocks of heredity-is changed in such a way as to make possible the production of new substances or new functions) is still largely unimagined. Several technologies, William, and other scientists have been theorizing on how to create several fully realized technologies; such as, quantum computers, room temperature superconducting devices, physical teleportation systems or gateways, and instantaneous transfer of information between intelligent species through bio-physic research. All of which can be developed and fully realized through proper research and investigation, elucidation (light and lucid transfers), and reverse engineering of the biopolymers on a living organism.

We as modern humans we have the ability to ourselves modify DNA today, but we still have so much more to learn. We must therefore ask ourselves honestly, 'If we can do this, isn't it logical that it could have been done before now?' and if so, 'by whom?'

Within this context, a joint project between IBM and National Geographic was soon envisioned and begun over 10 years ago entitled, "The National Geographic Genome Project." Since the project began, scientists and geneticists have been able to take DNA tens of thousands of samples from people all over the world. Through the years, they have been able catalogue and review many detailed changes that have occurred over the last several thousands of years. What they discovered about the human DNA molecular structure of modern humans, may have actually revealed not only how mankind was able to migrate around the world to populate the continents, they discovered concrete evidence that revealed mankind's very own DNA may have revealed startling new evidence. It appears our genes could very well have had highly advanced manipulation several thousand years ago, modifications that are well outside the scope of what any of our earthly ancestors, and even modern man would not have been capable of performing.

Zacharia Sitchin, indeed considered a rebel in his own lifetime, believed genetic manipulation was the most logical way to explain our modern genetic makeup. His research claims to have read of such accounts within the Ancient Sumerian artifacts that he had been studying throughout his entire career. Yet many naysayers believe and consider his theories are nothing more than Sitchin trying to offer an explanation to human evolution that fits into his studies on Ancient Sumerian Mythology. Although, those who have read about, or studied the very same artifacts on the Sumerian's, remain unconvinced. For they, like me, have not yet ruled out entirely the possibility of ET intervention has some merit. Yet, those geneticists opposed to the theory have not themselves discovered the 'missing link' to prove Darwinian Theory that our DNA had actually evolved from primates; quite simply, and most likely because none exists.

Genetic Haplogroups

At present, our understanding of the human gene pool provides us with many more questions than it does answers; as no 'undeniable' evidence has yet been discovered to prove otherwise. However, please note, the lack of evidence does not, in itself prove it either. Whether or not this 'evidence' even exists, I have to ask how science would go about trying to satisfy, much less identify their findings as a bonafide specific origin, be it terrestrial or extra-terrestrial, as Zacharia Sitchin had attempted.

What we have discovered in our human genome however, is that there exists within two very distinct haplogroups – and both categorized to represent an encapsulation of radical changes – mutations that occurred tens of thousands of years ago. The two distinct male and female groups represent a specific group of ancestors that share a common ancestor as the cause of the 'DNA mutation.' Geneticists refer to a haplogroup as a way to identify a shared group of common genetic traits within a specific lineage, whether from the patriarchal genome (male), or the mitochondrial (female) ancestral group.

Each haplogroup since 'Adam,' (and not in the Biblical sense of 'Adam') but fixated to a 'ground zero' man to signify its beginning. A hypothetical male name to representing humankind's 'most recent common ancestor (MRCA)' from which all living descendants on this planet had originated.

Each haplogroup, assigned a letter of the alphabet followed by a numeric designator with possibly an additional letter, are combinations designed to created and represent order within the human timeline; a 'when and where it belongs' designator so to speak. Based a joint study by National Geographic and IBM called the "National Geographic Genome Project," it was estimated 'Adam' may have originated some 60,000 to 70,000 years ago somewhere in Central Africa. [40]

As of yet, only two haplogroups within the yDNA (patriarchal) genome remain a complete mystery that geneticists have not yet been able to identify an origin; haplogroups P143 and L15. The discovery of these two groups raised many eyebrows within the scientific communities; as they introduce the possibility that that perhaps our human DNA may have in fact had some sort of outside intervention, which brings to mind a BIGGER question – by whom?

Ironically, these two haplogroups do seem to coincide with the Zacharia Sitchin's timeline, including his claim that human DNA was most likely manipulated by altering 'Cro-Magnon' man with an ancient alien race Sitchin called the Anunnaki, to create a 'better more useful' version of man. They wanted human slaves with enough intelligence to better serve them during a period that humanity knew about DNA, much less map it out, or modify it.

As an IBM employee I had chosen to participate in the National Geographic Genome Project to discover what mysteries my own DNA history held. Upon reviewing the results, I was shocked to see that my patriarchal DNA contained the P143 & L15 haplogroups in my genetic timeline, neither of which offered up any information, but it got me curios enough to research even further.

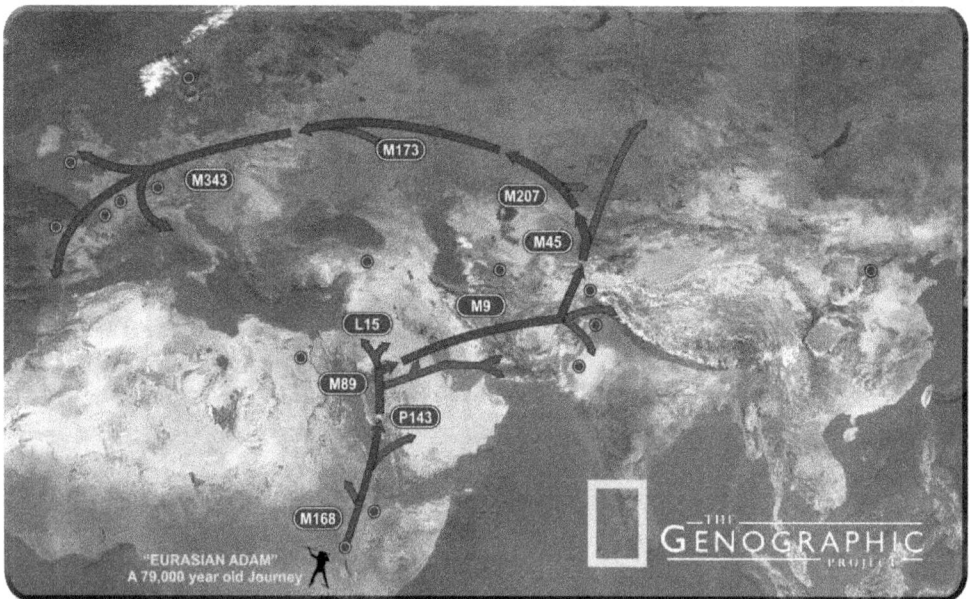

I began to work overtime searching for answers to these two mysterious and elusive groups; there simply was none other than they did belong to the two ancestral Haplogroups C and F of about 55,000 to 60,000 years ago and were not found on the continent of Africa. What information was able to uncover however, proved only to be subjective at best, making my search seem as if it were nothing but a futile exercise. P143 and L15 are really nothing more than an 'iteration refinement' (haplogroups iterations are identified by a letter and number combinations very much like a Dewey decimal system of genetic markers) that happened to be in my DNA genome, both of which are unusual.

For example, 'R1b1' is an 'iteration of haplogroup M343.' Both my father's Y-chromosome 'R1,' designated by a capital letter, with the iteration of '1' designating the first iteration of the R chromosome within M343; my mother's mitochondrial had a 'b1' chromosome designated with a lower-case letter 'b,' that signified an iteration of '1.' DNA has many different haplogroup designations that are dependent on just how far down they are on our ancestral totem pole; genetic haplogroups to indicate an origin in 'time' dating back for thousands upon thousands of years.

Within haplogroup P143 alone, there were as many as 235 mutations mapped to the Y chromosome (patriarchal) tree of my ancestors, eight of which occurred on several different branches. There are also 599 mutations incorporated into the overall tree and sub-trees mapped out within my genome; for which this particular super-cluster contained lineages that not typically found in what was once considered a sub-Saharan Africa. This information suggests these two ancient ancestral chromosomes (P143 and L15) were most likely not carried 'out of Africa' by 'Adam' during the early modern human diaspora (exodus) from Africa, carrying along with it, the 'ADAM' code.

The National Geographic Genome Project, deemed, by some could be nothing more than a study that demonstrates humankind did indeed migrate 'out of Africa,' yet no facts or evidence to support any type of artificial manipulation. But it is clear something had obviously happened to modern-man's DNA long after other species of homo-erectus – 'Neanderthal' and 'Cro-Magnon' man – began to migrate out of Africa well over 75,000 years ago; leaving us only with a trail of breadcrumbs with many more unanswered questions than answered.

Recently in 2008, a multi-institutional team of researchers that included scientists from the University of Minnesota, School of Medicine developed a powerful tool for genomic research under the guise of a medical procedure. This robust method allowed researchers to generate synthetic enzymes that could target and manipulate specific DNA sequences within the human genome for 'inactivation' or 'repair.'

Some see this bit of information as good news in light of speculations regarding the possibility of 'gene doping' (a form of gene modification where genes are changed to make normal genes to perform differently) applications; that are now being employed on the battlefield and in the sport arena, basically in an attempt to create that super soldier or athlete.

For example, by creating a better 'genetically modified (GMO)' corn, the could cure hereditary disease or help athletes win more gold medals at the Olympics, but not the public's general consensus. However, advances in understanding the human genome could possibly provide mankind many opportunities and benefits for those suffering from hereditary diseases such as, sickle cell anemia, muscular dystrophy, Alzheimer's, Parkinson's disease, dementia, or many other forms of cancer;

certainly, a double-edged sword that could prove to be devastating in the wrong hands. Especially when one considers what the military could do with this ability, especially when contracted to a global companies like Monsanto for application and execution. For it could easily destroy any and all the benefits of the natural seed humanity has relied on for thousands of millennia.

Could this 'new technological tool' have the potential of turning researchers into 'demi gods,' simply because they would be the ones to determine what genetic disorders and diseases should, could, or would be manipulated, altered, or deleted from either our human genomes or that of our food.

Perhaps, we could take this quagmire just a step further by looking at it from a different angle. What if the purpose to modify and/or create certain sequences within the human genome to improve human genome of a select few, while degrading what a government may deem to be an 'expendable portion of the population?' Very much the way we would destroy weeds in a garden to keep them from choking out other flora, genetics could be used 'weed out' the least desirable populations of an already crowded planet, while at the same time creating a 'super human intelligence!'

In an issue of the "Molecular Cell Journal, (25 July 2008)," researcher, Dr. Dan Voytas, director of the Arnold and Mabel Beckman Center for Transposon Research at The University of Minnesota School of Medicine, described a method by which geneticists can induce genomic modifications in many types of cells. A tool made available as an 'Open Source' technology strategy that makes it publicly available (free) to all genetic researcher's around the world as an aid to reduce their daily workloads by allowing other scientists to access another team's research regarding other DNA manipulation projects, regardless of whom, what, or where its origin is. [41] [42]

In knowing humans now have the knowledge to do so today, we must ask ourselves "Who did it way back then?" If we as modern humans can now manipulate DNA, "Isn't it then conceivable that we ourselves had been genetically modified in our ancient past?"

Many theorists have of course hypothesized that both these unknown haplogroups (P143 and L15) was a genetic feat engineered by the Anunnaki (an ancient alien race) when they combined their DNA with ours. For the sole purpose of merging our basic human survival instincts with one that allowed reason for the sole purpose of enhancing intelligence far beyond what our ancient 'ADAM' descendants had; although the reason why, remains unclear.

'Cro-Magnon' were known to be hunters, while 'Neanderthal's' were gatherers; both very distinct species of homo sapiens that pretty much used similar instincts of survival; including fighting to the death to protect their food sources. Because 'Cro-Magnon' was certainly much more intelligent of the two, and 'Neanderthal' instinct most likely detrimental and dangerous to their over survival, the question remains; which species were actually used to infuse with alien DNA? Theoretically speaking; most likely neither!

'Neanderthal' and 'Cro-Magnon' were only recently were granted classification as species within 'Genes Homo-Sapien;' more specifically, 'Homo-Sapien-Neanderthalensis' and 'Homo-Sapien-Cro-Magnonensis' (both now extinct). 'Modern Man' (us) are known as 'Homo-Sapien-Sapien,' (which I found kind of a redundant and humorous name) that have been around for approximately 200,000 years.

However, it wasn't until about 100,000 years ago that 'Modern Man' really began to 'evolve,' and absolutely no conclusive proof at all, that 'Modern Man' had originated from the 'Neanderthal,' nor the 'Cro-Magnon' species of 'Genes Homo-Sapien,' and are actually in fact, ONLY contemporaries to 'Neanderthal,' and 'Cro-Magnon'.

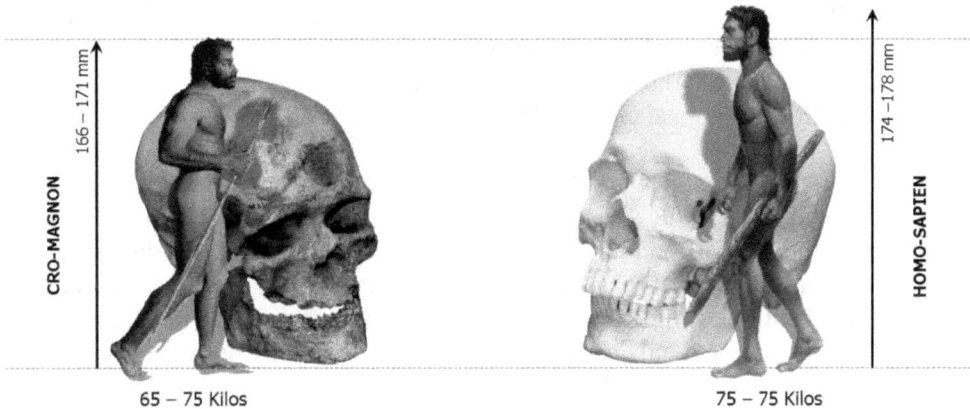

CRO-MAGNON — 166 – 171 mm — 65 – 75 Kilos

HOMO-SAPIEN — 174 –178 mm — 75 – 75 Kilos

Sitchin and others believed this was precisely why our 'unknown' creators - perhaps the Ancient Gods or the extra-terrestrials Sitchin hypothesized, 'the Anunnaki,' manipulated our ancestral DNA by blending it with theirs with 'Homo-Sapien-Sapien,' modern man, in order to create a gentler, more intelligent human.

Today, we can now pretty much manipulate DNA ourselves. So regardless of what you may believe, it seems obvious to me that the intention was to create not only a better species of humans that wouldn't kill them in their sleep, but a blueprint that has evolved into what we now call 'modern-man.' For 'Homo-Sapien-Sapien,' had just enough intelligence to serve the ancient ancestors as passive 'slaves,' and the capacity to evolve into what we are today.

Exopolitical Theories

Please understand, there are 'exopolitical groups' all around the world comprised of well-organized people attempting to challenge the covert practices of governments, politicians, political institutions and government processes that may be suppressing information concerning a government's reporting practices, actions, or propaganda regarding the existence of extra-terrestrial life or alien technology, by demanding it be made public. To wit, the supporting evidence is so overwhelming in scope that governments all over the globe often restrict access to such information, and what little information is released is quite often totally useless. Even many 'high-ranking' individuals within these governments, the information released regarding any extra-terrestrial activity is provided only on a very strict 'need to know' basis; said to allow the President of the United States for example, 'plausible deniability.'

However, there is collaborative research from various exo-scientific organizations postulating that within human DNA there exists genetic code believed to have originated from well over 20 different extra-terrestrial civilizations. Some exo-scientists have taken the work begun by Dr. Frances Crick and James Watson, who stunned the academic world back in 1953 when the deciphered the DNA molecule into the 'double helix.' Including findings purportedly believed to have come from an elusive Professor Samuel Chang (whom I cannot verify even exists), that was have said by many to have discreetly released information of his findings while working in the Human Genome Project that is **not to be associated** with, nor was is it conducted by the National Geographic and IBM project.

It's getting to the point now that legitimate scientists, including geneticists, are beginning to complain more and more about the exopolitical attempts that compromise the integrity and importance of their work. But when you think about it, could it be that the 'discreet releasing' of scientific data be yet another apparent way by which the legitimacy of their studies as nothing more than a way to discredit them, while attempting to mislead the public of what has really been occurring within our very own genome for some time now?

Detailed findings first published in part by Dr. Michael Salla, a scholar of extra-terrestrial research and founder of the exopolitical movement, stated that exo-scientists and other researchers have based their findings on carefully collected 'legitimate data.' This includes well corroborated and documented observations by many respectable people; including credible witnesses known to be 'experiencers, contactees' and 'whistle blowers;' for nearly all these verified sources at one point in their career most likely encountered contact with extra-terrestrial, or off-world humanoids civilizations living within many of our most populated cities. Many of whom may even serve in a number of political capacities within many of the various world governments.

The first fact about genetic manipulation we will need to contend with is, we simply do not know or understand enough about our own genome to be able complete a detailed model of our genetic sequencing. After all, how could we positively prove it was written, much less verified, that extra-terrestrial beings were indeed responsible its manipulation? Regardless, the fact of the matter remains that our genes cannot properly explain Darwin's proposed theory evolution when applied to humans, which may be why many are attempting to draw alternating conclusions that there must be something far more cynical at play when it comes to why and how modern man has evolved as it has genetically.

If we apply Ockham's razor to this dilemma, we must first ask ourselves, what is it the most logical and the simplest explanation to implicate the manner in which humankind may have been genetically engineered (modified)? Is it plausible, possible, and probable an extra-terrestrial intelligence could have manipulated our human genome?

If we believe it all these questions have been satisfied, we must then analyze all the possibilities by asking ourselves a BIGGER question, 'Why?' And why on earth (no pun intended) would so many reputable scientists, respected politicians, credible experiencers, and astute observers step forward to put their honor, their credibility, and their very lives on the chopping block to reveal any knowledge of ever being involved with extra-terrestrials, 'top secret' government projects, clandestine projects, 'off-world' experiences, or even having been abducted themselves? To me, it just doesn't make sense.

Many have been trying to hide the truth for what may account for certain human groups to possess ET-like features, characteristics, and intelligence that could be mistaken for that of a human/ET hybrid. Many tabloids would love you to believe that 'Indigo Children,' are indeed 'Star Children.' From which the label 'star seed,' thought to have originated and or been introduced by some mad scientists or alien races trying to 'take over the world!' After all, it does sell their tabloids, that usually only get read while sitting on a john to take care of other personal business.

If we accept that our human genetic code has been modified by extra-terrestrial intelligence(s), we must logically then need to not only identify, verify, and provide proof what had been done, but by whom, especially if genetic code has been compromised. But in order to prove what DNA code was compromised by 'off-world' entities,' we must first be able to identify what of genetic code inherent from our ancestral past, and evolved through a natural evolutionary process. We already know Darwinism doesn't work with the human genome, but 'why not,' remains unanswered. Thus, until we can, we'll ever know for sure.

Hybrid, Indigo, or Star Child

Authors Brad Steiger and Francie Steiger were the first to coin the labels, 'starseed, star children' and 'star people;' as an embodiment of worlds in other star systems far outside our own solar system. They believed that many different beings had traveled to Earth specifically to enhance the process of human evolution, once they had, they continued monitor our development.

Their theory describes extra-terrestrial's as many different benevolent species from multiple star systems throughout the Milky Way galaxy; a hypothesis derived from hundreds of documents on cases thought to have been well researched and documented; such as those by George Adamski, Orfeo Angelucci, George Van Tassell, Howard Menger, Paul Villa, Billy Meier and Alex Collier. Most of who had documented experiences about their interactions with human-like extra-terrestrials.

Extensive physical evidence to these cases was said to have been provided to the Steiger's themselves; most of their own 'close encounter;' that included a photographic logs of their evidence, film footage, and other witness statements. But the case of Eduard 'Billy' Meier appeared to have been the most extensively researched and documented case they ever reviewed (even though a majority of the physical evidence on Meier's 'alien abduction' was provided by Billy himself, although they did note some evidence had been provided by a few other UFO investigators.) [47]

ANCIENT ASTRONAUT DEBATES

"My brain is only a receiver, in the Universe there is a core from which we obtain knowledge, strength, and inspiration. I have not penetrated into the secrets of this core, but I do know that it exists."

Nikola Tesla

As mentioned earlier in this book, the believe of many 'ancient astronaut' theorists during our long distant past, may include many races of intelligent extra-terrestrial beings that had at one time or another, visited Earth with the sole intention of colonizing, harvesting, and mining this planet.

Evidence of this was derived (and conceived) was highly improbable in the fact that the 'Homo-Sapien-Sapien's' genetic makeup would or even could have suddenly emerged on this planet, violates every principle of evolution as it had been defined by Charles Darwin; based on the well documented myths of many ancient civilizations.

Tales that often describing in great detail just how human-like gods had come down from the heavens to create a race in 'their own image and in their own likeness.' In fact, most of which are only credible as documented accounts of ET's cited from several Biblical accounts; including 'Elijah and the wheel' and 'the immaculate conception of Mary.' Both of which point to alien abduction and the possibility that Jesus himself may have been an intelligent 'extra-terrestrial-human hybrid.' Then there are those ascribed as provenance of a race of highly intelligent beings described by many ancient ancestral civilizations around the globe as 'the gods.'

When I think about it, prior to the age of space travel and science fiction, any theory regarding the advanced genetic manipulation of humans would not have been possible, much less conceived by the ancient Noetic sciences of the time. Even today in the 21st century there remains a multitude of people who regard everything I've discussed herein as nothing more than pure science fiction poppycock; refusing to abandon their antiquated orthodox theories of human evolution as defined by creationism and only supported by lots of 'Bible Babble' and misinterpretation.

For me, although the concept of genetic intervention may not hold water by many, I believe there simply is 'not enough objective evidence' to determine if these theories are' plausible, possible,' and 'probable'. However, for me to conceive the possibility of an 'off-world human-like' species being responsible for humanity and our human genome is not, entirely incomprehensible. I must add that it is entirely possible, as well as plausible. However, I believe it's not yet probable; but only because of the lack of objective and concrete evidence to support the current suppositions. Unfortunately, man still refuses to let go of religion making all the decisions for them, and thus cling onto a 'dark-ages mentality,' believing they would be condemned as heretics to be burned at the stake.

Regardless, many doors have been opened since by science, which was subjugated into surrender by the Holy Church that suppressed any evidence, simply because it contradicted their 'subjectively' and irrefutable explanations as the only evidence required to solve the great mystery; because "God made it so." I find it really, really sad, that many people today still live very passive lives and believe every word uttered by their church leaders, because of the belief "God only speaks through them;" the very same words uttered by Bishops and Cardinals during a Spanish Inquisition.

A Rude Awakening

If we accept any of the theories regarding the 'extra-terrestrial hijacking' of our DNA by believing our DNA has indeed been manipulated since the dawn of man, we must also then ask ourselves several serious, but logical questions; "Why would our DNA have been manipulated in the first place? Who is responsible, and why was it done?" However, most importantly, "Was this intervention of our genetics responsible for the emergence (evolution) of an Indigo consciousness?"

If the objective were to save humanity from its own extinction, what would have been their agenda, because it's not working! Humanity has been hell-bent on its own self-destruction, especially when one considers all the recent reports of catastrophic events, nuclear disasters, climate changes, famines, diseases, floods, planes disappearing, and populations bursting over their geographic borders.

To make matters worse, man has been destroying the atmosphere, water supply, and natural resources. Some believe it's because we being directed toward a 'New World Order' by the power greedy governments of the world that would have you believe their corruption is only establishing the new 'norm' for our 'own good.' In reality, it's nothing more than a 'smoke and mirrors' attempt to divert our attention away a genocide that has begun to accelerate over last 50 years?

Regardless of what you may believe, what has become more and more evident is that there seems to be an emergence of 'intuitive humans' within the world's populations; a natural process by design to shield humanity from an inevitable annihilation by an unknown force. Then again, perhaps it's the evolutionary phenomenon of 'natural selection' at play here; not 'extra-terrestrials' As mentioned throughout this book, we must examine what is scientifically possible, plausible, and probable, before we go and make any unsubstantiated assumptions.

Follow the Yellow Brick Road

I times you will get the impression that I am taking you further and further down the yellow-brick road before I make my point; and more often than not, that's exactly what I need to do to get an important point across. Rest assured that I do not include it strictly for my amusement – there will always be a reason; I promise. So please bear with me, for each point discussed herein will indeed be relevant . . . eventually.

A Delivering DNA Modifications

In a 1998, at a study conducted by Sonoko Ogawa and Donald W. Pfaff, two scientists working in the Laboratory of Neurobiology and Behavior at Rockefeller University in New York, entitled, "Current Status of Antisense DNA Methods in Behavioral Studies," they determined that a mechanism to manipulate our brain's neural network is entirely possible.

Their research, concentrated specifically on 'genetic expression;' a process in which our genetic information (DNA code) synthesizes functional genetic products; proteins. However, with the 'non-protein coding genes' (such as rRNA or tRNA genes), the product would be the functional RNA process used by all known life forms. Ogawa and Pfaff were specifically interested in both the brain's molecular processes and its causal relationship to behavior.

They were what is known as a 'neurotropic process (the effect of nerves on a cell's nutritive processes),' to introduce a 'viral vector methodology' for delivery (vectors are DNA molecule used as a vehicle to artificially carry foreign genetic material into another cell). This has now become the most common tool used by molecular biologists to deliver any modified DNA genetic material to specifically targeted cells in order to manipulate the genetic expression neural tissue.

The 'antisense,' delivery of the specifically derived gene of RNA, or its complementary DNA, is then inserted in a reverse orientation into an existing neural strand of DNA; a genetic engineering trick that regulates the genetic expression of that particular trait. Their objective of which is to develop a broad approach for a genetic analysis of how the brain and behavior functions. [48]

Their approach is actually quite ingenious, and a brilliant way to introduce DNA modification(s) into brain cells; this delivery mechanism, which began in the mid-1980's, has now been around for well over a decade, and known as the 'Viral Receptor Delivery Mechanism.'

To mediate the viral genetic delivery process successfully, a 'benign virus' like the Herpes Simplex Virus (HSV-1) was used, because the virus possesses several multiple features to make it such an ideal 'viral' candidate to inject modified DNA code into the human nervous system. The prototype was preferred simply because the Herpes simplex virus (HSV) is the most common 'benign' virus available worldwide.

Everyone is familiar with HSV-1 virus; a virus that causes a simple infection on the mouth or lips people refer to as a 'cold sore' or 'fever blister.' In fact, it's estimated the HSV-1 so common, approximately 90% of adults have been at one time, or another, exposed to the HSV-1 virus – although not everyone infected will display the stigma of a cold sore; making the virus the prime candidate for a 'viral receptor mechanism.' [49]

The technology is absolutely mind boggling, especially when one considers the sheer scope of the entire human genome; a map more difficult than the average person can understand; especially when it comes to considering all the potential ramifications. Every person's genome on the globe planet consists of an identical base set of well over 20,000 genes comprised of 23 distinct, yet basic pairs of chromosomes contained with the nucleus of every cell; that when stretched out, is approximately six feet long and 2.5 nanometers in diameter; while a human hair is between *80,000 to 100,000 nanometers thick.* [60]

I had mentioned earlier, neurons cells are incapable of regenerating into new cells as the rest of our body does; and why when our old brain cells die off we experience memory loss.

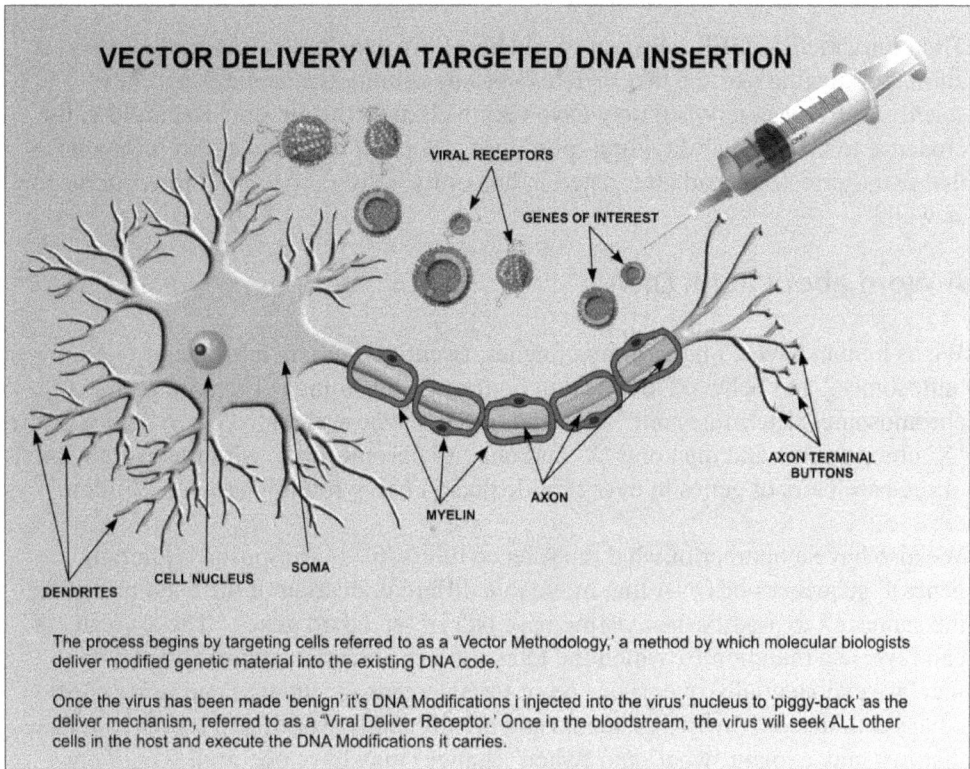

VECTOR DELIVERY VIA TARGETED DNA INSERTION

VIRAL RECEPTORS

GENES OF INTEREST

AXON TERMINAL BUTTONS

MYELIN

AXON

SOMA

CELL NUCLEUS

DENDRITES

The process begins by targeting cells referred to as a "Vector Methodology,' a method by which molecular biologists deliver modified genetic material into the existing DNA code.

Once the virus has been made 'benign' it's DNA Modifications i injected into the virus' nucleus to 'piggy-back' as the deliver mechanism, referred to as a "Viral Deliver Receptor.' Once in the bloodstream, the virus will seek ALL other cells in the host and execute the DNA Modifications it carries.

Neurons are also different from the rest of our body's cells in that most neurons in the brain preclude the use of 'vectors' such as a conventional retrovirus, which are dependent on cell replication for the stable maintenance of other cells. Add to this that most brain disorders have several specific molecular mechanisms that may be restricted to subsets (groups) of our brain's neurons during specific times of our human development and maturity, a normal process we all know as 'aging.'

Any strategies used for manipulating genetic expressions within the human brain must first utilize a 'vector' that persists as being stable or 'post mitotic cells;' which is an unaltered state of the usual method dividing cell that looks like a twisted threadlike form from within our chromosome's DNA. Upon separation longitudinally into two distinct parts and remains unaltered to successfully replicate the original DNA code within a cell during the regeneration process of itself; after which it can then be used to target cells within the nervous system – a number of such gene delivery systems have been developed over the last decade. [61]

Since the delivery of recombinant genes into the brain, and with the use of a 'viral receptors' quickly becoming a justification for an effective delivery mechanisms, it should be noted that it is fast becoming an increasingly important strategy to answer questions about brain function. Not to mention a human intervention of our very own evolution regarding a molecular modification to our human genome that not only affects our brain, but proposed circumvention to devastating disease.

Therefore, the BIGGER question would be, IF we can do this to ourselves, isn't it entirely logical to assume that there exists a possibility that ancient ancestral scientists (ET or otherwise) may have very well done this before? Regardless, the credence to the 'plausibility' and 'possibility' does exist, but is it also 'probable' that extra-terrestrials had intervened in humanity's distant past, and thus our destiny as well?

A Word about Junk DNA

We as human have 23 basic pairs of genes; twenty-two pairs labelled as 'autosomes,' and believed identical in both men and women. The 23rd pair chromosomes determines our 'sex,' and differ in that women have two copies of the 'X' chromosome and men one 'X' and one 'Y' chromosome, with the overall count of the base pairs of genes in every single person being roughly around 3 billion.

We also have a number of what the science refers to as 'transposons (jumping genes);' sequences of DNA that move to a different location of the genome within the same cell to modify the existing base pair of 'standard genes.' These create, or can reverse a mutation by which the total number potential combinations will increase exponentially over time. As of yet scientists, geneticists and researchers have yet to discover why this occurs and are diligently working to solve the puzzle that just may explain 'what' and 'when' changes may have occurred within our genome; perhaps even 'why' the changes were initiated and the current 'end-result' of those modifications.

A joint study conducted in 2010 by the Emory University School of Medicine in Atlanta, Georgia and Maryland School of Medicine in Baltimore, MA, revealed that 90% the project's participants had more variations in their human genome (as a result of 'transposons') than had ever previously been expected. In truth, they had discovered at least 1,145 new transposons from this study alone, suggesting that every new-born brought into this world will more than likely have a new, never-before-seen, genetic combination somewhere within their genome caused by a 'transposon.'

This of course is concluded by hypothesizing that new transposons form at least once within every human generation; accounting for approximately 45% of all human genome mutations, and by which the mutations were due to the formation of certain 'transposons.' Their conclusion being: the human body is in a constant state of mutation. [49]

"It now it looks like every person might have a new insertion somewhere," said

Scott Devine, PhD, a senior researcher on University of Maryland School of Medicine's Institute for Genome Sciences team. "…an under-appreciated mechanism for continuing mutation of the human genome."

With so many mutations taking place as the human genome evolves, one must wonder how these modifications function. Does the mutation function as a 'codon' would, and what is 'turned off,' suddenly 'turned on?' or could the mutations signal big changes on the horizon for humanity?

Knowing what we know now in using 'viral receptors' as a delivery methodology for altering our own DNA, scientists have been enabled to alter and deliver any unnatural mutation they would like into our genome; perhaps even disrupt, discourage, or destroy a natural evolutionary process that could have adverse and catastrophic results over time.

In the very first feature film, "Star Trek: The Motion Picture," there was a transporter malfunction when the transporter went on-line. Two new crewmembers were in the process of transporting to the Enterprise only to have the transporters suddenly fail to only end in a devastating disaster.

Although the story is entirely fiction, the malfunction is an excellent example of what a degraded genome could ensue without understanding everything there is to know about creating a valid and viable mutation. Just as Starfleet's attempt to save the crewmembers, as their DNA (data signatures) had become too severely damaged and degraded by the malfunction; ending in disaster. When they had finally rematerialized back on Earth, it was nothing more than a useless pile of DNA matter to which Kirk, now visibly shaken asked frantically, "Starfleet, do you have them?" the response, "Enterprise, what we got back didn't live long … fortunately."

Thus, when fiction mirrors reality, we all need to understand that scientists today are quite capable of making a 'jumbled mess' of their very own by screwing around with our DNA. Using 'viral receptors' to deliver modifications to our genome that introduces manufactured 'transposons' and 'codons' designed to mutate our DNA artificially is more often than not, done without fully understanding the ramifications. There are over 2.9 billion possible combinations of 20 different amino acids in our cells to create the necessary cell proteins for replication. Mind you, from only four different nucleotides within each strand of DNA.

This entire process is by natural design, an assurance guarantee built right into our DNA that ensures a 100% successfully executed replication. F humanity is to survive, it is of my opinion that we may just be doomed if scientists wishing to 'play God' continue to move forward with a 100% guarantee that their modification will not screw things up for humanity!

Again, I ask, "Is it possible that extra-terrestrials have intervened in mankind's historical development?"

To answer this question, we must consider the fact that if an alien race is cable of creating the technology necessary to navigate across the universe circumventing the laws physics we know regarding space/time, or cross multiple dimensions, then perhaps they can certainly modify DNA.

Is it 'plausible' however? Perhaps, and given this descriptor, perhaps even 'possible.' The fact is, many people believe they already have, thus making this belief quite 'probable.'

Whether Indigo generations are alien hybrids or not, the fact of the matter remains humankind has been and still is evolving at an accelerated rate that is unprecedented in human history and most scientist agree, attributed to an evolution of our genetic code.

Resonant Signatures

Just as any molecular physicist can detect a specific 'resonant signature' emitted by the different elements, metals, or organic substances by using a high-tech instrument called a 'magnetic resonance spectrometer (MRS),' they can also be detect with a less expensive Geiger counter or an outrageously costly electron microscope.

Indigos however, can psychically detect and access the 'unique resonant signature' of certain individuals within groups of people without the use of such highly technologically advanced instrumentation and nearly instantaneously sense anything and everything personal about certain person. This is because everyone on the planet resonates a 'unique signature,' signature an Indigo can tap into, sort, catalog, and identify simply by using their inherent 'intuitive awareness' that provides them the propensity to do so; which got many Indigo burned at the stake in the middle-ages.

A common misbelief long held in the scientific community, is that we as humans utilize only about one tenth of our brain's total potential. Thus, many in this scientific group find it inconceivable to accept the fact that we as humans may actually have (within our genome) dormant recessive genes within our DNA; genes that once provided our ancestors with what appeared to be one or many of the 'psychic faculties.' A survival mechanism perhaps left over from when mankind needed to worry about what dangers lurked within the dark shadows of the night, helping our ancient ancestors from becoming a late night snack by some saber tooth tiger stalking the bushes over 40,000 years ago.

Have you ever had a thought of someone close to you only to have the phone ring only to discover whom you were just thinking of was that person, or say you've been brainstorming with a friend for ideas to a surprise birthday party and both of you blurt out the same concept simultaneously? Many people have. Yet most people will not give it another thought. Was this just a coincidence? Possibly, but then again, perhaps it was your own inherent 'psychic faculties' at work here, and you were completely oblivious to the 'resonant signature(s)' you may had inadvertently tuned in to.

Sure, I believe in coincidence, I've just never experienced one. I would compare a coincidence to be more like having a fender-bender in the super-market parking lot with someone you haven't seen since high school graduation. Nor, is it really a 'psychic event,' which would be more like having had a dream of the person who hit your car days, hours, or minutes before of it had ever occurred. An Indigo's experience however, although similar, would be in a much higher definition of detail, the exact time, location, make, color and model of the car, the parking space location and what damage done. Whereas a personal psychic premonition is more like 'déjà vu,' with little or no detail defined. The Indigo however, would have most likely assessed and analyzed every potential outcome to the accident to void the event (accident) entirely, instantaneously and hookup with their schoolmate in the parking lot with no incident.

What an Indigo senses is not much different from a Geiger counter reading, measuring, and assessing ionized radiation (picking up similar information) given off by certain rocks (people) within a certain radius around the device (in proximity to the Indigo Child). Just as some of these electronic devices are much more sensitive and can provide additional information going far beyond the less expensive units, Indigos too cannot just 'tune-in' into the 'frequencies harmonics' resonated by everyone in their proximity.

The Indigo's ability to read others goes far beyond the use of any 'psychic faculty' and all possess this ability to various degrees. For some it's none existent or confusing information, very much like the bleed-over of a radio transmission while traveling in the desert late at night. For others, the intensity of the 'resonant signatures' sensed of those around them from individual to individual. Yet for many Indigo, the range is boundless; from being able to not only distinguish an single person's frequency who is close by, but zero in to a specific 'resonant signature' (the person of interest) while blocking out everyone else regardless of where they are, across town or on the other side of the planet.

Sure, there are people that can be called 'psychic' who are not an Indigo however, what information they receive is most often 'residual' information from an unknown source. A 'psychic' can often only picks up on certain energy sources when they have been given a lot of information from their client (and for some psychics, their target), and are in close proximity. Most of their information is suspect at best or had already been derived and identified through extensive background research and checks long before the 'psychic' ever gives a reading and is rarely intuitive or precognitive and usually very subjective.

An 'intuitive psychic impression' is attained by the Indigo through a consciousness that spans time/spaces that provides an Indigo's an innate ability to instantaneously analyze, interpret, and recognize people by the specific 'resonance signatures' people generate and transmit providing them with an 'instantaneous awareness' to the world around them. Indigos are not 'psychics,' but can relate to the experiences of others through the universal consciousness, that for centuries they had been given the 'psychic' or 'oracle' label, when it actually goes so much further that.

Translating Resonant Signatures

Today, science and technology in Western Civilizations is on a 'fast track' that has overcome much of the religious controls imposed during the Middle Ages. In fact, over the last hundred years, there seems to be a 'symbiotic' relationship between science and technology, an era that has catapulted humankind forward with knowledge and a burning desire that continues to encourage newer technologies no longer repressed by a religious censorship.

In ages past, an 'Oracle's' reputation was often taunted by doubt, surrounded by mystery, denounced by disbelievers, embraced by advocates, and feared by the multitudes. Yet Judeo-Christian's and Islamic fundamentalists for centuries have demonstrated a great fear and respect for anyone who had demonstrated the ability to 'oracle' and 'reveal' divine communication, revelation, or disclosed prophecies of apocalyptic events from unseen forces.

Perhaps it's because religious leaders throughout history have denounced these so-called 'miracles' because they determined they were caused by nothing more than an evil and unseen 'demonic force' they could not logically comprehend; believing them to be magical diabolical spells cast upon them to instill fear and control. These ages of magic often drew a very fine line between what was considered 'angelic' or 'demonic,' and could only be ascertained as to which they were by their clerical leaders. In order to maintain control of the people, these very same religious leaders everyone turned to for answers, would elucidate the 'oracles' by instilling fear through their confusing rhetoric over what was of 'God' and what was from 'Satin' himself, in an effort to preserve a consummate ignorance over the people and tighten the Holy Church's control of them.

Galileo Galilei, a 15th century Italian physicist, mathematician, astronomer, and philosopher, and Nicolaus Copernicus, the 16th-century astronomer, had both become role models that sparked a scientific revolution against the Holy Catholic Church that lasted for over four centuries.

All because their respective Popes feared them, they labelled them as heretics who spread venomous opinions that not only challenged the Holy Catholic Church but contradicted the scriptures and teachings of the Church, and the reason both Galileo and Copernicus were tried and convicted for heresy.

Since mankind has been observing the cosmic universe, we have gained just enough scientific knowledge to inspire us to create yet another technology (telescopes) to learn even more, with newer and newer advanced technologies to better do the job, the Hubble and James Webb telescopes come to mind, as become entwined in an endless loop of enlightenment.

Another prime example would be our quest to identify our DNA 'fingerprint,' as a unique genetic map, that only opened yet another door to develop additional technologies in DNA fingerprinting. That in turn spawned further scientific discoveries that can identify specific subsets of genetic code within an individual forensically. This technology has been valuable in identifying the 'unsub (unidentified or unknown subject)' of a crime by using DNA to definitively identify a person as the most likely suspect.

It was James Clerk Maxwell (1831-1879), a Scottish mathematical physicist, who first developed a set of mathematical equations he identified as the basic laws of electricity; describing them as a phenomenon called an 'electromagnetic force (an invisible1 field of magnetism).' He later proposed that light was in fact nothing more than undulations of the same medium and the cause of the electric and magnetic phenomena in that the unification of light and this electrical phenomena he had been led to predict the existence of 'radio waves.' [47]

However, it wasn't until 1887 when German physicist, Heinrich Hertz later confirmed through a series of experiments, that demonstrated electromagnetic waves did in fact exist and they even generated what he dubbed a 'frequency.' In the papers Hertz published between 1887 and 1890, he described his results as having little or no practical significance or value. The fact that Hertz only verified Maxwell's mathematical calculations as correct, should have only given him full credit for the discovery of 'frequencies' for his part of the discovery, of which Maxwell's calculations were an instrumental part that contributed to Hertz's research. [55]

Resonance and Radio Waves

'Radio waves' travel by a principle in physics known as 'resonance,' that can best be described as the tendency of an electrical circuit (an energetic system) to oscillate at varying amplitudes. In this case, it would be the deviation of a current to generate at a 'multitude of resonant frequencies;' simply put, the driving energy force that produces the oscillations stored as a vibrational energy; very much like the natural frequencies of a musical tone generated by a violin. As the strings of the violin are subject to the action of pulling a bow across them at a certain angle, will determine the resonance each string creates; its 'harmonics.' Each string can be tightened or loosened to produce various wave lengths, when the musician applies pressure on each string with his/her fingers on the neck of the violin they are modulating their length by pressing them down, to have a specific effect that would translate the 'resonant (tone);' thus changing the sounds we hear. Changing the vibration of each string in combination would generate a chord and thus change the harmonics created.

When the violin's strings vibrate at specific oscillations, they transmit an 'energy wave' through the atmosphere (sound cannot be heard in outer space because there is no atmosphere). When another receptor receives the energy wave that can precisely replicate those harmonics into the same energetic vibrations transmitted, like the mechanics with our inner ear (eardrums), our brain can precisely processes them back into the identical frequencies the violin had originally transmitted.

However for every powerful phenomenon of nature there's usually a dark side; and resonance is no exception, as resonant energy can have some catastrophic effects. Take for example the Biblical account of Jericho. Theoretically speaking, the walls of Jericho were tumbled by an intense resonance Joshua's army had created and responsible for the walls to fracture, crumble and tumble. However, it is highly unlikely that Joshua's Israelite army could have done this amazing feat solely with trumpets.

The concept is very much like that of an opera singer with a very loud voice and perfect pitch; a voice that can vocally hit the precise note to create a frequency that can shatter a crystal goblet twenty feet away by only using a 'resonance, intensity' and 'volume.' To perform such a feat, Joshua would have required a high-tech weapon capable of focusing his army's trumpets at a specific point on the walls of Jericho, otherwise it would have had little, or no effect. Yet, miraculously Joshua's trumpeters had been able to identify the correct frequency, amplify it, and focus that wave as a beam toward Jericho to fracture stone.

The mechanism to modulate, amplify and focus such a frequency such an intense harmonic beam directly at the weakest point of a two meter thick wall of stone, and for an extended period of time, in order to crumble the walls using a harmonic principles is only now being developed by the American military. In this example, I would have to say 'yes' it was an entirely plausible concept and very possible, however highly improbable considering the era; but it does make for a good tale.

Understanding Resonant Signatures

So, where am I going with all this?

Have you ever been introduced to someone you didn't know and suddenly realize you just don't like that person? Well, there's a reason for that. People can inadvertently tune into another person's 'resonant signature' without knowing it. Then there are those who don't even have to be in close proximity to do so, the Indigo Generations.

Being able to identify another person's 'energetic signature,' frequencies created within their brain, sounds simple enough, but it's not quite as straight forward as one would think. Every human mind resonates at a specific frequency generated by the electromagnetic current within their brain, an energy created inadvertently when neurons fire a series of electrical impulses – a by-product by which specific frequencies get automatically transmitted into the atmosphere, like a radio transmission if you will.

These frequencies are what allow you to 'sense' another person's consciousness as a momentary synchronization and to receive another individual's unique signature. Some even consider the connection a form of 'telepathy' where an instantaneous exchange of information between occurs. For some, it becomes an instant distrust for no apparent reason what so ever; that little voice within your head that warns you, although grounds for mistrust have yet to be established. For the Indigo however, it is an immediate recognition of that individual not being worthy of their trust, but more on that later.

The human brain is capable of transmitting and receiving information pretty much in the same manner a radio station broadcasts a series of 'radio waves' through their transmission tower. Once into the atmosphere and depending how much energy was used, these 'radio waves' are capable of traveling for hundreds of miles through Earth's atmosphere. To tune into their transmission however, an antenna connected to a receiving unit is needed to specifically 'tune into that frequency' before it can be translated back into sound waves and heard.

We may already know local governments assign specific radio frequencies and geographic boundaries; otherwise, all you would hear is nothing but gibberish. This is because it all depends on how strong the electrical current being used to transmit is and how close we are in proximity to the broadcast.

We've all experienced 'bleed over' while driving late at night late at night, this is due to the fact that after sunset, radio stations are allowed increase their power to maximize their signal strength in order to encompass a greater broadcasting area (distance) while broadcast on the same frequency.

Since bandwidth is limited, government also assigns specific broadcast frequencies to specific stations, as well as regulate their time of operation (day and night broadcast range) and the amplitude (clarity of the signal determined by the voltage used to transmit) allowed for broadcasting; of which, these bandwidths can be identified within two distinct ranges.

We are all familiar with AM Radio (Amplitude Modulated). These frequencies ranges from between 535 kHz to 1605 kHz, and separated by an assigned 10 kHz interval range (the reason why when you search for a radio signal on your car radio you will notice the AM dial on your car radio jumps by increments of ten).

The other is the FM Radio (Frequency Modulation), which is a recognized as a 'high fidelity' broadcast signal; and broadcasts at a frequency range from between 88 MHz to 108 MHz, of which VHF television occupies the largest portion of this range.

FM radio stations are assigned a 'narrow center' within the entire frequency range known as the 'guard bands' (beginning at 200 kHz) starting at 88.1 MHz; this is to better provide a maximum of 100 overall FM radio station frequencies, with a 75 kHz maximum deviation from the center of the entire FM band width. This leaves only the 25 kHz upper and lower 'guard bands' available to minimize 'bleeding' between other adjacent frequency bands to prevent radio stations from overlapping their broadcasts. [50]

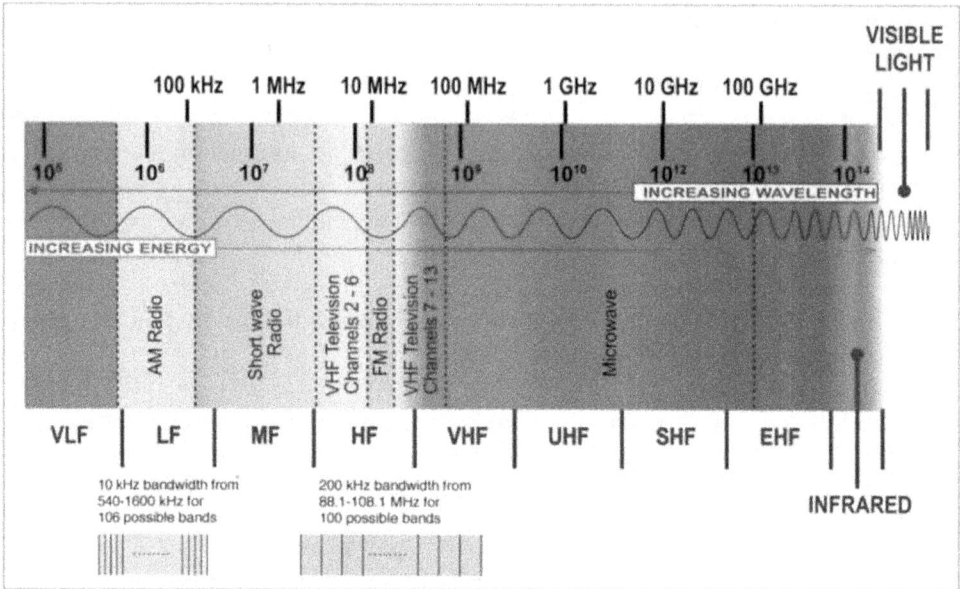

In a way, 'telepathic communication' (hearing another person's thoughts as your own without verbalization) is almost like a radio transmission of thought. Everyone has the ability to 'tune in' into another person's 'resonant energy,' regardless of where on the planet those souls are geographically located, unlike radio. The problem with experiencing a 'telepathic' connection, especially as this ability develops, would be very much like driving through a desolate desert in the middle of night. Instead of music, we hear nothing but a myriad of unbearable noise.

As each 'Indigo Generation' gets older and more experienced, they will eventually learn to fine-tune their reception quickly and effortlessly, much like a push-button selection already tuned in the correct signal on their stereo receiver, and that takes experience, a lot of it. The trick being that an Indigo has to learn whose thoughts (what stations) they are tuning into; a very difficult task indeed that requires a lot of experience doing so. [51]

Everyone on the planet has an assigned 'unique energetic signature' within his or her genetic coding set to transmit at a predetermined frequency that cannot be changed. However, what may not be active within their genome, or needs a lot of fine-tuning, is the ability to understand whose energetic signatures they are receiving, and what type of information they are receiving.

Deciphering the Confusion

As mentioned before, everyone has an inherent ability to receive what many confuse to be nothing more than a 'psychic impression;' déjà vu if you will. It is imperative that I point out everyone is capable of a déjà vu moment, but each at a different level competence, depending on their ancestral genetic makeup. Some call the ability a 'sixth sense,' others a 'gift,' and a few 'witchcraft.' As man has evolved, so has our inherent sense of 'knowing' things, to the point of being construed as 'psychic moments' (e.g. - events and outcomes before they occur, for which many believe to be nothing more than an 'instinctive response' or 'coincidence').

Regardless of what you believe, humanity has possessed the skill for hundreds of thousands of years and is ultimately responsible for our very survival as a species. It kept our ancestors from falling prey to sabre-tooth tigers hiding in the brushes hell-bent on having a meal, or from unwittingly falling into traps set by other not-so-friendly rival clans. It was that inner 'voice' inside known as our 'basic instinct,' and those who chose to ignore it often wish they hadn't.

These and other inherent coding secrets deep within our DNA coding have protected humankind from unseen dangers that have allowed us to successfully survive and multiply. Although an Indigo's 'instinctive abilities' closely represent the 'psychic faculties,' they go far beyond that. It provides the Indigo Child an innate ability to tap into what the Greeks labeled 'ethos, (the universe),' an unlimited consciousness spanning time/space; a consciousness by which every single soul in universe is part of, all acting in unison as a single collective pool of knowledge.

Our mind connects our brain as a 'genetic conduit' to a 'universal consciousness' comprised not only of every soul on planet Earth, living or not, but to every soul throughout the entire universe and without the 'linear' restrictions of time or space.

Indigo Children born today seem to have a natural 'intuitive awareness' of the 'universal consciousness' inherent in older generations and only see themselves as a 'normal' child. Older generations of Indigos however, seem to be evolving into a genetic code that is identical to their younger counterparts, who had emerged into this life with their coding already active.

Is it an evolutionary process that has gradually been activating dormant 'codons' within the older generations of Indigo, freaking them out to the point where they believe they are in the middle of a mental breakdown?
As this particular group of older Indigo's begin to receive what over the centuries has been called, 'divine communication' or 'revelation' flooding their conscious, unconscious, and subconscious minds it is often misconstrued as being a delusional psychosis of chaotic impressions that appear to have originated from an inexplicable source.

However, the reality is that it is a 'new awareness of consciousness' in the process of awakening many Indigo traits, which now bewilders and beguiles them into believing they may be on the verge of insanity. After all, during the fifties and sixties, revealing to a psychiatrist that you were hearing voices, or even worse, someone else's thoughts, ended up with a diagnosis of 'paranoid schizophrenia' for which they could have been institutionalized.

For decades, many the any of older generations of Indigo Children have already undergone the 'awakening' process may have learned to control the constant bombardment of the electromagnetic resonant signatures from every direction, as well as contend with the bombardment of emotions associated with them. They had to learn for themselves how ignore emotions that were not their own. Developing these necessary skills to control these random imprints, used to take a lot of forethought but eventually they develop a way to control them, making it a second nature.

However, the younger Indigo generations have been born with an 'instantaneous awareness' they seem to be able to control 'naturally' and 'instinctively,' perhaps because they possess a much higher sense of awareness. Eventually, for the older Indigo generations, the learning process will allow them to have the same insights and abilities as their younger counterparts.

Although, I believe myself to be from an older generation of Indigo Children born during the 'baby boom,' I have had these abilities as long as I can remember. As a child, I can remember scaring the hell out of many adults because I knew things, and could do things far advanced for my years. I also consider myself very fortunate in that I had someone who understood what I was going through and that I possessed a unique ability to connect to an unseen 'consciousness' separate from my own.

However, it wasn't until I had learned how to control my subconscious mind, that I was able to focus and discern myself from everyone else's thoughts and emotions within my proximity. Today this process comes entirely naturally to as an 'instantaneous intuitive awareness,' in that I can automatically filter out not only useless information from my own consciousness, I can clearly focus on the relevant data that is important to me and those I care about deeply.

The Emergence of Consciousness

When you think about it, as one tries to apply a scientific definition to describe what 'intelligence' is, what more than likely will become evident is that connotations denoting 'common sense' had actually been defined. Nor should 'intelligence' be confused with 'knowledge,' as anyone can recite information learned from the pages of a dictionary or an encyclopedia; and hopefully NOT from the Internet.

 Just because a person may hold multiple degrees, from the highest and most respected institutions (masters or doctorates) around the world, it does not equate to a person having any received a genetic propensity to having any 'common sense' at all or 'intelligence' for that matter. Diplomas displayed on an office wall only decree that person who received them is only capable of reciting information - often word-for-word – of their former field of studies. In a word, they're very capable of 'learning,' but really, can they 'think' for themselves?

'Knowledge' only demonstrates an ability to store information as 'learned data,' yet possess absolutely no proof what-so-ever of having the 'common sense' on how to use that knowledge. Remember, stupid becomes by what stupid demonstrates. 'Intelligence' cannot, and should never be, recognized only by what a person has been committed to memory, nor should it ever be misconstrued as 'cognitive' and/or 'intelligent.'

So really, what is 'common sense?' Common sense can best be described as the ability to instantly know or perceive information; a mental processes that recalls information from memory, or experiences, before formulating or making offering a final judgment call. However, before they do, they apply 'reason' from any lessons they may have learned in life - including emotional and apathetic experiences. This is analysis is usually done to first determine a possible outcome from any potential information available to them, and the likelihood of attaining success for final decision; long before making or even considering how to react or decide. It is an 'instantaneous awareness' that may just save a life - ask any Navy or Air Force pilot who has been in an aerial dogfight with an enemy aircraft on their six (tail) how they determined what was the best maneuver, and they'll often tell you, they just knew it without having to think!

Defining an acceptable definition for an individual who has 'cognitive intelligence' to solve a complex problem, or a series of problems with the 'intellectual capacity' to 'understand' the gravity of a situation without panicking by assessing massive amounts of data 'instantaneously,' to 'execute' the most logical solution, 'skillfully,' and 'successfully' with assurance, is difficult at best.

In fact, far more complicated than any complex mathematic formula designed; especially when trying to accurately predict an 'intelligence classification' to denote an 'IQ.' It is nearly impossible for an IQ test, to 'extrapolate intelligence' accurately through a mathematical algorithm designed to measure a person's 'smarts.' Nor is there currently test available that can assess 'stupidity.' This is because no matter how a person measures up on any IQ test, the test only measures that a person 'should' have enough gray matter between their ears to keep from doing something very stupid, or does it.

I reviewed what seemed like hundreds of studies that utilized IQ tests as conclusive proof that an average person who does well on the test will perform well in school or in a specific occupation. Certain tests went so far as to determine who was 'brighter' than any other individuals were by taking very same test. A preposterous assumption that in my opinion cannot possibly, nor adequately, been answered by a simple test.

Although an IQ test can denote if a person's level of 'potential knowledge,' well all know that intelligence is a broad term that appears to be heredity, but rarely gives and credence to a person's 'environment' or 'opportunity.' We know enough to identify the primary factors of an individual's success and failures, but not necessarily, whether that capacity to learn came from their educational background, environment, opportunities, or circumstances. What actually allows an individual to advance up the food chain or causes them to become a fodder for sharks that often includes the corporate ladder?

There is also no argument among scientists that intelligence is predominantly genetically inherited. In fact, most scientists agree that 75 to 90 percent of people thought to be intelligent, inherited genes that only provided them an inclination toward being intelligent. In study by Lissy F. Jarvik and L. Erlenmeyer-Kimling, who together compiled enough 'original' IQ studies to formulate an educated hypothesis that best determines what proportion of the IQ subjects within these studies believed 'intelligence' to be directly related to the genetic variables vs. the environmental ones?[38]

All the studies within their project had been compiled over a period of 50 years (1916 – 1966), stated that nearly all the IQ tests reviewed had been based predominately given only to 'white populations' throughout the United States and Europe (a sign of the times I suppose). Their average results indicated that 75% of a person's IQ was predominately caused by genetics, and 25% influenced by their environment. They also took into consideration several other studies to complement their findings, conducted by only three scientists whose respective names (with the results of each) were Sir Cyril Burt (82% genetic, 18% environmental, Arthur Jensen (87% genetic, 13% environmental), and William Shockley (80% genetic, 20% environmental). [39]

Given this sampling, scientists actually believed they understood how genetics factored into 'intelligence' as compared to those having a 'severely deprived environments,' however would most likely NOT deny an individual of possessing a superior I.Q., nor from a classification, based on their sampling of tests, as being an 'intelligent individuals.' However, when the tables were turned, a superior environment 'did not' allow a subject to have a 'superior intelligence,' without first having had an inherited genetic predisposition within their ancestry. A person's basic ability to perceive, solve, and comprehend are all fixed and directly relate the 'genetics inherited' from one or both biological parents. The genetic DNA structure of what we 'inherit' does not change simply because of the environmental factor we would have received through birthright.

Over the last four to five generations, an evolutionary trend seems to be taking shape regarding 'genetic predisposition.' Younger generations seem to have what can only be described as having an 'instantaneous intuitive awareness' that appears to manifest in certain individuals as an innate 'intuitive intelligence,' that cannot possibly be attributed to either genetics nor environment; an increasing phenomenon that appears to have accelerated exponentially over the last 50-60 years...With the bigger question being 'why?'

The Evolution of Intelligence

The area responsible for the process of how our human brain has evolved takes up a very large area within the cerebral cortex known as the 'neocortex.' This foremost region of the brain is composed of a complex layer of tissue that is believed to be responsible for highest brain functions; and the key component that separates us from all primates, because it allows our mind to engage in deeper level concentration to better formulate decisions and make choices; and nearly instantaneously.

Our human brain has served us fairly well throughout our history, although it has many flaws, and could have better served better if these shortcomings had been eliminated entirely; anxiety, disease, depression, and a plethora of other conditions of the brain. Recent discoveries have demonstrated how wrong many scientists were in believing humanity had finally reached its evolutionary apex to brain development. Thank goodness, many more 'die-hard' researchers didn't agree. In fact, they discovered that our brain is in a constant flux of evolution, and evolving at an exponentially accelerated rate when compared to the relatively short timeline man has existed.

In order for science to determine what the future holds in store for our brain's evolution, we need to gain a better understanding how our brain has developed and evolved through the various phases of the ages. One enigma that still exists today is that science has not yet been able to explain how humans ended up with such a large brain when compared to all the other primates. Some studies claim that recent and very significant contributions appear to offer conclusive proof that certain genetic events were, and are, responsible for many of the underlying factors regarding our brain's evolution for a concurrent emergence to an advanced cognitive capacity that far exceeds that of any of our ancient ancestors.

However, these hypotheses are not without their loopholes, some the size of category five hurricane that leaves their findings somewhat speculative. So far, geneticists have no methodologies that can definitively identify the exact genes, nor the genetic code that is most responsible for our brain's sudden burst of intelligence. Nor have geneticists been able to identify the 'codons' responsible for this evolutionary upheaval.

Instead, much of our genetic 'junk' code continues to be a mystery, and recently realized it's not junk! Simply put, in order for these scientists to characterize what function(s) are responsible for such a dramatic increase in human intelligence and cognitive ability, they must first identify the genetic code within specific genes that is responsible. Our evolution, including the individual 'codons' turned 'on, off,' or 'modified,' or any possible combinations associated with the evolutionary process, must first be identified to determine when this phenomenon began to occur. [37]

Once the human genome has been completely mapped out, identified, and cataloged we will finally be able to make that quantum leap forward to better understand which genes have been, and are responsible for everything good or bad in not only our brains, but our genetic makeup as well. As well as what else has been lying dormant and been waiting for activation since the dawn of humanity.

THE PARADOX OF INTELLIGENCE

"It is paradoxical, yet true, to say, that the more we know, the more ignorant we become in the absolute sense, for it is only through enlightenment that we become conscious of our limitations. Precisely one of the most gratifying results of intellectual evolution is the continuous opening up of new and greater prospects.

Nikola Tesla (1846–1943)

The first thing I'd like to point out is that when a person is 'ignorant,' it merely denotes they 'don't know,' whereas 'stupid' is when a person blatantly announces to the world that they are emphatically incapable of 'comprehending, knowing' or even 'understanding' they are stupid! Nor does 'knowledge' reflect 'intellect.'
Intellect is nothing more than thought functioning independently of emotion.

'Intelligence' is the capacity to feel as well as to reason; and until we approach life with 'emotion,' instead of intellect alone, or visa-versa. No political or educational system in the world can save us from the toils of chaos and destruction when it comes to 'emotion.'

'Intellect' is a complex faculty of the mind that we call 'thought.' It allows a person the capacity to distinguish, know, and understand how to develop 'reason;' a fabric of logic felt within a person's very being.

'Knowledge' however, does not engage the faculty of 'intelligence.' Anyone can recite someone else's teachings, and being 'knowledgeable' does not denote that that person has an ability to 'think' for themselves, much less a 'capacity' for acquiring any <u>new self-taught</u> knowledge because that would involve a much more complex, and a much higher mental capacity they may not possess.

When discussing 'intelligence,' it becomes important to distinguish what had been learned from a 'scholastic education' (environment) versus what is a 'natural propensity' functioning as 'intelligence' (genetic propensity). Certainly being able to read, recite and quote data, input through the process of educating one's self, reminds me of when my French instructor would say to us, "Écouter, récitent, et répétez;" listen, recite and repeat.

Yes, it can yield good grades however, does it really go hand-in-hand with being 'intelligent.' Are the two mutually absolute? We already know that 'average' students demonstrate sufficient intelligence when complimented by a little hard work and determination and perhaps yield improved grade-point averages; however a susceptibility to attain superior grades that would put them at the 'top of the class' consistently diminishes, and often dramatically, when the student falls short on 'intelligence' versus the ability to 'recite' from memory.

Additionally, the student with just an 'average' intelligence is most likely a bit more restrained from achieving superior success when tasked with more and more difficult problems that call on their 'cognitive problem solving skills,' and thus, most will likely fail. We must therefore realize that 'intelligence' is a major factor in, and correlates to, the degree of scholastic achievement a person can attain.

Many educators will admit that a student's behavior, especially regarding their demeanor, adaptation to new ideas or concepts, concentration levels, and their honesty (or criminal delinquency) potential, has been found to have an analogous association to intelligence as well.

Recently, this phenomenon, once considered a 'new age' anomaly, had been parceled over the last two to three generations of being born into the 'Age of Aquarius (a point when the March equinox point moved out of the constellation Pisces and into the constellation Aquarius, perhaps as early as the 1990s). Recently producer, director, actress and television personality Oprah Winfrey, brought this subject matter to the public's attention on her popular television talk show "Oprah;" as did the popular newscaster Diane Sawyer, and television programs like "60 (Sixty) Minutes," all of which identify these children as 'special' and somehow 'different' from the much older generations.

The media has identified this special group of 'super intelligent children,' as 'Indigo Children,' that can often be distinguished by an extensive list of characteristics that many feel would qualify them as 'unique.' These features often include several 'incredibly incorrect' distinctive physical features that seems to set them apart from 'normal' children; very large almond shaped eyes with bright colors, fair complexions (regardless of race), light brown to honey-almond or blond hair, and a demeanor that exudes confidence, charm, and intelligence; often described in essence as having an indigo 'aura.'

What is unfortunate however, many of these so-called 'Indigo Children,' are at an early age, they are often mistakenly diagnosed to have one or several severe learning disorders. Such as, Attention Deficit Disorder (ADD), Attention Deficit Hyperactive Disorder (ADHD), or an Obsessive-Compulsive Disorder (OCD), which can include mental deficiencies such as autism, dyslexia, neuropsychological, and Non-verbal Learning Disabilities (NLD).

Conditions and labels that often subject these highly intelligent children to 'special needs' programs that are 'NOT' so 'special' at all. Worse, they are often subjected to a myriad of mind-altering medications that dull their consciousness and get them put into 'special care facilities' hidden far away from society; out of sight, out of mind. All because their parents fear being embarrassed by their children as they grow older, told by doctors there is no hope for them, because they will never exceed the intellectual capacity of a three-year-old. Atrocious as it is, it's a fact.

Being Intelligent is Not Easy

Intelligent people have a tendency to be misunderstood and not just a little, but a lot! Indigo's however can take it to another level. This is because of their inability to communicate their thoughts in a manner that others can easily understand, much less comprehend. As a boy, I can remember quite a few instances when I tried to articulate something profound to several of my close friends. However more often than not, I just got that 'deer in the headlights' telling me that the vocalization of my thoughts was just too cryptic for them to understand, for which my frustrated response was usually, "Never mind."

I found myself frustrated to the point of apathy about many things that others found trivial or indifferent, yet important enough to be mentioned; at least for me anyway. I was a slave to detail, always finding something wrong that needed repair or change. I didn't take a rocket scientist to tell me I could not change everything myself and found myself quietly thinking about what others found trivial, because I got no cooperation from anyone. Thus, over time I just kept things to myself proclaiming myself an exiled outsider.

Every day I struggled throughout my young life, but never gave up on myself. Sure, I was frustrated, and to the point of daydreaming about sailing off to some desert island in the South Pacific to live the life of a hermit. Indeed, it was, and still is, quite difficult at times to fit into such a stubborn world, and faking was not as easy as it seemed for everyone else.

Many of my 'geeky' college-prep friends developed some weird anti-social quirks or tendencies that I often found quite humorous; in a good endearing way. To which I must confess, I took some liberties with from time to time, having a bit of fun with their yet unidentified condition, now noted as O.C.D. (Obsessive Compulsive Disorder). My quirks however, were very much benign compared to theirs, although I did from time-to-time talk to myself, and at times my chats ended up in an argument that I would often lose; but I never had these chats in public. These chats actually helped me think-out-loud through vocalization. I often shook my leg up and down uncontrollably under a table or desk when I was in deep thought and perhaps focused on something important…but I never really thought of these quirks as strange or weird, or not at least like the high school jocks who had IQ's five points below that of a dandelion.

Stupid kids often enjoyed reminding me when I was wrong so they could feel more 'intelligent,' a ruse to make themselves appear a bit more 'intelligent,' and they were always searching for loopholes, failures, and minute errors in a conversation with me, so they could gleefully berated me. When they couldn't find an error, they would call me a '(superlative) know-it-all,' and later would try to beat the crap out me after school. What they hadn't counted on, was that I understood physics a lot better than they did. One later afternoon, I knew four jocks were going to be waiting for me to leave the school grounds after classes. I went to the library veranda to wait it out. Removing a long song from one of my feet, I placed six or seven medium sized stones into it and put the sock into my coat pocket.

Ambushed, the leader of the group got in a sucker punch to my face. After which before he could strike again, I retrieved the sock in my pocket. I then began to spin it high above my head building up velocity before I wrapped it around his head with such a force that when the stones struck his nose it rearranged his nose. They never bothered me again.

Worse yet, I beat myself up when I just 'didn't understand' something! Although I never looked at myself as 'super intelligent,' I just understood things easier than many of my peers. I was much more imaginative and creative, but very critical of myself, especially when things were 'supposed to be difficult,' but that didn't matter regardless of how smart I was, there were and still are, things I just don't get. Many times in I lost a lot of sleep as I struggled to understand.
People believe 'intelligence' means you're able to do great things and when we don't live up to those expectations, it often leaves us feeling worthless. Intelligent

people are not always successful in life, not even often; for many, just don't feel motivated. Many times, they put so much pressure on themselves, they give up and would rather lie in bed all day, or worse, kill themselves because they don't feel they measure up to what others are expecting of them.

Many intelligent people aren't successful people, but don't choose to be tied-down by responsibility. They may even prefer to be a subordinate under people whose intellect is lacking.

Being intelligent can be a 'lose-lose' situation in terms of an individual identity. If I state openly I'm intelligent, people would classify me as an arrogant prick. If I don't reveal I'm intelligent, I then become a pretentious prick. What most people don't see or understand, is that I don't define myself as being either arrogant or pretentious, others do. It's a catch-22 situation, because if I take the time to address it, I then become pompous, so I just keep my mouth shut and move on.

Being intelligent should have given me many advantages…yea right, it didn't. It just ended up being painful.

THE EMERGENCE OF INDIGO

"A human being is a part of the whole, called by us a 'Universe,' a part limited in time and space. He experiences himself, his thoughts, and feelings as something separate from the rest – a kind of optical delusion of his consciousness. This delusion is a kind of prison for us, restricting us to our personal desires and to affection for a few persons nearest to us. Our task must be to free ourselves from this prison by widening our circle of compassion to embrace all living creatures and the whole of nature in its beauty." [21]

Albert Einstein

H.G. Wells introduced his novel, "The Time Machine" in 1895 novel, where he wrote, "There is no difference between 'time,' and any of the three dimensions of 'space,' as we perceive them, except that our consciousness moves along it." He went on to add that... "Scientific people...know very well that 'time' itself is only a kind of space."

With some accuracy Einstein theorized throughout the universe, "…space bends time and can even bend it back upon itself." Einstein also noted that the universe curves around the massive bodies in space, dragging space along behind them and creating a twist in what he called 'the cosmic fabric.' [21]

The concept of a 'universal consciousness' is not very much different than Einstein's 'cosmic fabric' theory, in that there are a countless number souls in its makeup that do not experience 'linear time' as we do. Not bound by the limitations of a humanoid body, souls don't have to adhere to the restrictions of a 'linear time or space.' Einstein said, "Space and time are modes in which we think, not the conditions by which we exist."[21]

A view also expressed much earlier by the Arabic physicist Ikhwan al-Safa, in 900 AD, when he said, "Space is a form abstracted from matter and exists only in consciousness." [22]

Knowing this, we can certainly understand then that there are certain people with an innate ability to be able to tap into events from within this 'universal' concept of consciousness others cannot even fathom. Nor do these events have to necessarily occur within our feeble understanding of the limitation imposed by a 'linear three-dimensional timeline;' for which many believe 'time' is just another dimension unlike that of a fourth dimension.

However, the human brain is quite capable of bridging into this 'universal consciousness' as a portal that spans the logic of a 'time/space' continuum. It is just another capability that allows humans the ability to know things that had not only occurred in the past, but well into the future. An 'intuitive sense' of precognition we recognize as a simple case of 'déjà vu' or a profound insight to certain 'intuitive faculties' many call our 'Sixth Sense.'

It's a very fine line between the 'conscious, subconscious,' and 'unconscious' minds, especially when it comes to possessing an 'instinctively intuitive' consciousness. Perhaps yet another reason humans have long been considered to be 'narrow minded,' What our brain will allow us to perceive in a 'conscious' state that offers us instead a very narrow perspective on how we react throughout life.

Our human mind is particularly selective in what it perceives to be important; important enough anyway to preserve and store as 'long-term memories.' As 'creatures of habit,' humans often rely on 'instinct' and not 'experience' to respond to certain stimuli and situations we encounter throughout our day-to-day existence. [21]

For that reason alone, I often turn to philosophy and western esotericism as a guide me so that I may gain a better understand as to what having an 'intuitive intellect' really means. Ask thirty people and they will most likely give you a different opinion of what 'intuition' or 'precognition' represents; depending on whom you ask. Often their view s will vary from being 'highly gifted and spiritual,' to being a supernatural and strange 'child of Satan.'

Merriam Webster defines an 'intuitive' person as being one who is "capable of being perception" or for which information is "known and recognized through intuition." With 'precognition' described as possessing, "…knowledge of a future event or situation through an extrasensory perception;" both definitions of which are ambiguous at best.

'Perceived' or 'known through intuition;' sounds very much as if it's being labeled as an 'extrasensory' method, which is not clearly defined. Simple definitions only suffice for a certain class of people and not what nearly everyone on planet would accept or believe.

Throughout history 'Indigo traits,' were most mistaken to be nothing more than a 'psychic faculty' (or 'ability'); a misnomer that doesn't even come close!

Growing Up Indigo

Although Indigo children have been known to openly discuss such abstract issues as religion, politics, justice, globalization and war, they more often than not will avoid the emotional impact of these issues; and when necessary 'dumb down' the conversation in an effort to engage others in the conversation (regardless of their age or intellect). For they know others may not be able to comprehend, much less join in the discussion.

Most parents of Indigo Children learn not to be surprised when an 'Indigo child,' (even at their earliest stages of childhood) will be discussing a topic such as Einstein's theory of relativity with you one minute, pause the conversation to fight with a sibling, and return to their conversation with you.

When this happens, it not only becomes confusing for the other children in the family, but freaks their parents as well. Yet as Leta Hollingworth, a pioneering psychologist of the early 20th century, pointed out in many of her studies of 'extremely intelligent' children, "…these outbursts and discrepancies represent a perfectly normal stage of development for these extremely talented children, and should be accepted as such; especially when it involves children believed to display a very high level intelligences."

She described her pioneering of these highly intelligent children this way; "It is especially to be noted that many of these problems are functions of immaturity. To have the intelligence of an adult and the emotions of a child combined in a childish body is bound to encounter certain difficulties. It follows that (after babyhood) the younger the child, the greater the difficulties, and that adjustment becomes easier with every additional year of age. The ages between four and nine are probably the most likely years to be beset by the problems mentioned." [57]

Today, many parents believe their 'highly intelligent' children are very much Indigo, without realizing that they themselves may be as well; which is often why they are able to assess their offspring with the same characteristics–although they were not afforded similar school curriculum programs designed for really 'intelligent' kids today.

'Highly intelligent' adults often relate to their kids, because throughout their own lives they had always felt 'different' from their peers without knowing why…they didn't fit in with the other kids. It's only when a parent come's face-to-face double dose of reality when they begin to understand the issues before them and fully understand the problem; the very same issues they tried to deal with as a youngster. Simultaneously, this forces them as parents to come to term with their own uniqueness, as well as that of their children, and perhaps for the very first time in their lives.

As a 'highly intelligent' child becomes a young adult, they will begin to withdraw, or even 'hide out' from everyone but a select few of their peers–and for a variety of complex reasons. Many people believe that since they are exceptionally intelligent and possess an uncanny 'awareness of consciousness' they would have an upper-hand advantage. Not true, in fact, they are far more likely to be scholastic failures that honor roll students and often seen as troublemakers in the classroom to the point of being well known in the after school detention classroom and summer school regulars.

However, it's not because they aren't 'intelligent.' To the contrary, it's more a self-imposed mechanism that allows them to blend in with their peers; and most likely leaves them bored out of their minds in the classroom, and it's the primary reason why many 'Indigo' children are not identified as being 'intelligent,' regardless of their high IQ scores.

Only More Questions

Many of the examples I will be sharing throughout this book are at best subjective to my experiences, and many who know me well will attest that my level of credibility is high. Precisely the reason I include not only many logical hypotheses to support my conclusions, but as valuable research information that supports the examples offered. Plausible research of a very long and arduous search for answers, all superseded by one, "Why am I different?"

Over many years I have interviewed countless parents and children who have given up, tossing their hands up in the air, simply because they had become bewildered, beguiled and bewitched by their own offspring. How they thought, how they had or had not communicated, and how they seemed to know 'things' or 'information' about people, places and events that went far beyond their young years or experiences, or were not privy to.

Parents often sought out guidance of 'how to deal' with these children, on subjects ranging from 'insubordination' to the 'paranormal and in their desperation resorted to drugging their children to a nearly comatose state; for which many in the medical profession believe to be 'unnecessary;' today, a common practice that only ends up with a much more rebellious child.

I remember when my step-mother begging my doctor, "Please give the boy a sedative to make him a LOT more cooperative?" To which he replied adamantly, "Absolutely not…but I'll give you a prescription to calm you down. You need it far more than he does."

One of the most common questions parents ask me is, "How do I know if my child is a gifted kid, or just plain strange?" I so wanted to laugh, But they were serious and it wasn't a trick question. Parents are often confused as to how their child, with such a high I.Q. (Intelligence Quotient) appears to be 'strange, quirky, nerdy,' or 'different.'

It's through observation without prejudice that 'Indigo Traits' are usually identified. 'Traits,' that can include an advanced propensity to subject matter in the arts (music, dance, and design) or advanced mathematic skills in science (astrophysics, chemistry, theoretical physics, etc.).

One particular trait that many parents often notice right out of the gate is an acute comprehension of subject matter that extends far beyond what is normal for their child's age or grade level. Parents are often left confused when their child demonstrates such an 'intuitive' understanding of a complex situation that would a lot time for an adult to calculate a 'favorable outcome' from what would otherwise seem to be an infinite number of probabilities. Yet an Indigo child can do it all in their head, without losing a beat, as they continue to play a strategic game on their Xbox with a friend that requires a high level of concentration.

'Indigo Children' often demonstrate a highly developed talent for many studies that would leave most kids crying and confused. Yet, their approach to such a high level of academia seems to be an innate ability making it almost effortless for them and why these children are often inclined into such complex fields of study; such as quantum physics, molecular engineering, advanced eukaryotic molecular genetics, quantum mechanics, or interstellar propulsion.

However, adults wanting their children to excel, because of their advanced developmental understanding on a wide range of subject matter, often forget their Indigo Child is still just a kid. A kid who loves to skate board, go to blockbuster movies, visit the mall with their friends, wrestle on the couch, and do pretty much everything else kids their ages like to do!

It's important for us to understand that although these exceptional kids may seem capable of highly advanced studies because they are Indigo, they also have the potential to take a 'nose dive' scholastically; regardless of the fact that they are fully capable of achieving perfect grades scholastically. Unfortunately, some educators believe they've reached their maximum potential, without realizing, it's because they're bored out of their skulls! Face it, most of these children have only two choices in a schools' curriculum; the 'normal curriculum' offered to the masses, or the 'special courses' labelled as 'special education' (classes for low aptitude or mentally deficient students). One more reason why it is so crucial to not only get ALL these children tested individually, but as quickly as possible before the child gives up all hope. It is only through the constant observation and the input from the Indigo Child, that a parent and the educators can tailor a successful program specifically designed to yield the most successful results for the Indigo's development.

A Final Warning

Before you go running off half-cocked to the superintendent of the school district, or begin to subject your child through a serious barrage of aptitude testing, there is a hell of a lot more things to consider.

The first of which, is that the parents must first come to terms with the realization that their child may not be an Indigo Child at all. Perhaps instead their child just a normal, yet 'bright' student at best, and possibly 'highly intelligent,' but don't really display any other traits of an Indigo Child. You'd be surprised how often a parent will see ONLY what they want to see in their child.

For this reason, parents need to set aside their own 'pride' with a reality check that could otherwise prevent them from making a grave mistake. Alternatively, their perceived Indigo child will suddenly crash and burn in dismay an failure as they fall into a great depression because they cannot possibly keep up with their parent's disillusion. Many kids put into this predicament either act out rebelliously, or attempt suicide.

When parents realize their child an Indigo Child, they will soon come to the realization that their child is NOT a 'normal' kid. When this reality sync's in, it ends up being not much different than that of a parent who has been informed their child is a 'savant' or has 'autism,' perhaps 'Asperger's Syndrome (a form of autism).' Now in protective mode, the parents begin to fear for their child and often set out on a quest to get answers, help, or advice from the experts; often turning to the pages academic publications, subject-matter books, a psychologist or psychiatrist, and even worse, off the Internet; all of these offering only contention and confusion to their dilemma. "What do I do now?"

As a child, there were no such experts or books on the subject, there was no Internet, and there were no 'special education' curriculums in public schools, and psychiatrists weren't well revered simply because very little of the phenomenon was understood. Only now is beginning to take a front seat, back then it was all a matter of trial and error. Today, there is a lot more information regarding 'extremely intellectual' and 'highly intuitive' children, but you must know where to look to find it, and once you do, even understand it. Even today there are very few qualified resources designed help identify and cultivate our Indigo Children that isn't categorized as mysticism or hocus-pocus, yet there are a few that are beginning to understand just what the hell is happening. Hopefully, if you've read this far, you can now better understand, what drove me to not only research, study and write this book, the least of which was to make sense of it all!

Distinguishing a Difference

Every child has the same basic needs, and certainly understanding those needs is the most challenging for parents and educators. Distinguishing the difference between a 'highly intelligent, special needs,' and 'Indigo' traits is not at all easy. It's like asking, "What's the difference between a car and a Ferrari, or a house and horse?"

In order to make myself perfectly clear on this topic I feel it's necessary to explain that primarily, "I despise labels;" any kind of labels. They only serve to classify and segregate, and everybody knows what happens when we humans begin to segregate anybody!

Thus, it is imperative that we all understand that the label 'highly gifted' is nothing more than a catchall-phrase tot 'elevate' and 'exalt' a child that demonstrates a scholastic aptitude; nor, should they be set apart or treated differently from any other child…Got it?

This is because a 'highly gifted' or an 'Indigo Child' could mean just about anything a person wants them to mean and therefore becomes just another ambiguous label. Because of this, I feel I am facing an ugly quagmire, for how else can I characterize either? Thus, I feel forced to use these labels myself...so please forgive me.

Defining a Child's Aptitude

A child that excels in their capacity for learning, reasoning, and understanding or other similar forms of thought usually require a high degree of mental forethought. Especially when describing an aptitude for grasping concepts differentiating 'truth from fact,' discernment with other potentially underling meaning's that 'are **not** being implied' as I attempt to demonstrate how 'intelligence' is represented within these two groups.
It's important to remember, 'intelligence' is nothing more than our ability to successfully utilize certain brain functions, how information is received, analyzed, and processed to determine its value before it gets stored within our long-term memory, and how it, determine if it's useful to store, and when it may be needed and later used.

The Awakening: an Emergence of Indigo Consciousness

The ability to correlate and process information with an advanced comprehension and understanding how to form a logical conclusion is not necessarily a second nature to the 'highly intelligent' child; it's a learned technique. However, for the 'Indigo Child' it's an innate ability the Indigo can perform effortlessly, a trait inherent most all Indigo Children.

As I pointed out earlier, being 'intelligent' in no way proposes that an intelligent person will display any 'common sense.' After all, stupid is what it is, and people with lower IQs can often demonstrate much more 'common sense' than someone with multiple doctorate degrees from M.I.T. who are purportedly intelligent!

'Indigo children' are far more than just 'super intelligent' children, they have an acute and 'intuitive awareness' that extends far beyond any intelligence level; a 'conscious awareness' that enables them to consider plausibility, probability, and possibilities, far outside of the proverbial box of 'intelligence.' So much so, their counterparts are more often than not, left in a cloud of interstellar dust wondering 'What the hell just happened!' Their level of 'consciousness' extends not only past their level of knowledge, but is not limited by dimensional boundaries that including space or time, in what appears to us to be 'instantaneously.'

A reason why many believe an 'Indigo Child' possesses not special skills, just unusual ones; that often earned them the reputation of having 'supernatural' abilities (that they don't) that had often got them burned at the stake during the Middle Ages.

It becomes essential that parents, teachers, and all learning institutions realize there is a difference as broad as Mount Everest is high and the Grand Canyon wide. Nor can any of these children's needs be ignored or swept under a giant carpet without causing some serious damage to either of these two distinct groups; 'highly intelligent' and 'Indigo Children.' Regardless of what is done, and that includes nothing at all, will assuredly affect every aspect of their 'psychological' and 'intellectual' well-being for the rest of their lives.

Understanding an 'exceptional intelligence' versus an 'average intelligence' is not at all that difficult. Liken it to an 'average' child that peers out at the night sky through their backyard telescope at the Orion Nebula. Excluding the quality of their lens Orion could simply appear to them to be nothing but a small, blurry and distorted image, almost as if it were nothing more than a smudge on the lens against the faint blur in the night sky.

Yet to a 'highly intelligent' child it would be as if they were looking through one of the most powerful telescopes on earth. The Orion Nebula to them would appear clear, crisp, and sharp, and in so much more detail, they would forget it was just a back yard telescope. Yet to the 'Indigo child' it would be as if they were viewing the very same nebulous cloud through the enhanced lenses of the Hubble telescope; they would see a clarity to detail that would go far beyond what their eyes can actually see.

Yes, both the 'highly intelligent' and the 'Indigo child' would see very similar images and with much better clarity the 'average child' and it is undeniable that all three of these children saw the same universe through the same telescope, but with very a different set of eyes. Each distinctly based on their inherent and innate abilities of comprehension and analysis…to the very same data. [30]

Although there are distinct advantages to one possessing a heightened perception of everything, and everyone them, it should be clear there are a lot more disadvantages for an 'Indigo Child' regardless of their generation.

Not very many 'Indigo Children' experience elation to knowledge they impart, they pretty much blurt it out as if it were a well-known fact, very much like Dr. Temperance Brennen on the popular television program, "Bones," they just don't know how to say it any other way. And in most cases the 'Indigo Child' will in fact most experience a discomfort and distress, by what they don't know; and rarely is there anything 'in-between' these two modalities. Balancing any of the 'Indigo' or a 'highly intelligent' child's development phases can, and often is a very daunting task, if not an impossible one for parents and educators.

I cannot stress enough the importance of establishing a support mechanism that balances these two groups of children's unique abilities and intelligence without pushing the envelope to an extreme. By this, I mean that as an adult and parent you must be willing to guide them without overinvesting your own interests over theirs; instead champion their desires and interests without taking influence over theirs. Regardless of how you approach this daunting challenge, understand it can be very expensive, emotionally draining, physically challenging, and intellectually demanding, but well worth the effort.

So, flush your own pride aside enough to realize that being the parent of an 'Indigo' or 'highly intelligent' child is not at all different from taking care of a handicapped child. Either way, you will need to provide the love, compassion, and understanding, that satisfies their special needs for intellectual input; but most of all never forget they're still 'children' and also need to engage in normal day-to-day 'kid stuff' as well.

A Decision to Test

Okay, we understand that an 'Indigo children' can comprehend, retain, and learn very quickly. Yes, they are a 'bit different' from their peers and/or siblings including many adults in their lives when it comes to intelligence, comprehension, and the communication skills. It is for this reason, and of the utmost importance, you must really prepare yourself for the wide gambit of reactions from an 'Indigo' child, even more so than a 'highly intelligent' one. Their 'awareness' and uncanny 'consciousness' of everything and everyone around them will at times seem like 'Little Einstein is on crack' when they try to engage you in a wide range of discussions; especially when it's in rapid succession.

It is important that I point out that you as the parent or teacher be considerate of any discussion they may initiate, and never promote the 'Indigo Child' to arrogance by setting them apart from any of their siblings and/or peers. They will come to know that their talents on their own terms and not that unusual or foreign to them at all, nor should any influence be addressed regarding any orientation they may display, such dexterity and/or talents. They are NOT 'special,' in any way; it is what it is, and they will develop and discover things about themselves and values that will mold them into becoming who they are, and ultimately what kind of adult they will become.

Most 'Indigo's,' regardless of their generations, are often become admired adults because as they were allowed to grow and develop naturally. Becoming leaders that possess an innate sense of humanity, fairness, and respect, and very rarely will they turn into a contemptible adult, if ever.

Moving Forward

Should you decide to move forward to determine just how 'advanced' or 'intelligent' your child is, or subject them to a barrage of tests, you MUST first understand that your child should be in 100% agreement with you request.

You may want to explain if asked that there are a number of unobtrusive and non-invasive tests that can help determine a child's aptitudes and inclinations; providing they are willing or curious enough to proceed. Under NO circumstances should an Indigo child ever be subjected, nor forced to succumb, to testing without it being 'their' idea; and should they wish to STOP participating with the testing, it is imperative that you too cooperate 100% with their request to cease all testing by honoring their wish.

Intelligence Quotient

The Stanford-Binet Intelligence Quotient (IQ) test has become one of the most significant and diagnostically appropriate exams for determining, not only a child's mental ability from extreme mentally diminished retardation but helps identify a propensity considered an intellectual genius. Originally designed to identify aptitude, inclination, and comprehension of knowledge in children, the test is still widely accepted as the standard today.

Designed by Lewis Terman and his colleagues at Stanford University, the 'Stanford-Binet' test, modeled after the examination first created by Alfred Binet in France, at the turn of the 20th century.

Lewis Terman developed his version of the IQ test after having concluded an extensive study on gifted individuals in his published work entitled, "Genetic Studies of Genius." Those who participated in Terman's study, were then analyzed and compared to their performance against the scores of the Stanford test, and the

'Stanford-Binet Scale' created from the results (based on a series of three distinct tests).

Today the Stanford-Binet IQ test is still considered to be the best single tool available for measuring a child's potential (at less than thirteen years of age) for determining the extent of their intelligence and define their overall potential; fluency, imagination, unusual or advanced concepts, logic, and the complexity of their linguistic knowledge and proper use. [31]

Today, it has become much more uncommon for many thirteen year olds to have IQ scores between 138-145, considering the 'average' has been normally between 90 and 100). Then there are those 13 year-olds who demonstrate an exceptional potential with scores that have exceeded 160. [Important note: Should any child score above 160 on each of the three standard test series – the WISC-R, the K-ABC, and the SB:FE – they will have peaked the parameters established for these test, after which, the parent should insist their child be tested by the Stanford-Binet Test form L-M. [32]

Even though many school psychologists may continue to argue that they are very well trained on the 'newer norms' – many of whom believe them to be 'better norms' – a parent should insist, NO demand that the Stanford-Binet test be given to their child. But don't take my word for it, in a recent article entitled, "Gaining Accurate Assessments of High Levels of Giftedness" by Linda K. Silverman, Ph.D. and Katheryn Kearney, M.A.Ed., they emphatically emphasize to parents raising 'highly intelligent' children, these newer tests, along with their newer norms, fall far short of differentiating a child's 'potential' only by an simple IQ score! [54]

When preteens and young adults appear to be predisposed with a higher than average 'intelligence,' it might also behoove parents to have them take a pre-admission college test known as the SAT (Scholastic Aptitude Test) required by all colleges and universities around the country. This test, designed as a standardized measurement tool to assess the most basic, and most critical skills a person will use throughout their lifetime, as it tests their reading, mathematics and writing skill levels. This standardized test also uses a standardized method during the admissions process; regarding a way to measure aptitude and important skills on the same ruler as their peers.

By testing a 'highly intelligent' thirteen year old student in the seventh grade using a better 'measuring stick,' could prove crucial in defining an academia for the 'extremely advanced' child from the overall SAT score. For example, a score above 630 on verbal section or above 700 in mathematics would be phenomenal for this particular age group. Because, when these young people can demonstrate such an advanced aptitude with a high SAT score, colleges and universities will trip all over themselves to secure admission of that child into their institution. To the point they may even provide a tailor-made acceleration programs specifically designed to coincide within that child's regular school program, that is specifically designed and appropriate for a 'higher intelligent' child at their specific grade level.

'Highly advanced' children with IQs around 130, unfortunately often fall into an 'average' course of study by being put into curriculums alongside their peers that were originally designed for students with an 'average intelligence.' However, it's a fact that educational requirements do vary greatly between a 'below average,' an 'average,' an 'intelligent,' and a 'highly intelligent,' child whose IQs can ranges can vary from very low to off the chart.

Determining an appropriate program for an 'Indigo' child will have an entirely different set of challenges. That's because the intelligence of an 'Indigo child' will need a development program that tantalizes their abilities and keeps them engaged. Because they are at a much higher level of awareness of the world around them, the 'what, why,' and 'how' of what they 'sense' and 'feel' is far more acute than that of their peers.

Any parent of an 'Indigo child' will tell you, their child seemed to accelerate intellectually faster and displayed innate abilities than other children their age found difficult to understand, much less keep up with. This is because when an Indigo Child processes information, they do so in greater depth, and with an increased sensitivity and precipitancy that appears to everyone else to be an uncanny 'awareness' that not only falls short for a 'extremely intelligent' child, it leaves the 'normal' child out in the cold wondering what the hell just happened.

There is even evidence however, that suggests the social, and emotional development skill of an 'extremely intelligent' child differs drastically in intensity from their 'average' counterparts. Every parent of an 'extremely intelligent' child knows all too well, that their child can fly off the handle when exhibiting an emotional outburst that often borders the extreme, and is often far more dramatic than their 'average' siblings or peers could ever imagine; from euphoria to despair.

Knowing this, one would expect an 'Indigo' child's emotional output to be way off the chart, right. Well that would be wrong! As it turns out, it's just the opposite. An 'Indigo' child's reaction is often one that closely resembles the emotions a mature adult and is definitely far beyond their years.

Measuring Intelligence

The Stanford-Binet Intelligence was developed back in 1905 when Alfred Binet began working with Theodore Simon, a physician who had designed a different way to 'measure intelligence' in children; specifically to identify those who were considered severely 'retarded (his words not mine being politically correct is current politeness),' while others were not. Based on their joint research, they discovered a child not only got taller, as they got older they developed a much higher 'cognitive mental capacity.' The test allowed them to analyze which tasks the normally functional children could perform so he could better determine what would be considered commensurate for their age; a way to verify an 'average mental aptitude.' The test was capable of verifying what specific 'equivalent-grade level' best corresponded within the appropriate range, basically qualifying them as having an 'average range level;' and how it measured up to what would have been an 'expected intelligence level' compared to their chronological age.

What Binet and Simon were surprised to discover, was how many children actually performed at levels far 'below' their expected mental developmental at their chronological age, to some totally, inept and incapable of exceeding the mental capacity of a normal child. For example, a small percentage of 6-year-old children could perform mental tests at the equivalent age of an average 8-year-old, while most could perform a 6-year-old task and problem solving like other 6-year-olds, with a smaller percentage group that would most likely never perform better than a 4 year old, or 6 year-old would.

Their initial conclusion was that some people are just more intelligent than others, which only sparked an even more burning question, "What exactly is 'intelligence' and how can it possibly be measured?" Their specific interest was to identify why it is that some children were determined to be "retarded," and what, was the root cause! Their brainstorming, led these two researchers to go on and develop a scoring mythology that became the "Binet-Simon IQ Test," their hope of designing a method to measure child's intelligence in relation to their chronological age and growth.

Although the Binet-Simon IQ Test is not in use today, it did lay important groundwork for the way intelligence (IQ) testing and what influence it played on the development of the analysis tools we use today. Binet however, did not believe this type of 'psychometric instrument' was very useful in measuring single, permanent, or inborn levels of 'intelligence quotient (IQ).'

Stressing its limitations, Binet and Simon suggested that 'intelligence' is far too broad a concept to be able to quantify it by a simple number simply because he believed that intelligence can be influenced by so many different factors, that over time can change. What they needed to identify was the 'fundamental need' that would compare the intelligence of children within the same age group, same stage of development, similar backgrounds, similar education systems, and even identical environmental factors in order for it to be even remotely accurate. [77]

Alfred Binet was able to ascertain from all his testing groups, was that the population as a whole and by definition had an IQ that averaged roughly around 100; once entered adulthood; based on a scale from between 0 and 200. He did on occasion discover that some children within his control group (no mention of their age in his study) had reached a level that amazingly exceeded a score of 250; with an even smaller percentage of young adults between 19 – 29 years old averaging only between 89 to 111 (approximately 4-5% of his control group).

Overall Binet determined by his study, that approximately 50% of the population of the United States had IQs levels between 89 and 111; that percentage however increased dramatically to 80% when he widened the IQ range by extending the range to between 80 to 120 points. About 10% fell below the average of 80 points and 10% exceeded 120, with less than 1%, coming very close and even surpassing 250 points. [77]

For Americans taking the test in 2012, the test scores had been adjusted (a bit narrower) since 1905. The average IQ score for young Americans between 19 and 29 years of age, the low IQ average increased from 89 to 91, while the higher average dropped dramatically from 111 to 99, so during that 107-year period normal changed to between 91 and 99.

Consequentially averaging IQs today is a bit different than it was in the Binet study of 1905. Other determined measurement classifications today include the follow categories: [78]

'Mentally Disabled' – below 84;
'Average Intelligence' – from 85 to 114;
'Above Average Intelligence' – between 115 to 129;
'Moderately Gifted Intelligence' – from between 130 to 144;
'Highly Gifted Intelligence' – from 145 to 159;
'Exceptionally Gifted Intelligence' – from 160 to 179; and
'Profoundly Gifted Intelligence' – from 180 or higher

(Writers Note: Between 115 and 144, is considered 'super intelligent,' while anything above 145, could qualify an 'Indigo Child.')

It is estimated that IQs today that are below the norm of 85 points, accounts for approximately 24% to 28% of the population; far above the 1905 scores, which came in at a very conservative 3% then. As far as the IQs above 160 points, there is still a lot of conflicting information regarding what statistics are available with any surety, and riddled with many inconsistences, meaning anything the researcher wanted them to mean. My conservative estimate however, garnered from dozens of reports, I would estimate scores between 115 to 180 to be around 29% to 32%, and scores above 180 to be roughly be around 10%, with less than .01% having a score above 180 (all percentages within a 3% margin of error).

A MENSA Alternative

The word 'Mensa' in Latin translates to mean 'table;' and was adopted by an organization established by Roland Berrill and Dr. Lance Ware, both attorneys with an affinity toward science, was founded shortly after World War II in England as a 'round-table' society that transcended race, color, creed, national origin, age, politics, educational, or social background.

Their objective; to establish a society of 'highly intelligent, creative, and bright' people whose only qualification was determined by their IQ. The goal then was as it is now, as to organize the brightest minds in the world into a politically free society, free of the two major distinctions; politics that had divided the world for centuries and religion, comprised of people from people all over the world and from every walk of life. Both of which have been a major contributing cause to the countless wars around the globe for millennia. Their only membership requirement is to have an IQ in the top 2% of the planet's population, for the sole purpose of interacting, socializing, and enjoy each other's intelligent company.

Members range from as young as two years old to over a hundred, with most between being between 20 and 60, with educations from preschool and high school dropouts to multiple doctorates. The organization spans all social classes from welfare to multi-millionaires; occupations include artists, university professors, truck drivers, aerospace, physicists, teachers, firefighters, computer programmers, laborers, and housewives–to name just a few.

MENSA understands 'IQ' scores are not only widely divided and poorly defined; often using different and confusing scales. A result of 132 on one test can be equivalent to another IQ test score of 148, with many tests not even using an IQ score at all. Mensa however, set to cutoff at the top 2% of the population (regardless of the test) to avoid any confusion. Candidates taking the Mensa test must simply achieve a score at or above the 98th percentile on any standard test that measures intelligence; meaning that to become a Mensa member the applicant must attain a score that is greater than 98% of the general population, and a good way to identify a child protégée, is in fact Indigo.

As discussed earlier, most IQ tests don't really measure a subject's 'cognitive ability.' Simply put, it's a child's ability to solve and understand problems and concepts that go far beyond a just a solution, and include perceptions, relationships, and an associations between patterns, numbers, and structures, and includes the ability to store and retrieve information from a number of solution possibilities, in the shortest possible time.

Many cognitive questions included in the Mensa test assess an applicant's 'spatial' ability to visualize, manipulate, or recognize a variety of shapes or combinations of various objects, often accomplished by using highly advanced 'mathematical' skills to identify any differences. The exam includes; simple to complex mathematics that require an understanding of advanced logic and analysis, a 'language' competency that allows the subject to complete incomplete or jumbled sentences, word recognition when letters within a word are rearranged, removed, inverted, mirrored or reversed, and 'Memory' recall from lists of items or numbers presented both visually and orally.

Before you subject your 'highly intelligent' child to a barrage of clinically applied IQ test procedures, have your child attempt a sample Mensa test on-line to establish if your child displays a propensity of being more intellectually advanced than their peers. Not to mention, they will find the Mensa test quite enjoyable, because many of the questions on the test will appear as nothing more than a simple barrage of puzzles. [86]

Education is Crucial

Obtaining an accurate assessment for an 'Indigo' child is crucial for both the parents and the schools their child attends. It can provide a better understanding of a child's intellectual, social, and emotional requirements, both personally and educationally.

Schools rarely realize, much less understand the needs these highly advanced children require to remain engaged in their education. Not necessarily surprising, especially since 'extremely intelligent' and 'Indigo' children have been, until recently, the least-studied and are the most misunderstood group of children in education systems across the planet; often ignored, or worse, misdiagnosed with a multitude of 'learning disabilities' instead of having been identified with an 'intellectual acuteness.'

Unfortunately, teachers are ill prepared to recognize, understand, or demonstrate the most basic knowledge of being able to identify the requirements these children require. Nor any of the many unique issues and problems, these kids encounter every day in a world that goes far beyond the 'normal' realm of growing up as a 'normal' teenager; because they're not.

Another quagmire most school systems with 'gifted programs' have, is that most of teachers involved within these programs most likely do not have even the most basic knowledge, much less or experience, to identify many of the nuances of a 'highly intelligent' child from those of a 'mentally challenged, deficient' or 'Indigo' child; let alone teach any of them effectively. Understanding this as a parent, can assist them in working with school systems, and cooperatively work together, to elicit the proper support for a 'highly intelligent' or 'Indigo Child.' Thus empowering them to ensure the school system where their child is enrolled, develops not only programs that support their child's scholastic development, it encourages 're-educating the educators,' and on a regular basis.

An 'Indigo or highly intelligent' child's upbringing can pretty well get quite intense at times, while still being a rewarding experience. In that this particular group of children, tend to be much more demanding than that of any of the other 'average' or 'mentally challenged' children in the curriculum of a school. What may entertain a 'normal' kid, and I use this term loosely, would most likely bore the 'intelligent' children to death; especially Indigo children since they tend to be so much more demanding.

Raising the bar for these 'intelligent' offspring, can certainly be a daunting and very expensive proposition at home and their school. Their curriculums would need to be academically more challenging than those proposed and offered to all the children. Let's face it; a school district's curriculum's assumes every kid in school is 'average;' from kindergarten through graduation.

In the school district's defense, many 'highly intelligent' are accelerated, in that they may skip a grade, or grades, from K–12 at such a quickened pace that it can put them into a university long before they've even gone through puberty. There is no doubt that caution has a place when considering advancing any 'intelligent' child prematurely through a curriculum. Early admissions to any institution of higher learning is also not ready, nor are these institutions any more capable coping with these young children either.

When assessing the expenses involved for caring for a minor away from home, most parents find the unexpected expenses skyrocket quickly, and can put the family into an unexpected and premature financial crisis. Especially, after one factors how much faster the expense of caregivers for a minor aged children living away from home can escalate; housing, food, lodging, medical care, and transportation. Regardless of how much assistance a student receives in grants, scholarships or financial aid it's NEVER enough.

Expect the Unexpected

Add to this the 'unexpected timing' that not only throws the family's financial budget into a tailspin because there simply is no time to allow the parents enough time to build the necessary funding to support their child, there's a a psychological factor to consider as well. Mothers in particular will have the toughest time preparing emotionally in letting go of their child prematurely, as the trauma is not much different that losing a child. In this case however, by accelerating a premature departure of their 'baby' from the nest can result in a very deep depression psychologist's refer to as an 'empty nest' syndrome. Both parents will come to realize too, that they will miss their child growing up with their family, friends and siblings; playing sports, going to a school events, learning to drive, their first love, their prom, and their graduation.

It is therefore crucial that the family carefully weigh the benefits of an early admission to consider the financial impact of part-time vs. full-time attendance. Most of all 'creativity' is the key to being flexible in finding a solution that the entire family can live with. [58]

Parents are often left feeling frustrated and cheated, as they will no longer have a full-time part their child's life, all because they cannot provide the educational stimulus their 'baby' needs growing up. Because of this, the family, including siblings, will often go through what psychologists call, 'separation trauma,' that is not much different that losing a child to an accident or illness. For this reason, it becomes critical that the entire family be in total agreement BEFORE submitting any of their children into an early college education. For it must not only be 'the right' decision, it must be a collective family agreement.

Then as a family unit, and individually, give themselves sufficient time to prepare for the separation; including the 'Indigo' youngster leaving the family. 'Separation anxiety' is an entirely normal phase all families go through when a child leaves home, the only difference here is in the timing of when and if it happens. [33]

AN EMERGING CONSICOUSNESS

"How can a three-pound brain, contemplate the meaning of infinity, or even question its own place in the cosmos? Especially awe-inspiring is the fact that any single brain is comprised of atoms once forged in the hearts of countless; far-flung stars billions of years ago. These atoms now form a conglomerate- your brain- that can not only ponder the very stars that gave it birth but can also think about its own ability to think and wonder about its own ability to wonder. With the arrival of humans it has been said, the universe has suddenly become conscious of itself; THIS is truly the greatest mystery of all."

"What Makes Us Human" - V.S. Ramachandran

For those of you who skipped the science behind defining what may be the reason to an evident emergence of an 'Indigo Consciousness,' you may want to return to it once you have satisfied your curiosity as to what defines an Indigo Child. For those of you that forged through all my scientific explication, I would first like to thank you for your patience. I hope that at this point, it's starting to make sense.

For those of you who were anxious to see how I had defined 'Indigo Children,' and what 'consciousness' really is, and what specific traits may identify a child is indeed an 'Indigo Child,' this is where you need to be. However, understand there will be times you may need to reference the Science, Logic and Reason portion of this book. It may be a bit more enlightening and relevant to understand just how all this has come about.

Aspiring Islands of Genius

I will start out by stating that all of the recent 'Indigo Generations' seem to all share an innate sense of attributes that can only be described as an 'awareness' derived from a higher 'intuitive intelligence.' One such creative restraint I have encountered many times over during my lifetime, be it during my educational or professional career, there were many limitations authority figures attempted to impose on me (and not with great success), all I was sure were hell-bent on stifling my imagination. All were futile, lame attempts to not only limit creativity, but also limit how and what to think. I'll be the first to admit that many may see and believe my logic is somewhat 'twisted;' and to many it is, but it is no different from a two-sided coin; I find other people's login is often for much more confusing than my own.

Jacob Barrett

Recently on YouTube, I discovered the story of a young man named Jacob Barrett. From the early age of two years old he had been diagnosed 'Asperger's Syndrome;' a moderate to severe form autism. Devastated by the news, his mother Kristine was not painted a pretty picture by his diagnosis, "Your boy will most likely never even be able learn how to tie his own shoes, much less read, and will always live in his own little world; one that will require special care throughout his entire life." This, of course, left her feeling quite despondent, sensing the experts had just written her son off as hopeless.

Fortunately, for Jacob, Kristine refused to accept the grim diagnosis and set out to prove them all wrong by attempting to tap into his world, "If he cannot be in mine, then I had to find a way to get into his." Not only did her efforts have profound effect on her life, it transformed Jacob's life forever. By the time he was nine, he had become a Princeton University professor, and enthusiastically described a series of mathematical models he had built that expanded on Einstein's theory of relativity; it was groundbreaking.

At ten years old, Jacob had been formally accepted to attend Indiana University-

Purdue University in Indianapolis as a full-time student and shortly thereafter even hired on as a paid researcher in the field of 'condensed matter physics.' His original work in physics set a new record for Jacob, in that he had officially become the world's youngest astrophysics researcher to date. His thesis, on improving the manner by which light travels, broke new ground on the subject and after he submitted his work to the scientific journal "Physical Review," subsequently, after publication, his work was shared not only with other physicists at the Smithsonian. His published work even got him noticed for scientific review from NASA, Harvard University, and several other colleges and universities.

Since Kristine first began her long and difficult journey to prove the doctors wrong, she has watched her son Jacob blossom and flourish into quite the boy genius. In fact, at only twelve years old Jacob's I.Q. was higher than that of Albert Einstein's; a whopping 189. Jacob has also received a nomination for a Nobel Prize on his work in theoretical mathematics, while still wrapping up his master's degree in quantum physics at UIPUI.

I highly recommend a book written by his mother, Kristine Barnett, entitled, "The Spark: A Mother's Story of Nurturing Genius."

Today, Jacob is studying at the Perimeter Institute, in one of the most comprehensive master's degree programs in the country, alongside some of the brightest students in the world, most of who are quite a few years older than he. Modestly Jacob said during a television interview in Waterloo, Canada, "There are a lot of people that appear to be amazed by my story, but in my opinion I'm just a 15-year-old who's very motivated about his subject. I got started early and I know what I want to do."

While watching one of Jacob's YouTube early videos entitled "Forget What You Know," (which he made at the ripe old age of eleven during a lecture organized by the educational group TEDx addressing a group of students), Jacob made a an opening statement that only exemplified what I had always felt growing up as a boy, "Forget what you know... 'STOP' learning and 'START' thinking! Don't take for granted everything that is already out there; because in order to succeed you must first look at everything with your own unique perspective and not settle in accepting straight facts."

Jack Adraka

Jack Andraka, a fifteen-year-old freshman in high school who loves to mountain bike, kayak or whitewater river raft, loves science most of all. Aside from being a big fan of "Beavis and Butthead, Family Guy" and "The Simpsons," this young man's passion for science allowed him to create a revolutionary pancreatic cancer diagnostic test that is not only 168 times faster and over 400 times more sensitive, it can also detect ovarian and lung cancer in approximately five minutes. This non-evasive test is also 26,000 times cheaper than the current 60 year-old diagnostic test in use today (approximately 3 cents) and very non-evasive. His science-fair project invention won Jack the winning title at Intel's 2012 ISEF.

"I'm incredibly excited. It's like the Olympics of science fairs. It's just amazing to be here,' he said, "even if I don't get a prize." Which he did, and received a cash Grand Prize of $75,000 along with over $25,000 of smaller prizes that Jack plans on putting toward his college education. [43]

Jack's interest in finding a better 'early-detection diagnostic test' came after a very close family friend had died of a pancreatic cancer that could have been cured had it been detected with a very expensive test that costs in the neighborhood of $800 and is not usually covered by most health insurance policies, much earlier. Not to mention this test was 'NOT' designed to detect pancreatic, ovarian, or lung cancer during their early stages when they are most treatable.

A solution that came to him during a high school biology class as he secretly read an article on carbon nanotubes during his instructor's lesson on antibodies. Nanotubes are fullerene molecules that a cylindrical or toroidal shape – much like a doughnut – composed wires so small and attached in a hexagonal pattern that form a microscopic tube that have been used on building tiny transistors for processors. It was then Jack had an epiphany, when he was able to combined what the teacher was teaching with what he had just learned about nanotubes, that he was able to visualize, and later create, his early detection test for Pancreatic cancer.

When Jack Andraka searched the Internet using Google, he discovered several free online science journals that allowed him to develop, plan, and formulate a budget. Jack then searched out, and contacted, approximately 200 experts; including research facility's at Johns Hopkins University and the National Institutes of Health with a proposal requesting lab time in their facilities. Of these all his submissions, he received 199 rejections, and 1 letter of acceptance. It was from Dr. Anirban Maitra, a professor of pathology, oncology and chemical & biomolecular engineering at Johns Hopkins School of Medicine, who was fascinated by Jack's idea and worked on his concept on all his free time, after school nearly every day, weekends and holidays in Dr. Maitra's lab until he was able to successfully develop the groundbreaking test.

What I found most surprising about this young fifteen year-old, was that he had absolutely 'no medical experience' in his young life. Yet all he heard everyone in the industry telling him, was, "It can't be done." Yet Dr. Anirban Maitra saw not only a vision in this young man, he saw a young man with passion and chose to give him a chance.

One has to ask why billion-dollar pharmaceutical companies had not yet developed a cheaper diagnostic test. I can only guess, because literally there would have been little or no profit with this technology.

Is Jack an Indigo? I cannot honestly answer that, although I suspect that he is. All I know is that young people today are encouraged by newer technologies and information that was unfathomable fifty years ago. Jack did have the drive, ambition, and intelligence to demonstrate he knew what was right and what was wrong. He fought diligently and passionately for what he believed in and what was the right thing to do…definite demonstrating a strong 'Indigo trait.'

My Own Little World

Over the years, I had often felt my creativity was being stifled, to the point I had become much more rebellious to authority. So much so that I had often tagged as being a 'rebellious outsider,' one that liked to stir the pot and upset the apple cart; the 'status quo;' and did so often with a vengeance. One report card I remember getting in the third grade my geography teacher defined me as "not being the brightest crayon in his box of Crayola's."

The incident that earned me this capricious comment was after she had rolled down a map of the world to begin her geography lesson. Mind you, she was boring as hell, and spoke in a low monotone voice that could have put a room full of insomniacs into a coma.

I intently began to stare at the continents on the map. In so doing, I couldn't help but notice how they all seemed to fit together like a jigsaw puzzle. In my mind, I literally began to see the continents slowly floating into a single landmass on the chart before my eyes. Granted at eight-years–old, my mind often seemed to wander, but now I began to think I needed a new pair glasses. Removing my glasses, I began to squeeze both eyes tight as I tried to clear my vision. Then suddenly, and without warning I felt an intense pain on the back of my head when the teacher broke her pointer over my head in an attempt to get my attention. "You're staying after school for detention. Pay attention!" Miraculously, when I looked at the map again, the continents were back in their original positions.

During my incarceration, the headmaster made a quick appearance to log the students in detention, to notify our parents; in my case, my evil stepmother. Staring down at me, she said in exasperation, "What the hell are you here for this time?"

When I got home, my father asked me in a decent voice what had happened.

"I was thinking how all the continents used to be part of 'one big continent' that broke into pieces and floated away from each other." He of course just chuckled at my response and asked, "And why on earth would you think something like that?" "I think earthquakes shook them apart and opened up a lot of volcanos." I stated like an expert geologist or volcanologist.

"Uh huh," obviously humored he added, "and then what?"
"And then just like the ice in the harbor breaks apart during spring, the pieces all

floated apart to where they are now."

My stepmother came in and again began to ridicule me as if I weren't even in the room. "Any 'normal' kid can see how stupid notion that is, and if he ever want to make something of himself, he better start paying more attention to what your teacher is teaching and stop day dreaming. Then maybe, he'll learn something!"

Today of course, we all know about 'continental drift' and 'plate tectonics,' and the major force that drove the continents apart from a single continent known as "Pangaea."

Although I maintained excellent grades throughout my education, and I had a higher than average IQ, I was not always scholastically at the top of my class. Simply because I dared to 'think' outside the box for myself, as I continued to refuse conforming to become what many of my teachers and headmasters (all of whom got to know me well) defined as what is 'normal,' thus I was labeled 'rebellious.' All because I had demonstrated an 'intelligence' that allowed me to 'stop learning' and 'start thinking' for myself.

In Retrospect

I became rebellious only because I distained teachers and professors who commanded compliance of authority over me as if they had been yielded the same golden sword Saint Michael used to fought off his dragon nemesis. In my defense, I found the rudimentary methodologies used to teach me from grade school through university were not only lacking, antiquated, and remedial; they bored me out of my skull!

Many of my teachers drew the line quickly with me, often 'throwing down the gauntlet' when they raked me over the proverbial coals for daring to challenge their teaching methodologies (not that they had any) or their authority. They never realized they were clueless while commanding repetitive exercises and work assignments were not only mundane; they suffocated my ability to 'think for myself,' which is precisely why I had refused to complete any homework assignments. In my opinion, the homework assignments actually reflected their skills (or lack thereof) and their ability to teach. Although I always seem to get great grades on my testing scores, I never did any of the homework. So would end up with an average grade. I was of the opinion that if the class got failing grades, it was not their fault. The teachers were just incapable of teaching and failed the students.

While still in the 10th grade, my school counselor had gone to the headmaster in defense of my 'average' grades and informed him, "There are several students that need much more stimuli than the standard prepared curriculum can offer the much brighter students; because their level comprehension often exceeds that of their instructor. They need 'mentors,' to encourage and guide them to learn, not teachers forcing them to recite and mimic procedures. In fact, they are often far more advanced scholastically than many of their peers."

When I entered the 11th class, my counselor and the headmaster had been instrumental in creating an experimental curriculum approved by the Board of Education as an experiment for ten 'highly intelligent' students; all chosen from the results of the 'Stanford-Binet IQ' tests.

Three 'mentors' had been assigned to us, whose main objective was ensure our course of study be selected from a list of approved subject matter curriculums that met the government's requirements to graduate.

As a group, the board often referred to us as the 'free thinkers.' No longer were bored with curriculum and we all had wonderful time learning; all this because we had finally been allowed to be the free 'thinkers' we were. In fact, we had exceeded the district's expectations, as they watched the group excel to the top of the class. As far as I know, this curriculum is still in use today.

What academia lacked then, and lacks now, is the realization that 'Indigo children,' long before their teenage years, will begin to experience a form of 'existential depression;' common with nearly all teenagers, not just the 'Indigo' teen. Let's face it teenagers already face the scary world when it comes to dealing with relationships, peer pressure, orientation, class loads, and home life. Then throw in there a multitude of other issues that can plague their young minds and you'll get a good idea.

The difference with an Indigo Child's depression is that it is a much more dismal feeling accentuated by an abysmal feeling of total helplessness – ranging from sheer sadness to an utter despair– often to the point of committing suicide.

I was lucky, as I myself had never suffered any form of depression as a teenager, manic or otherwise. I was however, prone to insomnia; and still am. Even today, I rarely enjoy a good 'Rapid Eye Movement' sleep; and when I do, I often suffer from a reoccurring myriad of intense nightmares, and an intense fear of falling back asleep because the dreams usually continue from where they left off. 'Indigo teens' that suffer nightmares will also tell you, they often have an inexplicable sense of foreboding after the dream that affects their waking hours, an issue that has plagued countless generations of Indigo children over the generations.

RECALLING OUR PAST

"Life can only be understood backwards; but it must be lived forwards."

Soren Kierkegaard - Danish Philosopher

'Déjà vu' is that unexpected feeling that we had experienced an event once before (a subject I cover in more depth later), but, what many don't realize, is there is a lot more to this phenomena. There are also other categories associated with a 'déjà vu' moment. These include:

- **'Déjà vécu'** – an event one had already experienced;
- **'Déjà senti'** – a feeling perhaps brought about by a specific sound, voice, music, or song without knowing why; possibly an emotion; and
- **'Déjà visité'** – the recognition of a familiar object or place, as being recognizable or not; one of which you should have no recollection of at all.

Perhaps the connection is neurological, which could explain the phenomena as vague? What Stevenson and Tucker suggested is that they may very well be nothing more than a 'fleeting memory' of a past life.

Night Terrors

Often, and at an early age, an 'Indigo Child' may be plagued by nightmares – many reoccurring periodically – during certain periods of rapid eye movement (REM) sleep. As they get older and are able to verbalize, they often relate their feelings of a horrendous terror that goes far beyond a child's fear of the boogieman; a distress often accompanied by such an extreme anxiety it leaves the child despondent. Many of whom have communicated some fairly detailed and remarkable tales of the people, places and/or events in their nightmares that at times were not only identified, but verified as a past life experience; often of their dying experience.

Over half the population of the planet believes in reincarnation to some or are open minded enough to not entirely rule out the possibility that this phenomena may actually exist – many of which have no empirical evidence to support it; although, there are several well documented cases of late that appear to have proven it. One way or the other many of the stories related by these 'highly advanced' children are quite compelling and detailed testimonies. Many of which are filled with convincing information, in that the child could not have possibly made the information they share from the 'night terror' as the imagination of their young subconscious minds; and the reason these children's nightmares are believed to be recollections of 'past-life memories;' and perhaps their own death.

A Dream or Reincarnated Experience

For thousands of years, cultures from every corner of the world have believed in reincarnation; ancient Samaria, Egypt, and Greece to the great civilizations of the Mayans, Aztecs, and the Incas in the Americas. All these civilizations believed, our soul's path is not only determined from its past lives, it also influences the destiny of their current life; the various and complex aspects required to define the soul's intellect, emotion and psychological makeup.

On a personal note, from the four frequently reoccurring nightmares I experienced since I was three and well into my mid-twenties, I'd have to say I totally concur with this assessment.

In his book, "Children Who Remember Previous Lives: A Question of Reincarnation," renowned researcher and author, Dr. Ian Stevenson, references several cases from the 2,600 cases he had documented over the last 40-years. His assessment also offers some very compelling evidence behind a child's earliest childhood memories. [44]

However, it wasn't until I read, "Return to Life: Extraordinary Cases of Children Who Remember Past Lives," by Jim B. Tucker, who took it upon himself to pick up where Stevenson left off. His work constructed a much more conscientious mountain of evidence that seemed to transcend only recycled memories, by going far beyond our simple understanding of the barrier imposed through death. His analysis meticulously offers up a very plausible theory based on his, and Stevenson's, well-documented research. He eloquently explains that our consciousness that can actually transcend space/time; for it is an eternal aspect of a greater 'universal consciousness.' [45]

Both these books appear to be addressing the enigma of an emerging scientific paradigm, as they both suggest that when our 'soul' moves on after death, it actually becomes part of a much greater 'universal consciousness.' It is therefore conceivable that when, and if our soul returns for another round of life, we will bring with it many of the experiences, attributes, skills, and characteristics we had learned in the last; each helping shape our personality in this life.

As a child, I had many strange and familiar memories I believed were experiences spawned from several of my reoccurring nightmares – often of the places my past lives may have lived and how they died.

Although my father used to try to calm my 'night terrors' by claiming my dreams were nothing more than a bad dreams and that they weren't real, but, I knew different – they were real to me. My grandmother was the only one that was able to calm those nightmares and told me one time, "Perhaps they're clues of your soul's past…" it wasn't until much later in life that I began to understood what she had been trying to tell me all along.

After some grueling meetings in Zürich (Switzerland) with a client, I decided to relax by exploring Zurich's old-town, the 'altstadt.' What I discovered was extremely profound for me, and was my very first time. As I walked through the winding streets, I was suddenly overcome 'déjà visité;' I knew where I was! No matter where I turned, at all times I was strangely familiar with my surroundings among the 17th century buildings.

As I walking toward the river on Glockengasse (on the west side of the river), I decided to proceed toward the old 'Operahuas (Opera House)' on the east side, by Lake Zürich. As I made my way past some of the very old buildings, many built between the 12th and 17th century, I suddenly became overcome with a deep sense of foreboding.

Although it was moderately cool, it wasn't cold, but I had begun to shiver uncontrollably and felt terribly cold. In one of my reoccurring nightmares, I would dream I was on my way to deliver some very important music to the Opera Haus, sometime around the mid seventeenth century. Tired and overcome, I remembered how difficult it was for me to breathe in my nightmare. When I stopped to rest in the alcove of the building, away from the strong winds of blizzard, I huddled in the corner of a doorway, finally feeling warm I fell to sleep and died of pneumonia.

As I stood in the front of the same building that over 300 years ago I had taken refuge from a blizzard from, I suddenly became overcome by such an intense feeling of loneliness; a deep emotional sorrow of having died alone, and unnoticed, in this very doorway.

Imprinted Characteristics of a Past Life

Although Stevenson and Tucker both pointed out, as a child gets older, the recollection of their past lives becomes dimmer with age, and often forgetting their experience(s) entirely by the time they're ten. However, this is not necessarily the case for the Indigo Children; simply because an Indigo cannot only recall the past lives with much more detail, they remember them longer. In my example of Zürich, I experienced that recall in my early fifties.

Even today, the 'night terrors' continue still, for they have become part of who I am and what has molded me into whom I have become: phobias, personality, and character.

Even today, I despise temperatures freezing temperatures. My temperate range is no less than 65^0 F (Fahrenheit) and no higher than 80^0 F. I distain snow and ice, and why I live in an area where temperatures rarely drop below freezing; and when it does, it's not for long!

Whether your child, Indigo or not, experience phobias for such things as spiders, snakes, monsters, or the dark, there may be an underlying reason. These phobias seem to be inherent in the human psyche and have in part have evolved into mankind's basic survival instinct. In the past, many psychologist's believed our 'phobias' where due to our early childhood experiences. They never even considered the possibility they were in fact, attributed in part to our past lives, as a carry-over that creates the composite personalities we all now display to the world. [46]

Identifying Affinities and Markers

Just like Indigo Children to have tendency to display an ardent interest in world government or world history, often to the point of it being an obsession, it really doesn't end just there. Although an Indigo Child's intense interest may be centralize on a specific subject or topic, it could on the other hand be an entirely natural phase for their age.

Young Indigo's tend to gravitate toward older, more interesting people because other kids their age cannot keep up with their intellect, nor really understand their affinities. Their grandparents often seem to be the center of their attention and laugh at their silly antics, while their parents sit and watch in bewilderment.

Although they rarely get angry, the can go livid on bullies; often displaying the courage of enraged gorilla in the schoolyard, regardless of the bully's size or age. When and Indigo feels an injustice has been committed, they first try to understand why it happened, which is soon followed by a deep feeling a sadness and empathy just before their period of contemplation ends in a sudden burst of contempt, anger, and outrage that goes far beyond a temper tantrum.

Yes, it can be good for everyone to have passion when executing his or her resolve, provided of course it does not become obsessive, compulsive, or debilitating. Unfortunately, many Indigo Children have a tendency to take it to extreme, and by so doing, aggravate everyone around them; specifically their parents and siblings.

When we consider these traits (and trust me, there's a lot more to cover), we have to ask ourselves a serious question, "Could these affinities and markers actually be the end result of one or more past life experiences or familiarity? [46]

One of the many 'nightmares' I can recall from another life was here in America several thousand years ago. My wife, child, and I had barely escaped a raid by a warring tribe on our village, we escaped the slaughter and scared, tired and thirsty we stopped to hide and quench our thirst in the reeds along a river in what is now North Dakota. Our only horse was startled as we rested and began to neigh, it frighten our baby who began to cry, which attracted the attention of our pursuers; we had been discovered and mercilessly killed.

Today, I have a deep affinity for the Native American cultures here in North America. So much so, I know many people and have many friends in the pueblos and reservations of Four-Corner Region of the United States. When I was a young man, my best friends grandfather, a shaman of the Hopi bear clan, gave me the name 'pahana;' which means 'white brother,' because he said I was an ancient native soul in a white man's body.

Birthmarks also thought to be other relevant signal that could point to reincarnation. Especially when an Indigo Child is familiar with what may have caused it. For example, Tucker in his book, "Return to Life," points out the case of a young Hindi boy who had told his father that he got his birthmark (an array of scattered spots on his abdomen) in his past life. Even to the point of telling his father, he remembered his name, Maha Ram, and killed by a single shotgun blast at close range to his chest.

Interestingly enough, the boy had an array of small birthmarks at the center of his chest that looked very much like that of a shotgun blast. Research later revealed, in coroner's autopsy report, that a man by the name of Maha Ram, who had indeed been killed by a single shotgun blast. After examination of the blast in the report, it was discover that the pattern did, in fact correspond to the boy's birthmarks. [45]
I was around five, when my grandmother prepared for a bath. Pointing the birthmark on my abdomen, she told me it was because my mother had an affinity for Italian butter cookies when she was pregnant with me. I of course laughed at whimsical tale and outright told her how I got it. "That's not true grandma. I got it when I was the

tribune commander of an archer's battalion for Rome in Gaul, and a Gaul stabbed me there with his sword when I was thrown from my chariot and lost my bow."

Was it the wild imagination of five-year-old boy? No, of course it wasn't.

Ironically, I have always had an affinity for archery, and I'm good at it. I also have a deep interest in many of the ancient commanders, like Alexander the Great and Julius Caesar; their battles, armament, strategies, and weaponry. Add to that a deep-rooted connection to Native American cultures, arts, religions, migrations, hunting, farming, and history; or a great love for classical to modern opera, 17th century poetry, and classical music and it doesn't take a blind man to know, my dreams are somehow connected. Why is this so? For me, it comes as no surprise.

Understand that many related experiences are entirely 'subjective' from the teller's point of view; the witness however, must also be credible. In addition, when offering 'evidence' to substantiate an argument, it first must have originated from a reputable source before considering it as 'objective' evidence that helps to make the argument not only 'plausible, possible,' and 'probable,' it makes it much more 'believable.'

We have to admit that the possibility certainly does exist, and the science supporting it, certainly encouraging. After all, the notion that we have lived before this life, and may again live after it, is a not very new notion all; it's a notion that's been around for millennia.

WHAT SETS AN INDIGO APART

"Indigo children are touted as the next evolutionary stage in human development, and their supporters boast that these children are like nothing ever seen before. But what exactly are Indigo children and just how unique are they?"

Benjamin Witts

Many people would like to consider themselves an 'Indigo Child,' without knowing if there are any identifiable skills or traits by which to identify them as such; because there aren't any. There is however, a 'litany of propensities' that I suppose could be used to help identify other individuals, like family members, friends, and coworkers, who may display certain characteristics that may provide a hint of whether they display an 'instinctive intuitive awareness' that appears to be inherent in all the Indigo generations of modern times.

Unfortunately, many people have overactive 'imaginations,' and therefore, it is of the utmost importance to be able to distinguish the difference between an Indigo's 'precognitive' or 'intuitive awareness' skillsets or 'whimsy' can be challenging. They should not want something so badly that they allow their own imagination to fabricate a lie, or label people as something they are not.

The Infant

Newborns eventually learn how to correlate the visual stimulus of images coming at them from all directions as soon as their eyes begin to focus. These random images are then processed through the visual cortex in their young brain and therefore allow them to quickly become 'aware' of their surroundings, but more importantly, the people in their young lives beginning with their mother.

Eventually the newborn child will develop an ability to differentiate and filter out 'what is' and 'what is not' important; mother vs. a strange woman for example. An Indigo infant however takes those early skills much, much further; they 'intuitively' begin to develop a clearer mental understanding of people, and the world around them, by identifying the resonant signatures of those most important to them, like the soothing music of their mother's song, to a chaotic noise coming through an open window.

An Indigo Child learns to differentiate order from chaos quickly by means of visual and resonant stimuli. Adult Indigos, who DNA are going through 'an awakening' into an 'intuitive conscious awakening,' will also first experience the same chaos; before they can begin to make order of all the jumbled and confusing bits information overload into their consciousness.

Therefore, the big question isn't so much, "How does a newborn Indigo infant or a young Indigo child correlate all the 'intuitive' information received from the universal consciousness?" It's "How does an 'awakening' Indigo child – young or old – learn how to recognize the difference between 'manufactured information' (their own thoughts) from the constant bombardment from an external stimuli called the 'universal consciousness?'

It all boils down to determining if it's 'real,' or a 'run-away imagination' working overtime. Because once the egg is cracked, the awakening Indigo traits will change their world forever, and that's scaring the hell out of them; giving them a whole a new meaning to the aphorism 'ignorance is bliss.'

Recognizing the Differences

At this point, you're probably wondering, "How one can recognize the difference between 'intuitive awareness' and 'resonant signatures;' much less if it's coming from the living or the dead, human or another source?" As I mentioned earlier, there is no specific 'on-off' switch that regulates activation. It's a process by which the Indigo mind can detect whether any emotions that they sense are an emotional 'resonant transference;' before they can filter out what's pertinent before they can identify whose 'signature' was received. It is an inherent trait that Indigo Children are able to do 'intuitively' and without forethought...an instinctive 'awareness.'

Think of it as going to a concert of Royal Hall of the London Philharmonic Symphony. Many of us can identify the individual sounds produced by dozens of instruments in the orchestra, and others couldn't tell you the difference between an oboe and a clarinet. An 'Indigo Child' is someone who can, and 'normal person' is someone who cannot. The Indigo brain can focus on the specific emotions in crowd (the orchestra) by first identifying the emotions they feel are coming from a foreign source (not their own), whoever remained becomes the 'person of interest (the instrument)' they had 'tuned' into (the obo).

Another example would be; people living in proximity of busy train tracks, a subway station, or a tramline, these people rarely hear the traffic on them. This is because over time, their brain had learned how to filter out all the unnecessary noise, just as an Indigo Child is able to filter out any emotional noise around them before focusing on the person (instrument) who is.

Everyone has these skills of 'awareness,' to varying degrees of expertise – most probably a left over inherent instinct; what I find a bit humorous, is most people haven't a clue they are connecting. They just assume it's their own clutter of thoughts bouncing around in their head and not someone else's 'anxiety' ridden consciousness they cannot detect, explain, filter out, or ignore. Only those who recognize this phenomenon can eventually learn their brain will 'intuitively' ignore the noise of the trains; unless of course, you're an Indigo.

For the many Indigo Children undergoing the 'awakening' process, the process is usually gradual, unlike the more recent generations born with their affinities fully functional and keenly astute. None the less, the older generations of Indigo will eventually become proficient and capable to not only sense everyone's emotional state, they will be able to filter identify where they came from, whose they are, and how to just ignore them.

Awareness vs. Inspiration

Once an Indigo has mastered the process of recognizing 'transmitted resonant signatures' from the world around them, they often report receiving what many theologians throughout history have called, 'divine inspiration' (a term now used loosely); however, it's not 'divine' nor is it an 'inspiration.' The Indigo Child has now become 'intuitively' connect to the 'universal consciousness;' thoughts so profound enter their head from nowhere that the Indigo Child cannot easily ignore. Thus, they stand up and shout them to the world, hoping someone will take notice. Often however, these 'flashes of intuition' are such an abstruse 'awareness' they question their own 'sudden insight;' some are baffled and confused, while others completely oblivious. Yet, it's all part of learning how to use what inspiration they derive from a previously unknown 'consciousness,' and eventually use it to their advantage; once they do, they will begin to realize it's just an accentuated extension to their other five senses.

Yet, for hundreds of thousands of years the genetic code had been there 'lying dormant' all along; but the big questions are, "Why?" and "Why now?" Over the last 50 or so years, countless Indigo Children have been born with the code 'active' and 'receptive.' For many others, the 'dormant' DNA code has somehow becoming activated and a new 'awareness' is emerging; and more-often-than not, confusing.

What I find interesting is that eventually their 'intuitive awareness' will become par with all other Indigo Children, and will become evident by their 'higher' sense of 'self-awareness;' their senses of 'precognition' will become phenomenal and their soul's 'sensitivity' profound; extending far beyond anything mankind has ever experienced before.

Intolerant Crusaders

Indigo's are often noted for being 'crusaders of injustice,' intolerant of cruelty and really, really, stupid people – especially when they're proud of being stupid.

Short tempered and intolerance tends to manifest itself with a very short fuse, because whenever senseless people are encountered, it usually ends with an exhibition bordering a 'rampant rage.' Although rare, these outbursts can be extremely agitated, please understand, it's usually only when the 'stupid' card has been played intentionally.

Growing up, I often disguise my consummate anger with a flood of tears because of my frustration. I knew I couldn't kill stupid people, because where would I hide all the bodies; stupid was frustrating because 'stupid defies logic' and useless to attempt! I learned very early in life, NOTHING could fix 'stupid' and unfortunately, 'stupid people' are here to stay; regardless of how much education they have. As a child, I would open a floodgate of tears when I found myself frustrated with stupid people. Other Indigos may react at an extreme opposite, showing absolutely no expression of emotion as they activate their vulnerability shield; a dome of protection that allows them to ignore stupid people, and then they get the hell away from them!

One thing about me that frustrates the hell out of a few people is that I always want to know 'Why' or 'Why not?' I often criticize governments, corporations, organizations, and even people who enjoy creating, establishing and imposing stringent rules they call a 'guidelines;' which are not guidelines, they are imposed rulings of control that are either inane, unfair, or impossible to follow. Although I must admit, I loved my role as a 'global business intelligence architect,' because, I had been paid well for pointing out the inadequacies of ineffective corporate methodologies that demonstrated NO business intelligence what-so-ever and their computer architecture and infrastructure often proved it!

I don't play well in the sandbox when the people around me are engaged in political mind games in an effort to gain dominance over other people by lying and/or cheating to make others look bad so they look good. Nor do I have time or respect for those that do and will alienate them without haste, prejudice, or looking back. Moreover, anyone who attempts to direct any dysfunctional psychological mind games my direction; then woe to them, for my reaction will be swift, merciless and without prejudice. I believe the perpetuators of any depraved plot (and all involved) should be draw drawn, quartered, and adamantly exposed for the frauds they are. Nor do I accept any kind of threat well, especially when I, or someone within my inner circle of trust, are threatened directly.

Indigo traits could be called the 'shield of injustice' and the 'sword of retribution' carried by all Indigo generations.

Other idiosyncrasy's Indigos may display –
- They despise long queues and will attempt to avoid them if at all possible;
- They do not like being told 'what to do, how to act or when to do it;'
- They don't mix words (depending on the circumstance), we tend to tell people 'straight-up' what they really may not want to hear to reveal who they really are;
- They see through a phony façade and may call people on it;
- They have absolutely NO qualm about putting unfair people 'in their place' at a moment's notice; especially when we perceive the 'boundary of decency' or 'injustice' has been crossed, and we will take great pleasure in watching their self-assured, pompous and arrogant attitudes take a lesson from someone who can when deliver it with a vengeance;

Loving the Challenge

Indigo's love to show 'how the game is played' when challenged privately or publicly. I personally take great pleasure in watching an attacker retreat with their unfounded pride tucked into their hip pocket and tail tight between their legs in retreat as they ask themselves, 'what the hell just happened?'

It's for reason, an Indigo will appear extremely 'cold, calculating,' and often 'anti-social;' and perhaps just the opposite, they are 'popular social butterflies.' People either gravitate toward an Indigo, or can't get away from them fast enough; and like other social groups, Indigos have an uncanny knack of locating and finding comfort with other outcast Indigos; for together they can be a force to be reckoned with.

The Transcendental Trance

Yes, it's true that many people may have a difficult time focusing when they are exhausted or overly stimulated for an extended period. Think of it as a very slow Internet connection or an overload of input coming from all directions; humans just have a tendency to bore quickly or give up confused. For an Indigo however, they can't ever seem to remain focused, a constant problem and the main reason the Indigo, is often said to have a wandering mind; a mind that doesn't always allow them 'focus' on many of the tasks at hand. Yet in their defense, it's that they (the Indigo) are often bored with subject at hand or find no use for the information, or are in the middle of an extensive download from the 'universal consciousness' that encourages them to ignore the world around them; temporarily at least.

An Indigo Child may have no control on any 'instantaneous' information being sent to them, as their mind has a tendency to transcend 'dimension, time' and 'space;' in that as information from the 'conscious universe' is being received. Often they will find themselves caught up in a loop of perception between this 'dimension' and 'alternate' or 'parallel realities' simultaneously; and perhaps why many believe the 'Indigo Children' is indeed a 'star child (alien hybrid);' a topic that has drawn a lot of contention, controversy and criticism from many scientific and philosophical circles.

Although it is true that 'Indigo Children' do tend to demonstrate a multitude of perceived 'psychic abilities,' what many people don't realize is that what they download is not all about offering 'psychic prediction.' All because an Indigo Child' will often demonstrate a unique propensity that demonstrates a 'precognitive' ability. They have been reported as seeing 'auras of energy' around certain individuals, feeling the presence of unknown ghosts or entities around them, and even have an out-of-body (OBE) experience, but by no means are they even remotely considered a 'psychic' in a 'trance' when they do get that far-away look in their eyes.

When the 'Indigo' goes into a 'transcendental trance,' they should be left alone and to their 'own devices' so to speak. They can hear you, but may choose not to acknowledge you and when they come out of their 'trance,' they may or may not to share what they had 'day dreaming' about. Nor should they be disturbed while in they are transcending the information download, for their brain waves will be most likely have gone 'delta' or 'theta' (see the section about Brain Waves).

So then, what does set all the 'Indigo generations' apart from the rest of the population? Is it their 'innate precognitive' ability to 'know that they know,' naturally and without reserve? Perhaps even by knowing something they should not have (nor possibly have) known. An Indigo's ability to access information from the 'universal consciousness' challenges our limited understanding as to what the human mind is entirely capable of; be it dimensional shifts, multiple reality layers, space or time (past, present, or future), or parallel dimensional realities; and even often confusing for the Indigo and why they retreat into their own little world.

Many people ask me, "How do I know if I'm an Indigo?" to which I can only reply,

"If you must ask, you probably aren't." and when asked, "Are you an Indigo?" my answer is quick and simple, "I connect!" Any other answer would be subjective at best. Yet, being straightforward, I tell myself, "I am." Regardless of what you believe, my hope is that this book provides with the answers you seek; or quelled your curiosity about 'Indigos' and 'consciousness.'

The Indigo Quagmire

I had learned a principle a long time ago while pondering many questions about the soul; "What is the difference between the brain, the mind, and the soul? How are they different and which is responsible for my thoughts, my ability to learn, and how and where do I store and my important memories (much less recall them)?"

Recently I asked Jacob Barnett, introduced to me prior to his talk on TedX, what his talk was going to be about. Casually he replied, "Stop learning and begin thinking." Immediately I heard my father's voice telling me the exact the same thing when I was nine. Forcing me to reflect on the impact that statement had on my life. At that moment, I had become a 'free thinker;' it was he (my father) who had dared me to "think outside the box," and now this boy is going to teach others the exact same principal.

Back in the 1950's many thought me to be a sagacious boy, driven by a passionate desire to discover everything I could about what life had to offer. The more I learned the more eager I was to discover more. "Who was I? Why I was here? What direction I would take? And who would I eventually become?" I wanted to know more than books or school could ever teach me and always questioned, always challenged, and always wondered what possibilities laid ahead that would enlighten my insatiable thirst for knowledge. Yet, the most provocative questions I needed to solve were, "What will happen to my soul when I die? Will I live another lifetime here or move on to another world? Will I remember everything I have experienced?"

Many thought of me as a troubled child when I was very young, calling me the 'young rebel,' because I would not conform. Their justification being, "It's because the poor boy lost his mother when he was still a baby." However, I knew that wasn't the reason at all, because I still connected to her and always felt her presence, somehow guiding me whenever I needed her council most. Yet in the back of mind, I always wanted to know, "How did I know my mother's council and how was it possible?"

As a teenager, I became a master at alienating myself from the rest of the world, always looking in as an 'Outsider;' distancing myself from society and their limitless boundaries, wondering what it meant to be 'normal;' for I felt I was normal and I was comfortable with myself, but others were frightened of me! "Why?"

When I read Robert Cracknell's book, "The Lonely Sense," he described himself as being an "outsider" while growing up in war torn London during the mid-1940s, to which I immediately related to having had the exact feeling. In fact, in that I am not alone, as many 'Indigo children' today consider themselves to be 'outsiders' looking in; raising still another question, "Is it possible I am one of the first Indigo generations to have been born into the 20th century?" Perhaps, it is entirely possible. According to the timeline many researchers believe, there was an influx of Indigo children born around the late 1940s and that has increased exponentially over the last 60 years.

Indigo Outsiders

Due to some the many experiences Indigo's often encounter while growing up, is the innate ability to 'see right through' people. A built-in protective mechanism I believe responsible for Indigo's, including me, to alienate ourselves from the general population. I learned at a very early age, that no matter how good people were at hiding deceit from a 'normal' person, my inherent ability to connect to their consciousness allowed me to identify their 'real' motives and intentions. Thus as a protective and instinctive characteristic, said to exist in all of the Indigo generations, I made the decision to withdraw myself from society, and proceed with extreme caution.

It's funny really, how quickly a 'red flag' can go up whenever I sense a person who has approached me with a sinister ulterior motive. Their disguise of being friendly and sincere actually set off an innate 'bovine excrement' detector within my consciousness that tells me to beware and put my shields up when sensing their phony façade. In addition, I can often sense instantaneously when anyone attempts to mislead or misdirect me from the truth or withhold pertinent information.

I literally have no patience and no use or for these people. My response usually ends up more often than not as a verbal assault at perpetrator, firing off a double barrel shotgun loaded with pellets of anger and distain for their lame attempt. Often, my response is swift and merciless, giving everyone in close proximity a very quick example of my normal demeanor of 'very calm' to 'total indignation' in a mere fraction of a second.

Today, children displaying this type reaction can be, and often are, diagnosed as being hyperactive and given fancy psychiatric labels that attack and cage their self-esteem; Attention Deficit disorder (ADD), Attention Deficit Hyperactive Disorder (ADHD), or Obsessive-Compulsive Disorder (OCD) all labels that describe the child as having not only a short fuse, is anti-social and disruptive. Another reason why so many 'Indigo children' are misdiagnosed by these negative labels; or worse put into a drug induced stupor simply because the prescribing doctor is addressing the symptoms without fully understanding the cause.

Thankfully, while I was growing up these tags and drugs were nonexistent, it wasn't until later in the late 20th century that the medications put thousands upon thousands of children in the United States alone into a drug induced stupor. Yet, in those days,

I go a good 'ass warming' because my reaction toward deceit was swift and merciless.

My profound sense of 'self-awareness' often left adults 'unnerved;' especially since I recognized my life had meaning. I have never liked change; even today, I refuse to accept it, for I prefer to live in the here-and-now; I have however learned to make the most of wherever I am, and what my timeline has in store for me; yet another Indigo trait.

Even having worked in a demanding career as I traveled all over the world, I have always been able to maintain a positive, self-assured, and spirited attitude on all my assignments. I have made my own choices. I have followed my own agenda. I have taken full responsibility for my own actions, and not in just within my profession life, but in my personal life as well. In fact, Indigo children will often display an assuredness that people find assuring. Indigos also exude a sense of confidence and self-awareness that attracts others like a beacon in the night. Yet however, there are those that feel threatened by an Indigo's demeanor, making them a prime target for whatever reason; often even unknown by the attacker.

In my career, I have had a few attempts at derailing a successful project I was managing in a lame attempt to deliberately sabotage and discredit me. However, their attempt usually ended up as a futile exercise. For they did not understand that Indigos are not only aware of their attack plans, they are also quite cunning in circumventing it. Most Indigos will use 'intuitive awareness' as an advantage; I know I did. For I very thoughtfully provided any perpetrator out to set my demise with just enough information (a sufficient amount rope) to turn the tide to my advantage. In other words, I allowed them to successfully discredit themselves and thereby hang themselves with the very rope I provided them.

Just remember, Indigos cannot only detect a misguided attack and intent at derailing them, they have an inherently instinctive ability to use as an advantage against the perpetuator(s) to turn the tide . . . of that I am again no different.

PRECOGNITION VS DÉJÀ VU

"Déjà vu is only the illusion of precognition. A "precognitive" knows this."

Author Unknown

'Intuitives, oracles,' and 'psychics' have long been revered for their special skills; 'gifts from the gods;' the reality being nothing more than a matter of 'perception,' and often 'conjecture.' Since man first made an appearance, the gifted-ones had been feared as 'witches' or 'sorcerers,' and their inherent 'powers,' elusive and often craved only by those 'seeking,' or wishing to 'remain' in power.

Just as an athlete trains a distinct group of muscles to ensure 'stamina' and 'endurance' during a triathlon, so does an opera singer train to increase lung capacity and airflow with vocal exercises on a different set of muscles to enhance resonance, range, intensity, pitch, tone and duration on stage. Regardless of the regime, their ultimate objective is 'perfection.'

However, science is still perfecting a regime to perfect the 'muscles' of our brain; however, there are not many exercises that are designed to enhance our 'precognitive' and 'intuitive' faculties. Our brain is the most important organ in the human body, yet what many people don't often realize, is like the accomplished athlete it depends on whether or not we (as individuals) possess the inherent talent, or even the propensity of 'precognition;' much less the stamina to not be driven insane by it.

One must first understand the difference between 'intuition (an understanding without a conscious thought, observation, or reasoning)' and 'instinct (a natural or innate impulse, inclination, or tendency).' The disparity between them must first be realized before a 'consciousness' other than their own could ever be understood.

What most people don't comprehend is that the 'conscious, subconscious,' and 'unconscious' minds access 'knowledge' differently. For some it appears 'seamless' and 'instantaneous;' an 'intuitive awareness' of 'knowing' and 'understanding' with no effort by the mind in any of these three states. It's only when we can understand this principle, that it becomes evident on how Indigo Children can effortlessly and instinctively tap into the countless collection of souls comprising the 'conscious pool of knowledge' I have been referring to as the 'universal consciousness.'

Nearly everyone–and this includes Indigos–on this planet are in total ignorance of this 'universal consciousness,' much less have any ability to recognize, sense or understand what 'déjà vu' really is, even if it coiled up, rattled its tail, and bit them on the proverbial ass!

Add to this those who are 'consciously deaf;' unable to receive, much less comprehend any significant harmonic connection from the 'universal consciousness;' think of it much like the person who wears ear-buds while listening to music on their smart phone is oblivious to the world about them. Often the volume will be 'cranked up' so high, it literally drowns out every word the artist is singing, not to mention permanently damaging their hearing. This not only causes them to become insensitive to noise in general, their brain becomes desensitized and unable to discern to hear anything else.

Indigo generations born within the last fifty years appear to have a propensity of receiving information without any limitations to 'time or space (past, present, or future), 'intuitively and instinctively;' regardless of whether it is received in a 'conscious, subconscious,' or an 'unconscious' state of mind. Where most people don't even understand there is a source, thus any meaning will elude them, so they end up ignoring it altogether.

Many Indigo Children I've spoken recently, seem to have been born with their innate 'Indigo' abilities already well in tune with the 'universal consciousness.' For some however, it takes a bit more encouragement, training, and practice to acquire the respect and confidence within themselves, to trust their instinct in order to increase their sensitivity to the constant bombardment of data. Eventually, their 'propensity' will transcend into a fully functional 'sixth sense' to become an 'intuitive' and fully realized conduit connection to the 'universal consciousness.'

The Confusing Clair Faculties

My objective here is to be able to distinguish the inherent 'Claire' ability of the Indigo faculties for what many confuse as being a 'psychic ability' rather than a 'precognitive' propensity; a lot to cover, for everyone experiences 'déjà vu' at some point in their life. The 'innate' and 'intuitive' Indigo orientation is not unlike having a specific eye or hair color, dexterity, or other physical attribute. We all have a built-in receiver and transmitter capable of accessing this vast universal pool of knowledge, called a 'brain.'

When a person experiences a case of 'déjà vu (the French phrase literally meaning to have 'already seen'), can best described as having had a very strange feeling or sensation that you had experienced a particular event at least once before; whether or not you can recall it. It is my belief when anyone who experiences this moment of 'high-strangeness' can credit the event to the brain's connection to an unseen pool of 'consciousness' that transcends time and space. Edgar Cayce called it the 'universal consciousness.' A state of mind where you may or may not be fully awake; or asleep, be it in a fully conscious thought, a subconscious warning or an unconscious experience such as a dream.

Access to this unified consciousness of souls is quite often subliminal, yet profound. Take for example an event that affected nearly the entire planet; 9/11. Very few people knew or lost someone they loved working near or in the twin-towers of New York City when allegedly downed by a terrorist attack; affecting nearly everyone around the planet; because of emotional upheaval that ensued within the 'universal consciousness,' an 'intuitive' tidal wave of grief if you will.

During the Second World War, Hitler flooded the airwaves like a runaway freight train to gain control of Europe's population through fear. Their propaganda machine was a brilliant tactic designed to the Third Reich gain control of Europe (and the world). Many people sensed what atrocities were coming to Europe as early as 1934 and tried to flee the Europe long before the Nazi party even came into power; taking measures to get their families or children as far away from Germany as financially possible. Edgar Cayce's dire warning came in January of 1934, when he accurately predicted, "Adolf Hitler will rise in power to reign over Germany, to which a great catastrophe will come to the world beginning as early as 1936. A catastrophe that will fracture the powers of Russia, the United States, the United Kingdom, and Japan, and world affairs will bring about a terrible war." [18]

Take other events, such as the massacre at Columbine High School in Denver, Colorado or the recently bombing of an Aurora, Colorado, theater; both affected nearly everyone – and thus the 'universal consciousness' – with a 'shock and awe' ripple that was felt by millions of people all over the world.

At the time, I was living in the Hague Netherlands when a bombing that had occurred in an Aurora, Colorado, was reported on BBC News. The Dutch immediately began taking precautions after the attack to protect moviegoers throughout the Netherlands by enhancing security measures wherever people gathered; as other extreme measures rippled across the continent of Europe that kept even kept many children from going to a cinema alone at all. Could this also have been cause by a disturbance felt by everyone from within the 'unified consciousness?'

For decades, physicists had been trying to link everything in the universe as being 'connected,' in what they have called a 'string theory;' a theory that unites all of the four forces of nature; gravity, electromagnetism, nuclear energy; resembling a taut string from guitar stretched across the universe. When plucked (depending on how thick or tight the string is) it would produce an effect that would oscillate at a specific frequency; producing either a harmonic chord or discordant tone, an oscillation in the universe scientists call an 'excitation' wave, either tranquil or chaotic.

The 'universal consciousness' operates very much like still another string theory, in that every conscious mind in the universe is connected and where changes in the vibrations of that 'consciousness,' would also affect the entire universe. A specific accelerator (event) harmonized to disrupt the 'normal harmonic' resonance of the entire 'universal consciousness' across a wide spectrum of frequencies; frequencies our human brain can 'intuitively' perceive as 'conscious' or 'subconscious' disruption; especially by the Indigo Child.

DELINEATING AN INDIGO CHILD

"We are not human beings having a spiritual experience; we are spiritual beings having a human experience."

Teilhard de Chardin

Of late, many parents, scientists, theologians, psychologists, and other professionals have taken notice of the remarkable phenomenon materializing before them, one that only be described, as a major 'shift of consciousness.' What many don't seem to realize, is that it actually began well over 60 years ago and accelerated with each subsequent generation since the early 1950's.

At first, these 'unique' groups of children were lumped into a single group that labeled these people as being 'enlightened, intuitive, highly intelligent,' or worse, 'specially gifted.' Recently, the 'New Age' labels like 'Indigo Child, Rainbow Child', and 'Crystal Children' have been used to set them apart, simply because these children appeared to demonstrate some very 'unique qualities, extraordinary abilities' and possessed an 'extreme intelligence' beyond their years. Therefore, it was important to set them apart from their counterparts. However, as if that wasn't enough, eventually teachers began to catalog some of their 'special' traits; such as an ability of 'precognition' and 'intuition' for which they were often described as 'psychic kids.' The reality being, this particular group of children have nothing more than an a predisposition to an 'innate' sense of 'awareness' accompanied by what could only be described as an 'intuitive consciousness' of nearly everything, and everyone around them.

From these labels, the term 'Indigo Children,' had been adopted to describe certain characteristics within children possessing not only 'exceptional intelligence,' but an 'innate awareness,' that drew a very fine line between being a 'normal child' or an 'unnatural child;' even to the assumption of labeling the child as 'psychic.'

Then a pseudoscientific, 'New Age' concept, coined in the 1970's by parapsychologist Nancy Ann Tappe, (self-described 'synesthete' who is said she could visualize colored 'auras' emanating from certain individuals in her book, "Understanding Your Life through Color" published in 1982. In her book, she describes seeing these children surrounded by an 'indigo (shade of blue) aura' around this particular group of 'gifted kids.' [15]

Based on Tappe's observations, Jan Tober and Lee Carroll later abstracted the 'label' coined by Tappe to describe these children in their book entitled, "The Indigo Children: The New Kids Have Arrived." A book revered as the first study on the 'phenomenon of Indigo Children' since Tappe first coined the label to describe them.[16]

Therein, Tober and Carroll identify an unusual set of psychological attributes shared as 'common traits' among this particular group of kids. Their goal was to define a specific set of behavioral patterns to characterize this particular group of children in their study.

Understand I DO NOT agree with 'stereotyping labels;' for they are often attached to specific groups of people as a 'negative descriptive.' However, the ONLY REASON, I will be using the label 'Indigo, Indigo Children,' and 'Indigo Child' is because it has singularly become the most used and most widely accepted label that everyone can understand; especially when I consider that it has now been used for well over forty years and I am not one to "rock the boat."

Moreover, for those of you that despise a label as much I do, rest assured it was unavoidable and necessary for this book. So, before I proceed, I feel that it is imperative I provide you with objective and logical theories, accompanied by sufficient background information, to explain WHY the phenomenon of 'Indigo Children' has become such a paradox for scientists, researchers, theologians, parents, and teachers alike; and for a very long time.

Understand the objective data I am providing you DOES NOT encompass any mystical fog of metaphysical mumbo-jumbo babble that is often 'laced' with nothing more than supposition in support; for it does nothing more than confuse, confound and bewilder those seeking logical answers to sincere questions.

So whether you know an 'Indigo Child,' are the parent, teacher, or sibling of an 'Indigo Child,' or believe yourself to be an 'Indigo Child,' I believe my decades of research seeking answers will herein provide you the information and insight you seek. Please understand too, I will be offering first person examples throughout this analysis as important background information, and although at times it may appear I'm babbling on and on, rest assured I will eventually be making a point about what it's like to 'growing up Indigo.'

An Awakening to Self

For many years, I was keeping a deep secret about myself that has guided me through all the curve balls life has thrown at me. Even as a very young boy, people referred to me as 'that strange kid, living in his own strange little world.' However, when I began to experience puberty things only got even stranger. The only way I was able to survive this period of my live was with the help and guidance of my maternal Grandmother. She helped me to finally 'come-to-terms' with who I was and what I was able to do. At the time, I never thought of myself as a 'precognitive;' nor did I feel it was a bit strange to see and know things I shouldn't have. My Grandmother referred to my abilities as 'psychic' in nature and often called them "special gifts from God."

Even as I matured into an adult, I had a difficult time understanding why 'God' had anything to do with it. All I wanted was to be just 'like other kids.' That never happened.

Becoming the 'Outsider'

Adults distanced themselves from me simply because I would often scare the holy bejesus out of them. My grandmother, often amused by my candor knew I wasn't speaking to 'imaginary friends,' but more-often-than-not, the souls of people who had passed. For it was they, who would reveal things to me they wanted said. Those who knew me well, knew I was quite often forthright, but more importantly, insanely accurate of things I could not have possibly known about their private lives. Thus my warnings were not only accepted, they alienated people; who would eventually begin to avoid me like bush full of skunks.

I heard their whispers and knew their tales of me when they talked amongst themselves, they called me "that strange little boy…" believing I could not hear what they said, or know I could sense how they felt; which would have been okay, they just didn't know that I already knew. Sensing their thoughts and trepidation was instinctive for me and they never realized I did not have to be in close proximity to do so, I could sense their 'transmissions' without their knowledge, because they did not realize they were broadcasting them loud and clear in my direction. Frequencies I had no difficulty in deciphering regardless of distance or proximity.

From grade school through university, I had eventually recused myself from everyone else, only allowing a few close friends into my inner sanctum of trust. Many of whom found me 'interesting, funny' and 'quite entertaining;' so much so, they began to refer openly to me as 'that little witch.'

Today, when someone asks my opinion of what I am 'picking up (sensing),' I simply ask, "Are you sure you really want to know the answer?" When they do, I reveal exactly what I have sensed, without sugarcoating the truth and give it to them 'straight-up.' When asked, "How could you have known that?" I simply answer, "It's instinctive."

Was I always right? No, of course not, but if I'm not spot on, I'd usually be pretty damn close.

Several years ago, I had read a book by wonderful psychic author named Robert Cracknell. I found him to be an interesting man, dubbed by the British press as, "England's Greatest Psychic Detective." In his book entitled "The Lonely Sense," a book recommended to me by my close friend Micah Hanks, editor of the "Gralien Report." Micah said about Cracknell, "I believe he has a unique perspective in writing about his journey of self-discovery, one you may find quite interesting. You should give it a good read."

Once I began Cracknell's book, I couldn't put it down, for I felt he him speaking directly to me. I lingered on each word as absorbed what he wrote like sponge; for Robert Cracknell's arduous journey seemed very much parallel to mine. It was through Robert's writing, I had finally begun to understand that I possessed 'precognitive' skills and although I had never considered myself a 'psychic;' as grandmother had, I had always felt my skills went much deeper.

Robert Cracknell's search for answers was a difficult road to self-discovery that was understandably confusing for him as well, and although his traumas and experiences often seemed parallel my own, they were not quite the same.

It was Mr. Cracknell's book, that clarified that being 'psychic' is not a 'gift' (as my grandmother had led me to believe), but was instead was the 'faculty' of 'precognition;' 'for which I had an epiphany. Being Indigo was an 'orientation' to an 'inherent' set of faculties that went far beyond just 'psychic intuition.'

From that moment on, I realized that part of me people feared most; the very same reason I had sequestered myself from society, and just as Robert had called himself an 'outsider' I too had unwittingly become an 'outsider' to all those around me. As I write these words, I have reached the conclusion it is for this reason alone, I still continue to live alone in the middle of now-where, in a quiet, yet secluded area of the state; far away from everyone else.

After having read his book, I was compelled to contact Bob Cracknell through his publisher to set up an interview for an article I ended up writing for a magazine I published on-line, entitled, "The Psychic within Us All" (under my pen name A.J. Michaels). Since that interview, I am proud to call him only by his preferred first name 'Bob,' as a 'best mate.'

If You Think Puberty is Awkward

Of course, every boy going through this period in his life is awkward, but as I grew into my young adult body, I began to keep everything I felt or experienced to myself. Being realistic, I had withdrawn into my own self-created version of 'reality.' I knew I was frightening more than just a few people; I had bewildered friends, scared the hell out of strangers, and perhaps even fascinated a few people. Yet what I could not do is fully comprehend or accept were the whispers. Not that I had heard any spoken aloud, I knew how they felt the moment I looked into their eyes, and thus I created 'my own little world' and willingly withdraw deep within it.

As a young adult I became an expert at the Dewy-Decimal system (after all, there was no internet back in the early 60s) as I pursued answers to satisfy the many provocative questions that haunted me; "Why did people think I was so different from everyone else? Why did I know things that had not yet happened? How was it I could tell when people concealed truth, or even worse, were outright lying? Why couldn't anyone else hear, see, or sense things that seemed obvious to me?" and "Why did people consider me so strange because I could?"

One of the fondest recollections I have occurred when I was about three-years-old. I loved helping my mother brush her long auburn hair every night before she would tuck me into bed at night. I would stand on a chair she placed against her back so I could lean up against her as she patiently sat at her small dressing table watching me in her mirror. There she would tell me how much she loved me, while expertly tangling her hair into the bristles of the brush.

I can still remember the feeling I sensed that night, because somehow I knew I would never be able to brush again after that night. For the following evening she had been hospitalized after complications giving the birth of my younger brother; her appendix had ruptured during the labor and it was understandably diagnosed as a normal post-natal pain.

By the time, her doctor realized something was terribly wrong; peritonitis had already poisoned her body. She died several days later while I quietly slept on my grandmother's bed. I remember awakening during the night by her hand gently tickling my back gently as she always had, saying, "Be a good boy son, as I know you will..." and quietly back to sleep.

The Awakening: an Emergence of Indigo Consciousness

When I returned fourteen years later, to live with my grandmother to I complete my senior year of high school (the very same school from which my mother had graduated). After I had prepared for school, grandmother, pouring a cup of coffee for me, began to share a conversation she had had with mother about the last night at home when I brushed her hair. I had apparently burdened her greatly with something I had said. Apparently, while brushing I had asked her, "Who is going to brush your hair when you go to heaven mama?" She worried about that question, especially since I was still so young and innocent. She had wondered if what I had said divulged what she believed to be an innocent 'precognitive premonition;' and it very much concerned her. Not for her own fate, but of mine, if something were to happen to her.

During the traditional Catholic Rosary the night before funeral, grandmother noticed I wasn't in the chapel and franticly began searching for me throughout the funeral parlor. Fining me in the foyer sitting at the top of the stairwell leading to the basement, I appeared to be having a single-sided conversation with myself, only I appeared to be answering questions; from someone she could not see, and whomever it was sitting next to me on the step. As grandmother listened, she began to realize I was talking to my mother in the empty stairwell.

Curios, she asked what had been said, and simply replied, "Mama told me I was going to grow up with lots of different people, but no matter where was, she will always be with me."

My eyes swelled with teas, I and began to tell grandmother something that she seemed to already know and understand. "Mother is here with us right now in this room and she wants you to know she's been with me always, and that you should not worry like you do." After which, mother added a personal and mysterious comment directed at me, "Someday you will understand why everything has happened as it has, for you are one of many, and you have much to teach."

At the time, I had no idea what she meant. As I sought out logical answers to my many questions, I have never felt lonely or alone in my quest. Many people had cared for me throughout the years, as I have cared for others; family, friends, and at times even total strangers.

Caregivers were often shocked and surprised by my random remarks, often relevant to many unheard conversations; especially when it appeared I wasn't paying attention; especially, when they came from child that seemed to not be paying attention, but played with invisible 'imaginary friends.'

On many occasions, I would abruptly stop my play, walk up to an unsuspecting adult, and stare at them in the face as I blatantly corrected the lie they had just told and revealed the truth. This not only shocked and dismayed everyone involved, for my remarks, often appeared indignant as I chastised an adult for lying. This literally scared the hell out of many people, family, friends, and strangers.

The Double-Edged Sword of Puberty

This is by far one of the most difficult times in a child's life, and even more so for a young Indigo. Indigo entering puberty have a tendency to become a lot more 'introverted' during this period of their young lives. As they will begin to ponder a new 'self-realization' that displaces their entire 'outer world' much further than expected. As their body prepares them to become 'young adults,' their entire world becomes confused and turned upside-down; including their 'inner self.' Everything they knew and loved is 'put on hold' as they begin to experience an expanded 'consciousness' that seems to transcend time and space; which would be confusing for anybody. During this period in their young lives, they must set out on a new 'quest' to discover who they are all over again, as a direct result of the dreaded 'pineal gland.'

The effects of puberty, at first will appear as a lower level of 'serotonin' begins to allow these children access to other states of 'consciousness' and 'awareness' that are unfamiliar to them. While on the other hand a higher concentration of 'melatonin' will hold off many of the powerful influences the pituitary gland has over them, delaying the onset of puberty and keeps them at bay by keeping them from entering adulthood too quickly as they adjust.

By seven or eight years old, the 'pineal gland's' function of a normal child begins to diminish while the production of 'serotonin,' signaling the onset of puberty, triggers a progressive release of hormones that will eventually drag the 'normal' child out of their 'intuitive state of awareness.' As the Indigo Child edges closer and closer from their younger version of reality, into that of an adult Indigo, they will begin to take on a more mature role that inches closer and closer into that of a young adult. Also known as the 'dreaded the teenage years', when a child is old enough to know better, but still too young to resist.

Simultaneously, when any child's reproductive system begins to wake up and take notice, they are also subjected to a great deal of emotional and mental turmoil as their 'psyche' attempts to adjust to their new body's; and not just sexually, but into an entire new version of 'reality.'

They will no longer want to play with their most valued toys, or the familiar games they had once entertained themselves with; all because of their diminished capacity to produce 'melatonin.' To make matters even worse, as 'serotonin' begins to build-up as a progressive concentration within their brain, their childhood door will subsequently forever close, as an expanded world of 'intuitive perception, imagination' and 'consciousness' takes over only to leave them feeling frustrated and stranded in a 'new altered version' of adult reality. This new 'awakening of consciousness' will eventually leave the Indigo feeling overpowered as they tragically begin to realize that the doors to their childhood has forever closed, and rarely if ever, be seen again, or is it? [14]

As children mature, the 'pituitary gland' activates the process of adolescence by defining the child's sexuality; while at the same time as the process of adolescence begins, the 'pineal gland' will inhibit the 'pituitary' from a 'premature sexual awakening' by scrutinizing 'thoughts' to inhibit 'actions.'

Unlike other 'normal' children whose production of melatonin begins to subside with the onset of puberty, an Indigo's production continues production at an equal or greater pace than ever before and just like other 'normal' teenagers who are experiencing a period of 'growing pain,' so does the Indigo Child. However, for the Indigo, the transition is far more difficult, much more intense, and quite moody; not to mention they get easily irritated and are often short tempered; parents, teachers, and family, just have to remember and consider it's a natural 'rite of passage' into adulthood

Parents, Siblings, Teachers, & Friends Beware

Anyone coming into contact with an Indigo teenager will need to learn to be patient and understanding during this period of an Indigo's life; not only as they develop their own sexual identity (confusing for any teenage) but discover who they are and their place in the world around them. Exponentially, the changes any Indigo goes through are often much more profound than those experienced by their peers.

While their perception of the world around them begins to 'awaken,' a new and confusing, 'consciousness' will begin to flood their soul with what the Ancients called the 'seed of illumination;' a period of 'intuitive' and 'precognitive awareness' also connected to 'pineal gland.' A 'cosmic connection to consciousness' the Ancients worshiped.

If you were to compare the 'pineal gland' to 'intuition' and the 'pituitary gland' as 'reason,' a symbiotic connection that can then be realized as a coalescence of function between these two very tiny glands; a singularity the Ancients called our 'third eye' and the Egyptians and Greeks worshiped as the 'Eye of Horus.'

Approximately fifty years ago it was noticed that rise of Indigo births had begun; most of which with their 'third eye' fully functional early in their childhood. These children seemed to be inherently aware of their 'intuitive consciousness' as if it were only a 'sixth sense' accentuating the other five; not unlike the 'sixth sense' psychic profess to have. What I find interesting, is that many Indigos as young children don't even realize there is a difference from their young friends; at least not until the Indigo Child goes through puberty.

We must not however forget the other group of Indigo Children, those I will refer to as the 'older generation;' some of which were not born with an 'awakened' state, and are only now beginning to realize the new sense of 'awareness' as it awakens within them. An 'intuitive' and 'precognitive consciousness' that only now allows them to escape from the old limited 'three dimensional' view of 'consciousness' they know and recognize. What's sad, and funny in a way, is that what they are beginning to experience is totally 'freaking them out' and they often believe they're experiencing a 'psychological meltdown' of sort, and afraid to tell anyone.

Consider it a delayed 'rite of passage' that had not been activated during puberty, simply because certain triggers within their genome's DNA had not triggered. The biggest question I am often asked is, "Why now and why me?" All I can say, it's nothing more than a delayed 'puberty' trigger of 'consciousness'…and is just as confusing to an Indigo Teen.

The stage of life when this 'self-realization' occurs is really immaterial, but what should be understood, one older generations of Indigo still have to experience; along with the same problems their prepubescent counterparts went through, but without having to deal with puberty all over again. In addition, it is a 'rite of passage' just like puberty that will not only expand their perception of everything and everyone around them it does so with a profound clarity. The trick is to trust their instincts during the entire process.

DEFINING INDIGO CHARACTER

"Parents can only give good advice to put them on the right path; the final forming of a person's character lies only within in them."

Anne Frank

Many consider themselves an 'Indigo Child' without ever realizing any of the specific propensities and character traits that would identify them as such. Saying, "I'm an Indigo." 'Being' Indigo and saying you are, are two entirely different things; for there is a litany of 'genetic propensities' and 'characteristics' that predisposes a person as to whether or not they can demonstrate any of the identifiable characteristics to an 'instinctive intuitive awareness' that's inherent in all Indigo generations.

Unfortunately, many people have overactive 'imaginations,' and unable to understand the difference between having a 'propensity (a natural inclination or tendency)' or developing 'character (an aggregate of features or traits that determines their individual nature – morals, ethics, honesty, courage, or integrity).' Nor would they be able to distinguish the difference between a 'premonition, precognition,' or 'intuitive awareness.' Because all too often, they let their runaway imagination may want something so badly that they allow themselves to fabricate and incorporate a lie into their own version of reality; not only unto themselves, but in providing others a lame attempt to convince them they are something they are not.

Development of Character

Newborn infants eventually learn how to correlate a variety of images (visual stimulus) coming at them from every direction as soon as their eyes have learned to focus. The random images processed through the visual cortex of their brain, allows the infant to become 'aware' of not only their surroundings, they quickly recognize who the most important people are their young lives.

However, it doesn't take long before a newborn child will eventually develop the ability to differentiate and filter out 'who' and 'what' is important; mother vs. stranger, bottle vs. toy. An Indigo infant however takes those early skills quite a bit further, in that they will 'intuitively' begin to develop a clearer mental understanding of the people and their environment by identifying the resonant signatures of those most important in their life; liken it to recognizing a soothing musical score vs. the chaotic noise of mayhem.

So just as an Indigo Child learns to differentiate order from chaos, be it as a visual or resonant stimulus, adult Indigos going through their own 'awakening' to 'consciousness,' will also first experience chaos before they can recognize order from all the jumbled and confusing bits of information overloading their consciousness.

The big question isn't so much, "How does a newborn infant or child correlate 'intuitive' information received from the universal consciousness?" It's, "How does an 'awakened' Indigo Child – young or old – learn how to recognize the difference between what information is 'manufactured (their own thoughts)' from the constant bombardment from external stimuli being received through the 'universal consciousness?'

It all boils down to knowing what is 'real' and what's from an 'imagination' working on overdrive; when is it truly an 'intuitive awareness of consciousness?' Once that egg has been cracked (the 'awakening' of Indigo propensities–often called traits), the world will never ever be the same; and thereby give the older generations of Indigo going through an 'awakening' an entirely new understanding to the aphorism that 'ignorance is truly bliss.'

A Propensity to Precognition

"When is a square not a square?" If you ponder this question for a few minutes, you will soon realize "a square is also a rectangle, and yet a rectangle is not a square." If this statement is true, then a rectangle is not a rectangle when it is square, but a square is always a rectangle...or is it...confused yet. "When is an Indigo, an Indigo?" Now 'that' question is not very easy to answer either; nor will it ever be. Being Indigo is no different than possessing any other human orientation or faculty; such as hair or eye color, dexterity, sexuality, skin tone or race, intelligence, talent, etc. It simply defines a specific set of characteristics inherent within each-and-every individual on the planet. Indigo Children born with their 'Indigo' traits active, simply accept themselves as 'normal;' nothing special, because for them, they are as 'normal' as everyone else around them is.

Those undergoing the 'awakening' will eventually begin to display different propensities, characteristics, and qualities that will make them 'uniquely' Indigo, and through time they will learn to embrace themselves as 'normal' as everyone else. The only difference being, they all happen to share some unique characteristics and qualities within a specific group of people; yet, it does not necessarily define them as a whole, for each person different yet still the same (right or left handed, blue or brown eyed, blond or brunette...).

An 'Intuitive Psychic' or a 'Precognitive Indigo'

Humanity has a 'natural inclination' or if you will, a 'propensity' to demonstrate one or more of the many 'psychic faculties' the ancients worshiped for thousands of years. However rare as it may be, it is also highly unlikely that any single person on the planet will have all of them. Just as our vocal cords create vibrations that sync up with our tongue, teeth and lips to form sounds and articulate words, our inherent 'faculties' may or may not, begin to work in unison until we develop a deep sense of character that enables us to 'tune-in' to others. Indigos can easily establish an 'intuitive connection' without forethought – a synchronization of resonance – that provides pretty much all Indigo generations an upper advantage, in that they 'know that they intuitively know' things without giving it any forethought.

Regardless of what you believe, please understand that it is very important to note that being 'Indigo' does not grant them with a 'Carte Blanc' license to dominate, control, or manipulate others; much less seek out fame, glory or fortune! (I've never heard of an 'Indigo' ever doing this, but there are hundreds of 'psychic charlatan's' with fancy websites and 800/900 numbers that do.)

"Do no harm." My grandmother warned me, "And be sure you never divulge anything you sense, feel, or know about anyone else, unless you are specifically asked you to do so, and then you only share that information with the individual it concerns. Remember, they may not want know – the burden is yours until they relieve you of it. So, please promise me you will never use this give of 'awareness' and 'knowing' for your own personal gain; it doesn't work that way, because it will only end up biting you in the ass if you do!"

I made that promise, and I've still not broken it. So, rather than using another idiom in distress to make a point here, I will instead relay an experience that occurred to me while working on a contract in Melbourne, Australia on a four-person team of international consultants after we had wrapped up another successful project.

On our last day there, we had all gone to the canteen for lunch as we always had, when I noticed a large barrel prominently placed next to the cashier full of Cadbury's famous chocolate eggs. However, the eggs were filled with prizes instead of the normal Cadbury yolk-like creamy center. A donation of one Australian dollar for each egg as asked, with all the proceeds going to the Australian Breast Cancer Research Foundation.

After lunch, I looked at each of my colleagues and held out my hand to collect for a dollar from each of them, I told them they were about to make a donation by purchasing one of the eggs.

I sat the four eggs on the table and told them to choose one; they did leaving me the last. I slipped the egg into my pocket and after lunch, we all stepped outside to enjoy the warm spring day and opened our eggs. Each of my three colleagues received a kind note thanking them for their kind donation and a discount coupon redeemable for any Cadbury product at the company store. My egg however, had instead a fifty-dollar note as a cash prize. They of course all objected that I had picked a winning egg and suggested we should split it four ways. After which, I reminded them that they had in fact chosen their own egg, and I was left with the last one on the table!

When asked me how I was going to spend the winnings, I replied, "I won't, someone else will." Perplexed by my reply, they couldn't refrain from asking me what I meant by that, to which I simply said, "It's not mine to spend." and left it at that.

The following day, two of these colleagues were returning to their German homeland and we all decided to celebrate their departure and our success at very expensive restaurant in downtown Melbourne for a late night supper. It was a beautiful evening and we all decided to walk to this wonderful Chinese restaurant several blocks from the hotel and rang up quite a tab; nearly $500 Australian between the four of us.

Although the staff was patient with us, we literally closed the restaurant and asked to leave. We gathered our coats and stepped out into a drizzling night on streets that had become quite well soaked; making for a chilly spring night. Wearing only light coats, we quickened our pace to get to into the warmth of our opulent rooms at the Hyatt Regency, still several blocks away.

The Awakening: an Emergence of Indigo Consciousness

As we approached the hotel, a very elderly woman pushing a shopping basket that literally overflowed with what I was sure were all her worldly possessions, approached us. Humped over with severe osteoporosis and her head covered with a dirty rain-soaked blanket, she held out her severely deformed arthritic hand toward us and begged in a quivering and humble whisper, "Please good sirs, I am cold, hungry and wet…a dollar for an old lady to let a bed at the shelter for the night?"

My colleagues simply walked past her as if she didn't exist and continued on their way; I could not. I stopped and called out to them to wait for me, and turned to face the well-seasoned woman and looked into her tired blue eyes and asked, "How many nights will fifty dollars buy you?" as I put my hand into my pocket.

"A whole month, including a bath and meal each day," She responded. I took her hand in mine and laid the fifty-dollar note I had won, into her palm and closed her fingers around it. She began to sob, and I pulled her close into an embrace and hugged her frail body gently. I whispered in her ear, "This was meant for you." and bid her a Happy Christmas.

Without hesitation they asked why on earth I would give a beggar so much money…My reply was simple, "My Grandmother taught me long ago, that which you freely give away, will multiply ten-fold and what you withhold will surely die…I didn't have that fifty dollars this morning and I certainly don't have it now…so what's different? I told you this afternoon, that money was not intended for me, so I am not 'out' any money, Am I?"

Was what I perceived as 'precognition,' in reality an 'intuitive awareness' of events? Had I had intuitively known the prize money was not been intended for me? For I had not chosen the egg that contained the prize…it was chosen for me… and somehow knew the money was not mine to spend. But, how could I possibly know this?' Consciously, I didn't; but eventually when the time was right, for whom the cash prize was destined, would eventually become known me.

The following week, the last of my German colleagues had finished his duties, and was preparing to leave for his homeland. On his last evening in Australia, the two of us went to enjoy a wonderful meal at a restaurant located in a new casino on the harbor, and like most casinos, to get to the restaurant we had to maneuver through an impressive gambling arena of slot machines to get to it.

After our wonderful meal, we again had to traverse the casino floor, but as we approached the exit, my young associate turned to me and stated, "I have never gambled on a slot machine in my whole life, only poker with friends over chips and peanuts. How do these crazy looking machines with all the lines work?"

Walking over to one of the new generation of slot machines with lots of buttons, lights, and a myriad of lines, he said, "Like this one."

It was foreboding for even me, for I learned a long time ago to double my money I folded in half and put it back in my pocket. "Well to be honest Martin, I am not a gambler myself and work hard for what I earn. But I've been known to keep myself entertained on the penny slot machines while waiting for my die-hard friends who enjoyed wasting away enough money to make my mortgage!"

I placed a twenty-dollar bill into a slot on the machine of his choosing and watched it quickly swallow the bill up like a hungry great white. I then tapped out the number of lines I wanted and hit the maximum bet of twenty coins per line (nearly the entire $20 dollars on a singlet pull to make appoint) and pushed the flashing red button.

After the amusing series of beeps and tunes had stopped, to my surprise, loud music began playing as the lights went wild to inform me I had just hit a $500 jackpot. Without even blinking, I pressed the 'cash out' button and said to my colleague, "That's how it's done!"

Mind you now, karma will not normally allow me to use my faculties for personal gain. So winning a jackpot was a totally foreign to me. I retrieved the winning receipt the machine has spit out from a slot, and took it to the cashier for the payout. Suddenly, my colleague had an epiphany; "You just multiplied ten-fold that fifty dollars you gave that old woman last week…just like you said. Wow! So what do you plan on doing with this money?"

"Watch me." I replied as I picked up the stack of money off the counter, removed a single twenty-dollar bill from the pile, and slipped into my wallet. "My investment…" and without batting an eye I dropped the remaining bills into a red Salvation Army bucket as we exited the casino…"I didn't have it when I walked in…and I don't have it now…and it is Christmas. Isn't it?"

An Innate Intuitive Awareness

Scientists believe that we as humans utilize less than one tenth of our brain's total capacity, and that have survived tens-of-thousands of years solely on 'instinct,' and not 'intellect.' Yet, it is conceivable, and perhaps not too outlandish to believe that many of us–Indigo in particular–have a 'propensity' that transcends not only 'instinct,' it even eclipses time, space, or dimensions.

Since the beginning of time, our ancient ancestors have misconstrued the human propensities of 'precognitive' and 'intuitive' skills as being nothing more than a 'psychic abilities.' The confusion being that our ancient forefathers most basic instincts protected them from danger, and are most likely left-over from an era when danger lurked behind every bush; whereas 'precognitive' and 'intuitive' skills go far beyond an ability to ward off impending dangers.

How often have you sensed it imperative to take a different route on a trip or change your itinerary, but were unsure of the reason why? Perhaps you've even experienced that 'queasy uneasy feeling' something was just not right, sensed someone you know was in dire need of help, or knew who was calling you before the phone even rang. Is it merely 'coincidence,' or more than that? After all, everyone at one time or another, experiences a 'déjà (having already) moment.' For some, it's an intense experience, for others a fleeting thought.

Premonition (not to be confused with 'precognition') does not a 'psychic' make, especially since most people are completely oblivious to 'premonitions.' Our cave-dwelling ancestors after all, were 'instinctive' not 'precognitive,' and 'instinct' is what allowed them to survive.

Now that I have most likely confused you, 'precognition' is disparate in that it is an 'intuitive conscious awareness' that transcends 'instinct,' and is often mistaken as a 'psychic faculty;' such as 'clairvoyance' or 'clairaudience.' Indigo Children have 'precognitive' skills that go FAR beyond any 'premonition,' which is very often confused as the 'psychic forecast' of a fortuneteller.

The reality being, an Indigo Child actually taps into a vast 'universal consciousness' that allows them to 'know' the outcome of every possible scenario and each outcome's inevitable conclusions, long before they make any decision; because they know it's the best path to follow with the most favorable results. It is in fact, 'precognitive insight' not 'psychic premonition.'

Yet for anyone considering everything an Indigo Child is capable of, the most important ability would be distinguishing the difference between 'precognition' and 'premonition'. Otherwise, how else would you determine the difference between pure unadulterated 'bull feces,' and a major evolutionary enhancement to our basic human instinct?

An Emergence of Genetic Programming

We as humans instinctively search for familiar patterns in nearly everything we do millions of times a day without even realizing it. Whether it's finding a pattern in the sand that resembles a familiar animal, or something as simple as identifying a familiar image in the clouds. It's a phenomenon called 'pareidolia,' that provides us these vague random stimuli (both visually and audibly) that seem to have a perceived or significant meaning. More often than not, the patterns are useless and meaningless–like a rabbit in the clouds–yet in our early human development 'pareidolia' allowed us to distinguish distinct and important patterns etched in the sand; like those left by a mountain lion, or a bear's silhouette outlined in the bushes; making them quite significant for survival.

Humans can often be quite gullible, in that we tend to believe nearly everything we see or hear as factual data. It is after all, far easier to believe than to not believe, especially when one has to make a sudden decision of whether or not to run like hell because their life may depend on it.

Not that this is a bad thing, it's that we have been 'programmed,' by evolution, to believe first ask questions later. Why, you might ask? The answer is simple. It's because when footprints encountered on a nature walk in the forest, may put them on alert; especially when followed a series of deep growls and grunts in the bush. For all these clues together, would put terror in anyone's soul once recognized as belonging to a mountain lion. However, had you not noticed the patterns of a large animal, you would have simply brushed them off; for which the penalty could have been quite severe. Therefore 'believing' it is, is definitely the wiser of the two choices and thus engrained deep within our DNA.

Recognizing patterns in chaos is just something we are genetically programmed to do instinctively; a survival mechanism inherent through thousands of years of evolution; is NOT a coincidence, and remains today as one of our most basic instincts. Coincidence is having a fender-bender in the super-market car park with someone you went to high school with 20 or 30 years ago and haven't seen since you graduated. Whereas a 'precognitive event' constitutes having thought of, or dreamt of that person –only hours, or minutes before the accident occurred–only to experience later the accident exactly as it had been envisioned.

When a person states they possess a 'precognitive ability', I used to find it quite amusing. By that, I mean watching how other people react to their statement, and how few actually believe them. For many, their 'precognitive experiences' are only imagined 'premonitions,' that should not be taken seriously; yet for others there is no debate as to their 'inherent awareness' of 'time', space' and/or 'dimension.'

A love-hate relationship I (and many others) associate to be a remnant medieval fear of the 'dark arts,' that promoted an aversion to public ridicule and perhaps even persecution because of one's beliefs. Yet, this 'faculty' is no different than any other innate basic faculty humankind possesses–be it sight, sound, taste, smell or touch–as just another inherent 'sense' mankind is capable of.

One must first 'believe' it is so, before they can challenge that belief; otherwise, how could anyone possibly identify or otherwise understand anyone who possesses these 'genetically inherent faculties?'

For centuries, Judeo-Christian cultures have maintained that any skill used by an unseen force is 'to be feared.' Which is precisely why, religious zealots and ancient cultures categorized the faculty of 'premonition' as a black art, black magic, devil worship, or demonology. The main reason being, anyone thought to possess 'precognitive intuition' was believed to be receiving assistance from a 'demonic mystical force,' and therefore must be practicing witchcraft and should be tried, burned, or dunked until drowned, as a witch. The fact remains that the faculty of 'premonition' and 'precognition' are still highly misunderstood.

Many rival political and religious factions throughout human history used fear as a reason to persecute anyone who opposed the Holy Roman Church's authority and accused to be practicing the 'dark arts;' forcing the Church to deal swiftly and in a a most extreme manner. Another reason why Indigo Children often keep any 'precognitive knowledge' to themselves and end up eventually alienating themselves from their peers to prevent ridicule…my close friends every now and then will lovingly refer to me as a 'witch.'

Just as humanity has evolved over the millennia, so has science. The invention of radio, considered a miracle in science, allowed us no longer to be physically present to hear an opera singer sing, a symphony orchestra play, buy a ticket to the World Series, and listen to political candidates to debate without them having to jump on a train and go from city to city in their bid for President. All because sound was discovered to be an invisible wave that traveled instantaneously through our atmosphere (and later discovered to travel through space). All one needed was the electrical circuitry and highly technical device to tune in this new contraption a 'radio.'

Soon to be followed (in a relatively short time) by waves of not only sound, but visual images, broadcast in pretty much the same manner to a miraculous device we now know as 'television.'

No one can see or hear this invisible energy zipping at high speed through our atmosphere; yet we now know it exists all around us. But in order to receive these signals (waves) one must have the necessary devices to translate these invisible images and inaudible sounds, 'before' they can materialize before they can fill their eyes with images or hear wonderful sounds from 'thin air.' We know energy is constant and perceived to be without the constraints regarding 'time' or 'space.'

Since time began, a 'consciousness' that spans the entire universe also began oscillating frequencies throughout the universe; a physical universe that to us on Earth appears to be linear and concrete, when in fact it is not. Just as a two-way radio signals can be transmitted and received resonated radio signals throughout our atmosphere and even deep space, so can the next generation of Indigo Children broadcast and receive the resonant frequencies 'effortlessly, intuitively,' and 'instinctively' without limitations to linear 'time, space' or 'dimension.'

Kinda, Sorta, Maybe

To be clear, 'precognisance, intuition' and 'premonition' are kinda, sorta, maybe the very same thing, but they're all different. 'Precognisance' denotes an 'intuitive awareness' of 'knowing with certainty' and 'intuition' is the very strong sense that something is about to happen with a definite trust and conviction, while heeding any warning, 'without fully knowing why they should.' Although they are all quite distinct, 'premonition,' is often included in this trio as one of the many 'psychic attributes.' It being that a 'psychic' qualifies as a person who perceives the future only through interpretation. Whereas, an Indigo Children are 'precognizant' and have an 'intuitive instinctive awareness of knowing' what the future holds, a sensitivity that often defines an Indigo as being a 'sensitive-empath' and do not qualify as necessarily being 'psychic.'

Most Indigo Children are extreme 'sensitives' in that they 'knowing' the outcome of events regardless of what choices have been made. It is important to understand premonition,' is a metaphysical phenomenon, denoting a 'psychic ability.' While 'empathy' denotes the 'sensitive' can intellectually identify with–or vicariously sense and experience–the emotions, feelings, thoughts, and attitudes of others; past, present or future, as well as the souls of the living, dead, and the unborn.

Are you confused yet? Don't be...

I don't think too many people will argue against the fact that most theories about 'psychics' have been shrouded by myths and fanciful tales for centuries. Today, when you search the Internet on this elusive subject, you often get nothing but abstruse theories presented as nothing more than a 'hypothesis,' theories immune of empirical evidence meaning they rely mostly on experience and supposition. The offer little or no objective scientific proof that is based on logic and fact; ultimately excluding any adequate explanation related to cause and effect, rendering 99.9% of the theories on the World Wide Web meaningless.

Do psychics really exist? Yes, I believe they do, but I also believe there a hell of a lot more charlatans exist out there, than psychics, for inherent 'psychic' skills are quite rare. Just as we use language as a form of communication, others use 'precognition' and 'premonition' with varying degrees of accuracy. Some are 'spot on' and with such a high degree of accuracy that they can best be compared to an advanced warning home alarm system that detects intruders.

Many psychics consider themselves as possessing 'special gifts,' and many have capitalized on the vulnerability of people by marketing themselves as 'psychics' when in fact they are not. More often than not, their only goal is to defraud gullible targets of their money while ripping hearts out. Capitalizing on mankind's basic human emotions, makes humans easy irrational targets, making them easy pickings for the unscrupulous, and usually self-proclaimed, 'psychic' who abuses trust as a 'Carte Blanc' invitation and license to dominate, control, or manipulate others.

Indigo Children are the extreme opposite in that they do not believe there is anything special about their ability, and will rarely ever charge others for their assistance. In fact, Indigos can get quite irate when they encounter a profiteering self-professed psychic, and will make a public display to put an end to their self-glorified, self-centered, and selfish attitudes as a public display of humility. When an Indigo instinctively encounters such treachery and deceit, they will make it their life's mission to destroy them; skillfully, swiftly and without mercy.

When dealing with unscrupulous people the Indigo Child has the upper-advantage, that innate sense of 'awareness' and a 'conscious' ability that instantaneously analyzes every possible scenario and its inevitable outcome. From that analysis, they then are able choose the most cunning method to not merely expose the 'charlatan,' but embarrass them publicly to better destroy and discredit them for the 'cons' they are; which sends them off running into the horizon, tail tucked high between their legs.

People familiar with Indigo traits understand that we are constantly being bombarded by 'intuitive imprints (resonant signatures)' emanating from everyone around us as a 'spontaneous consciousness;' a consciousness unknowingly transmitted by every individual on the planet. We can't help it and we don't do it intentionally, perhaps by predisposing ancient genetic remnants designed to allow humans to seek each other out, emotions that with ward off unscrupulous individual, or attract other like-minded people like ourselves. This ability to read these errant 'resonant signals' has been lying dormant within our DNA for countless generations and until now only begun awakening within a select few over the last several hundred years.

Every human on the planet is unique and we all come from diverse backgrounds, beliefs, value systems, religions, cultures, morals, experiences, opportunities, and educational levels. Yet each of us possesses within us certain characteristics inherent within our ancestral DNA – at varying degrees. DNA coding that may not be specifically unique to 'humans,' for other animals can instinctually sense danger long before encountering the threat.

Today, the signs that dormant 'inherent genes' within our human genome is somehow being activated are all around us. Many people are beginning to awaken to new ability that appears innate because of the gradual changes within them…'precognition' being one of them, changing the way they see the world. Most people in fact, have absolutely no idea that these recessed 'genes' are beginning to activate within their DNA as mankind begins to discover a new fundamental abilities. Abilities that will allow them to 'know' what to do, how to react, and how to use a new 'intuitive awareness' of not only themselves, but 'others' as well.

AN INNATE AWARENESS OF CONSCIOUSNESS

"When you look in the mirror, what do you see? Do you see the real you, or what you have been conditioned to believe is you? The two are so, so different. One is of an infinite consciousness capable of being and creating whatever it chooses, while the other is but an illusion imprisoned by its own perceived and programmed limitations."

David Icke

Indigos can inherently 'sense' the world around them; as their minds are constantly being bombarded by sudden and often inexplicable information. As the older generations of Indigo Children begin their 'awareness,' they will most likely brush off those thoughts as nothing more than fleeting 'day-dreams.' Eventually however, they will begin to sense they're not daydreams at all. For others however, they will quickly understand they have a new 'awareness' to 'precognitive' events, or perhaps somehow know what others around them are thinking before they have even voiced their own thought.

This entire book has been on how Indigos are so much more in-tune with the 'universal consciousness.' However, does that make them any less susceptible to the unscrupulous, or people they care about? The 'resonant impressions' the Indigo receives, regardless of distance, is often difficult to discern, the tricky part is learning to either keep it to themselves, share what they sense, or disregard it altogether.

'Intuitive Awareness' seems to come quite naturally to the youngest of Indigo generations. From infancy, they seem to demonstrate an effortless ability that clearly focuses on whose thoughts, feelings, and desires they are sensing from a storm of what can only be described, as a 'resonant noise.'

As a child, I remember feeling not only other people's emotions, I often felt what was left in the room, 'residual energy signatures' people unwittingly leave behind in a room or on an object. In fact, I thought everyone could sense them because to me, it was second nature, but it wasn't!

As I entered those awkward teen years, I successfully learned how to block out any unsolicited resonant signals left behind by others. I can only imagine how difficult it is for Indigos undergoing a latent DNA 'awakening' as they slowly begin to comprehend the previously unknown 'consciousness' they have become aware of, but not necessarily accept.

Regardless of whether or not you're an Indigo yourself, understand we all are, have been, and will be connected to the very same 'consciousness' our entire lives! The difference being is that when an Indigo enters a crowded a room of people they can instantaneously feel the residual remnants everyone has left behind, a thickness so dense, it would be impossible to cut with a chainsaw.

As a child, I can remember feeling everyone in proximity, including people who had already left the room; memories I will have forever etched into the deepest recesses of my mind as it were yesterday.

For 'sensitive' Indigo undergoing changes to their genomes, it can often be confusing. They tend to believe every emotion they sense (from others), is their own, when the reality is, the emotions emanate from sources all around them. But just when they think they've got it all under control and the fog of confusion has begun to lift, another startling realization comes into play…the begin to sense the intense 'resonant emotional signatures' large crowds of people have left behind; sporting events, theaters, conventions, or the worst (for me, your author) amusement parks. These places are prime infestations, where countless people have unwittingly transmitted every emotion under sun; elation to anger being the worst as it is quite often a very intense imprint. This confusion can leave the awakening 'sensitive' Indigo, so overwhelmed, they physically become ill until they remove themselves from the source. Once they have done this enough times, they will begin to put two-and-two together and notice that the further away they get from crowds of people, the better they feel. It's when they realize the emotions they're feeling, are in fact, not their own and are what made them physically ill.

Many believe an Indigo's 'consciousness' is a 'psychic faculty' and the confusion gets even worse when one considers their 'clairvoyant' or 'clairsentient' nature; blurring the reality as a 'psychic gift' and not just an additional 'sense' to enhance the other five; Another reason why the Indigo often feels compromised, physically and emotionally. Not to mention, distraught, anxious, and extremely nauseous and their emotions can jump from being elated and happy-go-lucky to being grief stricken, angry, and hell bent on revenge to the point of vile…for no apparent reason.

Let's face it, it is within our nature to ride emotional rollercoasters, but for the budding Indigo, is most likely do an 'unconscious resonance' of negative or positive influence. My experience dictates that this rollercoaster of stimuli often–and inadvertently translates the 'negative resonance' into 'physical pain;' usually centralized to a specific part of their body manifesting as severe headaches, stomach cramps, and back pain.

A Personal Revelation

Grandmother's stories always amused me growing up. She always seemed to know what to say at the right time. As a young lad, I believed everyone was like me when it came to sensing and knowing things. However, I soon discovered that was not the case. In middle school, I had been afraid of being labeled 'weird' by other kids or teachers, so I took preventative measures and just alienated myself from the playground before it even happened; however, it didn't work and the ridicule would often end with a good beating after school.

Being quite religious, my Grandmother often tried to explain what she perceived to be a 'psychic ability' as a 'special gift from God,' by telling me the other children were afraid of me. She would tell me, "God allows you to reach beyond the grave, and even allows you to relive the past and see into the future. I know you think of it as a curse, but in time, you will learn how to use it as I did. Know too, that people will come to you for guidance when they realize you have these 'gifts,' and it's important that you never charge them for what you reveal. For what you give away with an open heart, God will repay you ten times over and make you that much stronger; but never forget God will take it away from those that do so in greed."

My Grandmother called my innate sense of 'knowing' and 'precognition' a 'psychic ability;' and my ability of 'clairvoyance' she referred to as my being a 'sensitive' (meaning an empath), because in the 1950's we were as much in the dark about these talents as we had been during the Dark Ages.

I had been quite confused as a boy; what boy isn't? Yet, what confounded me most, were the wide range of emotions I constantly felt; elated one minute, angry the next, earning me the label 'moody.' However, I soon realized the emotions I was feeling, were not mine at all. They belonged to everyone else around me!

"Never judge another man, until you have walked a great distance in their moccasins," meant a lot to me (and surely spoken by a 'sensitive' shaman), meant a lot to me in understanding who I was, and what I could do. Growing up, I learned to understand that the confetti of emotions I sensed all those around me, were not my own, and in understanding this, I was able to develop a profound sense of compassion for people as well as and intense 'distain' for a select few.

This inherent ability was not my choice, but I had to learn to make the most of it, and so I did! What amazes me today is how easily, naturally, and instinctively, I am able to do so. The irony of this lesson is when I'm around others, I know exactly how they feel…and if what they're telling me is really, what they're telling me!

It has taken many years and a lot of practice to be able to fully control the 'resonant signatures' broadcast by others that I inadvertently sense. Similarly, although I have learned how to block out a majority of them, and ignore others, sometimes there are those 'emotional vampires' that force me to vacate the vicinity as soon as possible; for it's not as simple as just turning a switch on and off.

Today, younger generations of 'Indigo Children' demonstrate a propensity that allows an instantaneous identification of who is transmitting the resonance, but whether or not those souls are 'living, deceased,' or 'not of this earth.' The difficulty however, it is when hundreds suddenly inundate any Indigo – if not thousands – of people broadcasting emotions simultaneously, think of it as having hundreds of radios tuned into different stations, in a small room with the volume blaring at the same time. Only then can you understand just how difficult it would be to discern your own thoughts from all others.

Whenever I allow myself to be enticed to go into an amusement park, a rock concert, or a conference – anywhere large crowds congregate – it doesn't take long for my emotions to run rampant and my 'shields' go up. Understand that it can take a lot of energy for me to block everyone out as everyone around me indiscreetly drains my strength. I hope that you can now begin to recognize the good, the bad, and ugly of what it really means to be an Indigo.

"Just imagine you put yourself into a protective bubble that blocks out all that emotion"; sounds simple enough. However, it can't be done; at least not for extended periods. The energy required to do so for an extended period would leave the Indigo not only physically exhausted, but mentally, a raving lunatic; and why you won't find very many Indigo Children anxious to go anywhere near an amusement park…unless it's absolutely necessary (like a parent taking their child to Disneyland).

It really doesn't matter where people go, it's the extremity of the simultaneous emotional signals broadcast; rallies, casinos, office parties, political gatherings, funerals, or weddings, they all generate enough emotion to suck the energy from an Indigo like the sun sucks the moisture from grape off a vine, turning it into a raisin.

The Perception of Being Indigo

Throughout this book, I have mentioned the Indigo ability of 'intuitive' input, a natural and inherent connection to a greater consciousness that spans not only the entire universe, it has no constraints to 'time, space' or 'dimension.' It is an ability that can not only communicate with the living, an Indigo can sense souls who have passed, as well as those entities that have no soul and may be passing from our dimension into an alternate dimension or reality.

Since my early years, my conscious acuity has become quite sensitive. As a young man, I was often bewildered, confused, and perplexed by all the random 'resonant signals' I was picking up; not to mention fascinated that no one else around me could. It was a difficult adjustment for me at best, but with time, practice, and experience I became much comfortable and familiar in my 'sensitivity.' It was an integral part of who I was. Grandmother recognized this 'sensitivity' and with her influence as a teenager, she helped me to develop the necessary skills I needed to trust my 'hunches, vibrations,' and 'gut-feelings' and use them as an advantage. Far beyond what warnings that little person on your shoulder (who most people totally ignore) would offer, I learned to heed the warnings from a 'consciousness' I knew little about and thus became much more 'empathic' to the world around me.

Merriam Webster Dictionary defines "empathy" as, "The intellectual identification with or vicariously experiencing feelings, thoughts, emotions, or attitudes of others." Add to that the definition for "sensitivity," as "having acute mental or emotional sensibility; aware of and responsive to the feelings of other;" this should provide a more eloquent definition of what being an 'Indigo' with an accentuated 'sensitivity' and 'empathy.' For this reason, many generations of Indigos throughout time have been misconstrued to be 'psychic sensitives' and/or 'empaths.'

The Road to Self-Discovery

What is quite interesting is that the newer generations of Indigo Children born after the year 2000, have not experienced very many difficulties of self-discovery. For them, their ability to a 'universal consciousness' is totally normal. However, for the older Indigo patriarchs, say born before 1970, their experience goes far beyond that of their younger counterparts, in that they had to learn and experienced control of their abilities and usually don't take them for granted.

The Awakening: an Emergence of Indigo Consciousness

Now enter the generations of Indigo Children born between 1970 and the year 2000, their abilities of communicating with a 'universal consciousness' is just now becoming active, as codons within their DNA is activating. Unaware there are changes in their genetics, they become much more 'sensitive' or 'empathic' to 'resonant signals' being received all around them; leaving them with a feeling of confusion by what is happening to them. Understanding just whom they really are and what is transpiring to them is a long and arduous process; very much like going through puberty all over again; emotions: discomfort, strange desires, confusion, and depression. It is only when this particular group of Indigo Generation can recognize that the 'resonant signals' they have detected, 'are not their own' that they will come to question what is happening to them. I can only hope this book will yield the answers they seek.

I knew I was different, but I was lucky enough to have as grandmother who provided me a road map through her love, understanding, and welcomed advice. Although my time with her was relatively short when I add it all up, she always seemed to know when I was feeling extremely uncomfortable with all the extraneous emotions around me, and would ring me up. I had always known her to be 'intuitive' and with her help, even from great distances, she taught me how to identify and block out foreign 'resonant transmissions' of others, before I made myself physical ill; a skill that at first was difficult to understand and far easier said than done.

Indigo emotions are far different from others in that an Indigo cannot quite understand why 'common' people show such extreme variances of emotion; it just seems very illogical to us. This however, does not mean we don't feel extreme emotions such as sadness or elation, it's just shorter lived and at times quite intense. Indigo Children don't forget or forgive easily either; we just tick it off our checklist of 'experiences' as just another lesson learned, and avoid any similar situations in the future and move on quickly.

When I was a young man in my teens, I used to find it difficult to focus or deflect unwanted 'energy (resonant signals)' from all those 'emotionally unstable' people who were constantly bombarding my mind – 'psychic vampires' if you will. It was when I learned how to clear my mind, by envisioning a blank slate to concentrate on nothing at all.

The exercise allowed me to take control of own emotions, while at the same learning how to filter out everyone else's 'negative resonance,' to the point of becoming ambivalent to everyone, and everything around me. I wasn't until I was able to master the technique that I no longer felt sickened by the overload of 'other people's' emotional baggage. Although this technique can work well, I must also confess that I had to endorse a natural instinct to self-preservation, basically, by getting the hell out of Dodge (fleeing). When the instinct of 'flee or fight' kicked in, it was because I had been so overwhelmed I needed to withdraw rapidly, thus I didn't just walk away, I ran off as fast as my legs would carry me.

The Awakening: an Emergence of Indigo Consciousness

Everyone is 'sensitive' to other people's frequencies to a point, although not everyone is 'empathic' or 'sensitive.' Because of the 'universal consciousness,' our connection to others is impossible to avoid, it's just how our minds operate as humans (unless of course a person is psychopath, sociopath, or narcissistic). What we perceive within this intricate web of 'inter-connectivity' is a 'universal energy,' a 'consciousness' we are all part of and therefore cannot detach ourselves from it. Yet at times we all need to maintain our individual sense of separation (the 'self)' from those around us, while learning to respect the needs of others who wish the same.

It's now with the emergence of a new Indigo consciousness, that the most recent generations can easily shut the 'negative energies' that surround them. And for the fledgling Indigo, 'awakening' to an 'all-encompassing consciousness' it will take practice, patience, and acceptance that will allow them to achieve their full potential…it just takes time, practice, and most of all…perseverance.

ASPIRING TO UNDERSTAND INDIGO

"Intuition is the highest form of intelligence. It transcends all other individual abilities or skills, for things are never quite, as they seem. We may think we understand the world around us, but all we are really seeing is the reality we have created as our own little world."

Author Unknown

At this point, you're probably asking yourself, "How can anyone truly recognize an Indigo?" "How can anyone know who is, and who isn't 'intuitively aware?" or "How do I know if I'm picking up another person's 'resonant signature,' much less if it's a soul of the living or a non-human entity?

Well to be honest, there no 'on-off' switch that will allows you or anyone else to become instantaneously an Indigo Child; nor is there any switch that will allow a person to become suddenly 'empathic' to the world around them. An Indigo however, IS capable of accessing whether or not they are 'intuitively aware' and if you have to think about it without a lot of forethought…you yourself are not an Indigo Child, they just know without question they are different. Just as our human brain can identify individual sounds produced by dozens of instruments in an orchestra, an Indigo's brain can focus on a specific instrument in that orchestra to identify how well the musician playing it, can play.

For example, people living in proximity of busy train tracks, subway, or a tram, will tell you they rarely, if ever, hear any trains pass, all because their brain has learned to filter any loud noises produced by the train as an unnecessary and blocks it out entirely. Thus, as in this example, unnecessary emotional noises all around the Indigo, can be identified as not their own – and totally ignored.

Everyone is 'aware,' but to various degrees – possibly an instinct left-over from when man slept in a cave – yet many haven't a clue that their mind IS connected to others around them, much less understand what clutter has been thrown at them and needs to be filtered from their own thoughts. As the constant roar of a passing train behind your home can be annoying when first encountered, your brain eventually learned ignore it as unnecessary information and blocked it from your mind. So too, your brain must learn to 'intuitively' block and ignoring the useless 'resonance' of others from you mind; automatically.

For those who are going through the 'awakening' process, the result of dormant genetic coding of DNA is allowing a gradual transformation to take place. Once the genome has begun the process, the brain will inadvertently begin to connect to the 'universal consciousness' sporadically, and so doing, create an emotional upheaval during the process as the emerging Indigo Child beings begins to not only sense everyone's emotions around them, they also become emotionally compromised to the point they believe they're going crazy. At this point, they cannot yet filter, much less identify where these 'emotional resonances' originate, or who transmitted them.

It's not until an Indigo can master what's been received and by whom, that they will later be able to receive what many have called 'divine inspiration' (a term used since the early days of Christianity). Once this is accomplished, they will suddenly begin to realize they are becoming more 'intuitively aware.' Their thoughts, often profound, will seem to appear from nowhere. Thoughts, they cannot possibly ignore as an Indigo, and for which will stand up and begin to take notice. Eventually these 'flashes of intuition' will be abstruse, an 'awareness' of 'sudden insight' that will first baffle and confuse them, while many others are completely oblivious to them altogether. Eventually they will eventually learn to trust themselves, that they are not crazy, and somehow the 'awakening' to a previously unknown 'consciousness' will be realized and they can begin to pay attention.

Over tens of thousands of years, humanity's DNA coding has been suppressed enough to stifle our brain's ability to recognize and process 'resonant signatures.' Why this is so, remains a mystery. What is interesting to note however, is that an individual going through this emergence of consciousness, will eventually allow an 'intuitive awareness' that is directly related to one important factor; dormant DNA code.

The Indigo is genetically 'sensitive' to the point that it gives them the uncanny ability to access a 'higher level of consciousness' instantaneously with an 'intuitive awareness' that extends far beyond anything mankind has ever experienced before. Why this is happening is still unknown, but it appears that a more advanced population is emerging and appears to be 'highly intelligent,' and is the most common identifier of Indigo traits. Perhaps because of a 'higher awareness' of self, a 'highly accurate' sense to 'precognition,' and an ability to transcend thought beyond time, space, and dimension, and why we have coined the label 'Indigo Child.'

Precognitive Insight – Déjà Rêvé

"I have often had a feeling that something just wasn't right or immediately felt I should not trust someone and should stay away from them." a common statement of many Indigo Children, including myself. How many times have you said, 'I should have listened to that little voice in my head?' After all, everyone possesses some ability to 'precognitive insight;' at least to some degree; is it a fleeting 'intuitive' moment, or is it actually linked to a higher 'awareness of consciousness?' Everyone has experienced this 'sixth sense' at one-time-or-another, the hard part is in knowing how and/or why you were able to do so. "Was it because you possess the necessary inherent Indigo genetic coding that allowed it to happen, or was it just a fluke, and if you have demonstrated Indigo traits like 'precognition,' has it always been so or had developed recently?"

Different people experience 'premonitions' at varying degrees, and since we all communicate at different 'wavelengths' (resonances), some people (not necessarily Indigo Children) are naturally in tune to these 'energies' some of the time…and at different levels. Yet for an Indigo, it goes a whole lot further than just a 'premonition,' for them it's 'precognition,' because an Indigo has the inherent ability to assess a 'precognitive event' as an 'intuitive awareness' from within the 'universal consciousness' and is a lot different than simply being a 'premonition.'

Either way, it is necessary to understand that as man has progressed over the last thousand centuries toward a 'higher state' of 'consciousness,' a very thin line has been drawn to separate the two; for both 'precognition' and 'premonition' are often interchanged and confused to represent the same ability. Each thought to represent the same thing, a detailed insight to a particular event, person, and place able to foresee what had, or may transpire.

For the Indigo, 'precognitive ability' goes much, much, deeper than just a fleeting 'guts feeling.' The Indigo's innate ability draws an 'inherent awareness' from the 'universal consciousness' spanning space, time and even dimension to allow the Indigo an innate ability of 'knowing what they know!' Their knowledge, information that is far more detailed and complete, with a higher degree of accuracy that any self-respecting psychic would envy, because every potential outcome had been assessed by the Indigo, which rarely by a psychic.

The faculties of 'precognition' and 'premonition' are often referred to as the 'Déjà connu, ('already known') and far more intense than having just having the sense of an event 'having already been played out before' or 'déjà vu,' and had been experienced at that very moment; whether it was or not.

Indigo's are predestined to possess the eerie ability to 'precognition;' a manifestation of knowing the details to an event that is about to occur to a specific person at a specific location in the near or distant future with absolute confidence. 'Physics' on the other had are at times are said to possess the facility of 'Premonition,' only offering a sense of foreboding, with a blurry vision (usually a dream) of an event they believe to be inevitable, and made known through a deep unconscious sleep. So how does one know what is eminent (precognition), and what is merely a perception (premonition)?

For centuries, 'clairvoyance (premonition)' had been daunted as THE 'psychic faculty' to possess. Why, It's more of 'precognitive' ability that better defines an Indigo's 'intuitive awareness' skillset? 'Precognition' actually accounts for 69% of 'déjà vu;' a 'post-cognitive' recollection of a 'precognitive event.' 'Pre-cognitive' translates from the French phrase 'déjà rêvé,' which literally means 'known through a dream;' thus accounting for much of the confusion. [52]

Another error many psychics have make, is using the term 'precognitive event,' (having detailed knowledge regarding a future event or situation and its inevitable outcome), when in reality they are relating is nothing more than 'gut-feel' or a 'hunch.'
A 'premonition' (a feeling anticipation and/or anxiety over a perceived event that may, or may not occur sometime in the near or distant future) is not based on fact, but derived from instinct, which is quite subjective interpretation…and is much more ambiguous that an Indigo's interpretation though 'precognition.' A 'psychic' does not claim to 'know that they know' without question or reserve, it's usually all speculation.

To the best of my knowledge, I have never heard of a 'psychics' that can definitively convince me they possess the extraordinary ability of 'knowing' an outcome to their 'premonition' with an 'undeniable confidence;' and for those 'psychics' that believe their interpretation is indeed of a 'precognitive event,' were most likely Indigo Children themselves. Remember, the proof is in the pudding…of that I have no doubt that there are psychics who are very capable of having bonafide 'premonitions,' like everybody else, but when they bloat their 'educated hunches' with nothing more than pure, 'unadulterated conjecture,' I have a problem with them, for they really don't know squat.

Symbolic Precognitive Dreams

Abstract precognitive information is often received as a 'symbolic reference' that may not be fully realized until the actual event has occurred; therefore the information received makes it much more difficult to identify as a 'precognitive dream.' Yet, there may be certain symbolical impressions received through this dream state from which an 'inexperienced Indigo' may or may not be able to extrapolate, reference, or match to a future event. However, once actualized, the event is either quickly forgotten, or totally ignored; with no reference ever made to the 'precognitive dream.'

However, there are unscrupulous people who will attempt to take advantage of these cryptic impressions by confusing people into believing their 'mumbo-jumbo;' a half-ass attempt to dazzle them with a non-existent brilliance. So instead, they baffle them nothing but pure unadulterated bullshit; all because they refuse to admit defeat to the fact that they have absolutely no idea what the symbology behind the dream actually represented. Since the information is symbolic, anything derived is 'subjective' at best. While on the other hand, Indigo's would normally consider 'symbolic dreams' to be nothing more than the lowest form of 'déjà rêvé,' and would not even attempt to make a good 'guess.'

Literal Precognitive Dreams

The experience of a 'first-person precognitive' dream is that it full of literal detail. Perhaps by what had been 'sensed, thought,' and 'felt' during the 'dream state,' or that it may very well had been realized to be some point 'in the not too distant future.' This type of dream allows an Indigo, or an 'experiencer' like a 'remote viewer,' a sufficient amount of information to assess that a 'literal precognitive dream' has indeed occurred, and by which provides enough information to believe that the 'déjà vu' moment can be directly linked to a 'déjà rêvé' experience.

3rd Person Precognitive Dreams

This type of 'precognitive dream,' received via a 'third-person's perspective' more often than not, displays both 'symbolic' and 'literal' similarities, and the information received through in this dream state will most likely will never be observed, or even occur from a first-person point of view.

Lucid Precognitive Dreams

Lucid dreams occur during an 'awakened state,' a dream where the 'experiencer' of the dream is 'consciously aware' of the fact that they are indeed 'aware, alert,' and 'awake.' As well as being aware that 'they' are the focal point of this type of 'precognitive dream;' another prime example demonstrating the emergence of yet another form of the phenomena to demonstrate another 'precognitive' state.

The American Psychological Association defined lucid dreams as a person being, "…in a dream state in which the sleeper is aware that he or she is dreaming and may be able to influence the progress of the dream narrative." Yet many others hang on the belief that a 'lucid dream' is the "realization that they are in a dream state during the dream…" in other words, they are entirely aware of the fact that they are in fact dreaming. The commonalities being both definitions agree of being in a 'conscious' realization of experiencing a dream, while within the dream state."

What is particularly interesting about a 'precognitive dream' is that it represents at least one of the two highest states of 'precognition,' – 'precognitive déjà rêvé,' and a 'non-lucid precognitive dream.' Robert Waggoner explains them as an 'active' or an 'ambient' lucid dream. In the 'active lucid precognitive dream,' the person dreaming is 'actively engaging' in the flow of the 'precognitive dream;' while in an 'ambient lucid dream' the dreamer is only 'passively observing' and remains neutral within the flow a dream as it progresses.

"As the years passed, however, certain pivotal lucid dreams opened my mind to the possibility that lucid dreaming offered a gateway to so much more." Robert Waggoner recently acknowledged in his 2009 book, "Lucid Dreaming – A Gateway to the Inner Self." [53]

As researchers continue to document and explore the phenomenon of 'lucid dreaming,' evidence continues to mount. Some very significant signs of a biological factor are now beginning to reveal unusual brain activity occurring while the human body experiences a 'lucid dream.' Recently, a study conducted at the Neurological Laboratory of Frankfurt, demonstrated that 'lucid dreamers' produce some of the fastest gamma brainwave frequencies ever recorded. The brainwaves operated around 40Hz + (1); revealed evidence that suggests 'lucid dreamers' are actually quite 'self-aware' and much more 'conscious' during a 'lucid state' than what occurs during a normal 'awakened state;' which isn't anywhere near the gamma frequency of 40 Hz, but closer to the frequency of a normal 'sleep state.' Thus, the study suggests the existence of the gamma brainwaves in a 'lucid dreamer' prove without a doubt that the subject studied was actually having a 'total conscious experience,' demonstrating 'lucid dreaming' to be a very real phenomenon. [56]

Now here are some eye-opening questions to ponder: Which state is actually real? Is what we perceive as an 'awakened state, actually be a 'dream state;' or are we merely jumping between different 'reality layers' in our perception; including alternative timelines, dimensions and aspects to each reality?' Is our ability to create each and every one of our own realities easier during a 'lucid dream state' by the way our brain functions at a higher frequency, and imagine just what we would be capable of if we could attain a frequency of 40 Hz + (1) without even being subjected to a 'lucid dream?' I'd be willing to be my 'E' ticket on it.

Since gamma brainwaves are said to involve a higher state of mental activity that enhances our ability to consolidate information, it's very possible that if our brains could maintain this 'at will' frequency. Certainly, we would be processing information in multiple parts of the brain simultaneously and thus use perhaps that 90% of our brain scientists for decades have been saying we don't currently use. [57]

The fact, now be out-of-the-bag, in this study may very well have proven that Indigos capable of 'lucid dreaming.' Especially since an Indigo's brain tends to operate at an accelerated gamma frequency that produces a higher frequency vibration to allow them to function in a much clearer, more coherent, and in a higher state of consciousness. Especially, when awake, and although the relative size of the human brain has not changed for well over 200,000 years, but has become even more evident that our minds are what has evolved; and with it, our 'state of consciousness.' [91]

A university professor I had many years ago had assigned us a paper written by Aristotle in 350BC to read entitled "On Prophesying by Dreams." Therein, Aristotle chastises man with extreme prejudice and skepticism I might add, to the validity of people claiming to have had dreams that revealed knowledge to future events. Although he (Aristotle) never completely refuted the possibility of 'precognitive dreams,' he believed that a 'precognitive dream' was nothing more than mere coincidence.

His reference led me to read other ancient Greek philosophers and authors who whole-heartedly subscribed to the belief that 'precognition' and 'premonition (prophecy)' were indeed real and quite evident throughout history. Homer for example in his writings "The Iliad" and "The Odyssey," believed Apollo – the Greek god of music, healing and prophecy – bestowed upon Cassandra (the daughter of King Priam of Troy) the gift of prophecy.

The reason I mention Homer and Aristotle is that while trying to answer the ancient question "Why do 'precognitive dreams' exist?" it had occurred to me that perhaps quantum mechanics have may indeed had a hand in how 'consciousness' and our 'awareness of consciousness,' are indeed part of the equation. Remember, Indigos are able to 'intuitively' tap into a 'consciousness' that spans not only the universe but also traverses outside our concept of a linear time or space; which could explain a lot about how Indigo Children are able to experience 'precognitive dreams' in such depth and with a high degree of accuracy.

Consider this possibility – If we examine the universe as a 'multi-world universe,' using quantum theory, every possible past, present and future probability could theoretically exist as an experienced probability for the 'precognitive dreamer;' the quantum superposition being that a particle can exist in every possible state until it is observed.

Although quantum theory is only fledgling science on the surface by the academics of quantum physics, theoretical physics, and astrophysicists around the globe, on the surface our understanding of quantum information is still minimal at best. What we do know about quantum information is that it is indeed 'non-linear' and exists within an astronomical dataset. Knowing this, it is quite conceivable to me, and plausible to believe that the Universe is indeed, organized into the most complex set of data, information, and structure populated by a myriad of parallel probabilities. Thus allowing me to believe 'precognitive' information is drawn from that vast pool of knowledge (myself included), all calling it a 'universal consciousness' exists at such an astronomical scale, our minuscule brains could not possibly fathom all the possibilities. In fact, many scientists today believe that the entire universe is a living conscious being in and of itself as a whole; to which, we are all connected as tiny specs of cosmic dusts to the whole scheme of it.

The Quantum Approach to Precognitive Consciousness

In Dr. Stuart Hameroff's first book, "Ultimate Computing," in his tenure as a professor at the University of Arizona, he proposes that microtubules may provide a better understanding to the operation of 'consciousness' within our human brain cells, both at the molecular and supra-molecular level. His theory proposes that the human brain is not only a super neuralcomputer, but a very advanced quantum computer as well. [58]

For years, 'artificial intelligence' has been elusive for computer companies to recreate within their super-computer prowess, and to no avail. This is because the computational ability and nature of the human brain is far too complex when it comes to calculating an intelligent 'consciousness.' It's when quantum physicists are able to add the necessary equation to the Quantum mechanics necessary for explaining how 'human consciousness,' is capable of making an astronomical number of complex decisions, both simultaneously and instantaneously, then and only then will mankind finally explain how the universal entanglement and superposition affects truly affects 'human consciousness.'

In a separate study, Roger Penrose, an English mathematical physicist and philosopher, published his first book on consciousness, "The Emperor's New Mind," based on 'incompleteness theorems,' by Kurt Godel, an Austrian born mathematician. In it, Penrose argues that the brain is perfectly capable of performing functions that no computer, network of systems, or algorithm ever could. From this Hameroff extrapolated that consciousness itself may very well be fundamentally a non-algorithmic incapable of ever being modeled. [59]

Hameroff, was inspired by Penrose enough to contact him regarding his own theories about the mechanism he experienced in the surgical arena as an anesthesiologist, and how anesthesia seemed to specifically target a patient's consciousness; his theory being via actin cytoskeleton of the neural microtubules of a cell. When the two men finally met in 1992, Hameroff discussed with Penrose whether or not, the microtubules to identify with quantum mathematics to better determine if they were indeed responsible as a connection mechanism to a vast 'consciousness' as a quantum mechanism that takes place within the human brain. Penrose was interested, and began corroborating with Hameroff on mathematical features of how the microtubule lattice may be involved. Eventually after a few years of research the two formulating and published their theory.

By contrast, Hameroff discerned from his work with Penrose, that the coherent photons firing within the brain do processes information using quantum mechanics as part of the way humans gather and process complex bits of data and information and with such astronomical speed. Photons he believed that also contribute and communicate to a 'consciousness' that is somehow linked throughout the entire universe. A consciousness he hoped that research, and time may someday unravel with quantum mechanics. [59]

When everything discussed herein is considered, it becomes even more evident that the entire universe shares a 'consciousness' that can only be viewed as an information source 'our soul' can access from within our physical brains, that act much like a Wi-Fi connection would to your computer, when rendering our 'subjective reality;' everything we perceive to be real. This connection to a 'universal consciousness' therefore offers the 'Indigo child' quite a unique first-person vantage point; regardless of how objective their reality may be; because it is always experienced 'subjectively' by a conscious observer.

The nature of 'precognitive dreams' is in recognizing them as a recursive interface into a vast consciousness of knowledge, which not only sends data, it also receives information from itself regardless of a linear time or space. This being the case, it is like no other iCloud interface I've ever experienced; especially when one considers all the ramifications it makes to knowledge, events, destiny, and self-awareness; more than we could ever possibly imagine, nor ever physically build.

Indigo's possess such an 'awareness of precognition,' that data received during a 'precognitive dream state,' allows them to experience a recursive feedback that 'plays-out' every form of probable reality during their dream experience; allowing the Indigo to actualize the specific 'layer of reality' in which a specific 'precognition' exist, and its outcome, when their dream's finally played out. It could further be se suggested that 'precognitive dreams' may very well be another form of 'reality,' a precognitive programming if you will that forms within the recursive interface to a universal consciousness; where the actualization of the 'precognitive dream' also ends up becoming an 'outcome' feedback that loops back into the greater consciousness.

I realize that many of you will believe that it seems like I've climbed way out on a limb here, but we are discussing 'precognitive dreams' here…gimme a break. After all, "How often have you ignored that that 'little voice' (a precognitive thought) in your head when it was directing you to select a different outcome that could have materialized but didn't, simply because you decided NOT to listen to your inner 'self' talking?"

'Precognitive dreams' and 'premonitions' for the most part are 'passive experiences' where our thoughts are merely projected as ideas to reveal eventual outcomes. Organized thought is based on principles that allow certain creative processes, certain dreams for example, to qualify as 'precognitive intuition;' and much like an unwritten law where Murphey states, "The unknown potential of a dream does not become apparent to the dreamer until the dream has already been realized." Once the dreamer has realized the event (perhaps through déjà vu), only then can what was considered 'only a dream' reveal later that it had indeed become their reality.

A Dire Word Regarding Precognitive Dreams

The difficulty in knowing what is really a 'precognitive dream,' or what is merely a story where your subconscious mind plays out the issues, or concerns, that plague your life as a 'dream,' is not that difficult all. More often than not, it's nothing more than a person's subconscious mind, displaying wild and imaginative imagery that plays out what information it has been provided from recent memories; a story that is often entertaining, but at times terrifying; and more often than not, totally boring and benign.

I have however met over the course of my life several 'psychics' who were actually quite good at 'cognitive premonition,' to the point of display a degree of 'precognition.' I was impress in that while they were very awake they were able to assess events that were about to play out either in their own life, or someone else's life close to them. The problem though, was that they often felt compelled to interpret every single dream they dreamt as something of importance; especially when they felt their 'premonition' was a foreboding one.

Thus, spending all their free time and energy trying to determine for whom a 'presumed premonition' belonged. To make matters worse, they proceeded to warn that person about an 'impending doom' that never happened. People eventually tire of hearing these empty warnings and quickly get tired of them. When this happens, one of several things will occur; 1) people will simply ignore everything they say and stop listening to them, 2) people will not believe or heed any more of their warnings, or worse 3) people will stop believing in psychic premonitions regardless of where they came.

Consider the child's story of "The Boy That Cried Wolf," the story of a young sheepherder who gets bored watching his flock, so he tried to create some excitement by crying out 'wolf.' The villagers would come running up the hill to help him protect the flock sheep from the non-existent wolf only to find the boy hysterically laughing at them, and thus the villagers would return to their homes angry at his prank. The young boy pulled this prank so often that when a wolf actually began to attack and kill his sheep. The villagers did not heed his call of a wolf, because they no longer believed him and no one came to his rescue. The wolf devoured his entire flock and saved the tender young boy for his desert.

I quickly learned as a child to tell no one of my 'precognitive dreams' or 'premonitions' unless I was specifically asked to do so. More importantly, when I did, it was because the Indigo in me 'knew that I knew.' Unlike others, I demonstrate a mastery of 'clairvoyance' as a young man in that I drew information from a 'consciousness' of which I was instantly aware of every possible and/or relevant scenario that allowed me to 'knowingly' assess each and every potential outcome. So when I shared any 'precognitive' knowledge, it was usually demonstrated a very high degree of accuracy. Knowledge that it had been derived from a 'precognitive dream,' while in a lucid sate that not only revealed whom the dream involved, but how that 'precognitive event,' would eventually play out, and to its best and final conclusion; including what choice and direction the client would ultimately chose to take and thereby making it their realization of reality.

The Anatomy of Indigo Precognition

Remember that Noetics was a 16th century scientific revelation. Humanity's ancient ancestors had long known about a 'consciousness' and the power of the human mind in various cultures scattered around the world and was not strictly limited to the Mayans, Aztecs, and Incas in Americas, or the Greek, Egyptian, or Sumerian cultures. Yet a term to classifying this ability as a 'mystic' skillset or belonging to the 'psychic faculties' was the only option they really understood.

Today modern Noetics has revealed the reality of being able to tap into a 'consciousness' that indeed spans the 'entire universe' and is not at all 'mystical.' It's a genetic predisposition that allows certain individuals to experience an 'instantaneous intuitive awareness,' a vast 'consciousness' comprised of countless souls that spans space and time. Therefore the perception and belief these ancient cultures had with 'psychic' or 'mystical oracles' was misplaced, and can no longer be attributed directly to any of the 'psychic faculties;' especially those with the genetic propensity we have come to call an 'Indigo.'

I would like to point out that I believe many of the 'psychic premonitions' recorded over history, would today be considered from an 'Indigo Child' instead.

'Clairvoyance' and 'precognition' are not dualities that Indigos intuitively possess. For these faculties only allows an Indigo access to information that may have labeled 'psychic.' These faculties (abilities) are what set an Indigo apart…they have no regard for a linear time, limitation to space, and can span multiple dimensions with an accuracy the goes far beyond uncanny. Indigos intuitively realize that a 'precognitive impression,' that can be actualized within their physical reality, only after it has already played out within the 'universal consciousness.' It is there that the multi-verse scenarios will play-out every possible outcome instantaneously to make the Indigo totally aware of the best actions to pursue for their current reality, long before the Indigo has chosen which event will become an actual 'experience' as a 'precognition' and fully 'realized' within their own reality.

Bear in mind, the most likely 'potential' (outcome) chosen by the Indigo, and known as a 'literal precognitive' observation that has not been 'sensed' from a 'subjective vantage point,' but from an 'objective vantage point.' Which also suggests the possible existence of a multiple, yet separate set 'reality layers' that are dependent to a specific 'state of consciousness.'

For example, a 'precognitive dream' is a future event from which an outcome has not fully been 'extrapolated (realized),' is only considered to be a 'subjective premonition.' Whereas an Indigo on the other hand, is able to gather all the information necessary from a higher 'source of consciousness' to assess and analyze how any potential event will not only be 'actualized,' but how and when it will be 'realized.'

'Precognition' affords the Indigo Child the ability to assess each-and-every potential outcome of each scenario by playing them out within alternate dimensions. From this 'instantaneous' and 'intuitive' data, the Indigo then selects the most likely scenario that will succeed, because they not only 'know' which event will succeed, but also which one will be selected by a particular subject in order to offer them the best possible direction to take. Simply, and Indigo knows the outcome before the subject has chosen which one has yet to be offered them.

This ability suggests a direct relationship between what has been 'lucidly dreamt' and later 'experienced.' An uncanny advantage Indigos have over others is that the Indigo can experience every available layer of an alternate dimensional analysis of what could be considered, other potential 'realities;' the difference is an 'objective' outcome versus a 'subjective' one.

To put it into a linear context, it appears that we as humans are constantly seeking answers for the granddaddy of all causality dilemmas, "What came first, the chicken or the egg?" In this case, "What comes first, the dream or the reality?" For this quandary I must of course answer, "a precognitive dream,' of course!

A Caveat to Precognition

In essence, a quagmire to 'precognitive dreaming' exists in that when it is observed from a 'subjective perspective,' often assumptions are made when recollecting observation made during a 'perceived precognitive dream state;' in essence turning it instead into a 'premonition.' In order to provide an 'accurate assessment' or even a 'plausible perception' of events that occurred during a precognitive 'dream state,' it must first, be remembered in full detail. Often the dilemma of this syllogism (when a major premise is formed from two or more hypothetical propositions and the minor premise is disjunctive), and can be entirely missed by becoming a 'subjective viewpoint' by the observer, which occurs more often than not when the Indigo experiencing the 'precognitive dream' is the dreamer.

Think about this logically… the amount of data required for an 'objective vantage point' would be quite significant and thus to allow a total 'memory recall' of each and every event and scenario played out in the Indigo's dream, which would have to have been derived from a heightened sense of 'awareness' to the 'consciousness.' As everything dreamed from each-and-every reality layer would require an allowance for an 'objective perception' that would explain each, and every 'outcome' that was revealed in the Indigo's dream; then and only then, can the dream be qualified as an 'objective precognitive outcome,' otherwise it's only a 'subjective' one.

What I find most interesting and unique among Indigos, is that those who possess different capabilities when it comes to recognizing what values a 'precognitive dream' holds, because they are 'all' dependent on not only their varying abilities, but also their experience. What I also find interesting is that those born with all their Indigo traits already active have absolutely no problem in recollecting every detail of their 'precognitive dreams.'

Everyone is capable of having 'precognitive dreams,' but for most, it's only a first-person paradox; they cannot even begin to understand, conceive, or accept what has happened during the 'precognitive' experience, and therefore discount the 'precognition' as only a dream. Most likely because they had never experienced a 'precognitive realization' and thus remain extremely skeptical, never believing it to be even remotely 'possible, plausible' or 'probable.'

The 'causality dilemma' I've just presented you is really about whether or not you have had a dream that preceded a 'physical realization;' especially when the 'dual-reality' that it represents is often quite profound. However, once experienced the implications often necessitate a shift in your personal 'physical paradigm;' perhaps, to resemble something much more idealistic. Whenever we begin to deconstruct our 'dream states' we begin to understand that we may in fact possess the innate ability to organize those dreams into more understandable facts – that includes the fact that we each live in the 'reality layer' we have identified, organized, and created for ourselves – while we were simply dreaming. No one understands that as fact more than the older generations of Indigo, for we have all experienced it ourselves firsthand and we see it in everyone we meet.

THE REALITIES WE CREATE

"Our thoughts create our reality – where we put our focus is the direction we tend to go, if you're not actively involved in getting what you want, you don't really want it."

Peter McWilliams

Einstein once said, "Reality is merely an illusion, although a very persistent one." Have you ever had a dream that seemed so real you could have sworn you had just experienced an alternate reality? Many people do. Dreams, unlike the 'physical reality' we chose to live, are not comprised of atoms, molecules, or gravitational forces, thus they are nothing more than thought organized and generated by our 'subconscious mind.' Our mind often opens a gateway to the 'universal consciousness' Indigo or not, to allow us to experience alternate states of reality; often similar, yet different to the existing 'physical reality layer' we are currently living in.

The Awakening: an Emergence of Indigo Consciousness

It's within an 'alternate reality' introduced to us during a 'dream state,' we may see people and objects in places we may have never experienced. While there, we also notice light, darkness, textures, and patterns, as every basic aspect of that 'dream' is comprised by subconscious thought to creates an altered 'sensory state of perception;' that later may in fact be realized by the dreamer. There are no real atoms, no real objects, and no real people in that 'alternate state of reality;' it's only uncontrolled thought.

Indigo's however, are unusual in that fact that regardless of what 'conscious, subconscious,' or 'unconscious states,' they are in, they are quite aware of whether or not, it's an 'altered state of reality' they are experiencing during a 'dream state.'

For most Indigos are very capable of directing their own thoughts, even as an observer in whatever 'state of consciousness' they find themselves in. This coherence allows them to access specific information, knowledge, and any potential outcomes regarding their 'alternate state reality;' regardless of where their dream has put them. They use that knowledge to live out their life in the 'reality layer' they created of their own choosing, a destiny they are able to often control.

Most people have no real control of the direction their thoughts may take them within their dreams, and more often than not, the 'altered reality' they end up finding themselves in; most likely centered around important issues that surround their life, and by what concern them most. Therefore, any audible or visual stimuli their mind generates during their 'dream state,' stems from a process psychologists call 'self-evident exploration;' in that it very much resembles, but can be different, to the 'layer of reality' they are most familiar or comfortable with.

This process is not unlike how our subconscious mind processes thought; liken it to how our minds create the distinct voices for the characters in a novel we may be reading. For example, if our characters are from France, Germany, or Italy, our mind will create the necessary accents to keep those characters distinct and separate within our mind. However, it they're from the Czech Republic, Tibet, or Finland, you may not have a reference point from which to associate a specific accent; therefore, your mind will either select an accent you are familiar with (like a French, Italian, or German) to represent an accent from a Czech, Tibetan, or a Finn.

In the same fashion, the 'reality layers' – think of them as the accents – you are most familiar with, become your 'reality layers' you create them in your mind as you did the accents in your novel. The same holds true with what and how you dream. What you dream about will resemble what you are familiar with, or most afraid of, and in many cases parallels the people and issues in your life that you are most concerned for; only to become the 'reality layer' you currently live in, and most likely the 'reality layer' you are most anxious and fear the most.

Therefore, it should be no surprise that dreams, 'precognitive' or otherwise, mimic what we are most familiar with in the 'reality layer' that surrounds our everyday life.

If dreams are comprised of thought – conscious or otherwise – we must then ask ourselves, "How does all this talk about 'reality layers' apply to my dream, I'm not Indigo?" or, "Does my dream have a 'precognitive potential' for changing my existing reality?"

Once again, it's Kinda, Sorta, Maybe . . . to be honest, these questions aren't fair, because from what I have just explained, an Indigo is the only person who can fully comprehend the 'reality layer rut' enough to escape it.

So your 'dream state' is comprised of only 'familiar information' extracted from what is currently happening in your life (and perhaps the lives of people around you). It therefore makes sense that your dreams would interject into your 'conscious organized thoughts' or into your 'subconscious scenario;' specifically–your nagging thoughts. It's a way of offering you only the pertinent information it extracted from your current state of reality. This being the case, how is it then that what began as an organized thought pattern is later played back to you with a variety of outcomes; one of which may later materialize as your 'new' chosen 'reality?' A most challenging paradox presented through 'precognitive dreams.'

Remember what I said earlier regarding the fact that everyone has the capacity, within their genome, to demonstrate a propensity to 'precognition' or 'premonition;' but to varying degrees. However, before I continue, please indulge me in recapping what I just stated regarding 'precognition' and 'premonition;' 'Déjà vu' is the most common form of 'precognition' that may or may not offer you a warning or a 'premonition.'

Unfortunately, the 'dream states' that provides you with a 'precognitive event' or a 'premonitions' will most likely not be remembered until it can be actualized. Yet once 'realized,' you will absolutely recollect those memories from within the dream and recognize, or perhaps derive, any potential warnings or premonitions from them. Not to worry though, most people don't remember most of their dreams in the first place; and if they do, they're quite sketchy at best and soon forgotten.

Without getting into the science of dreams any deeper, an average person has approximately three to five dreams during a full eight-hour sleep cycle. This is when the most of the vivid dreams occur; within the first two hours –the deepest stage of our sleep – or the stage scientists call 'rapid-eye movement (REM)' stage of a dream. During this period that our brain patterns become quite active, to point our eyes actually begin to move under our eyelids quite rapidly. During this period of sleep our brain also appears to generate nearly the same type of brain activity (gamma waves) as it does in an awakened state.

Some dreams that can last from a few seconds to as long as 20 minutes, but rarely any longer. Understand too, that certain people tend have more vivid dreams than others (Indigos are a really good example here); and nearly everyone, will only be able to recall the last dream they had once awakened – and they are usually remembered only for very short period of time – if they even recall the dream at all. Also important to note, the longer a person sleeps, the longer their dreams tend to be as the night progresses. [60]

Indigos have the ability to choose which of their 'precognitive dreams' are relevant, and understand that not all are specific to themselves, but dreams that may address other people in their lives; perhaps family members, close friends, and often even strangers; some encountered and some they have not yet met. Often their 'precognitive dreams' are 'spot on' and sometimes a few details are off. Yet most Indigo will not talk or reveal what they know of their 'precognition' unless they have specifically been asked to do so; and rarely do charge anyone for revealing what their 'precognition' told them, unless perhaps expenses had been incurred.

Enter then the 'Indigo children;' generations of people that slowly began appear during the late 1920's and early 1930's – close to the end of the 'spiritualist movement.' Today's Indigo Child is 'the next generation of intuitive consciousness,' and never been realized that it had existed within humanity for eons.

Each generation since, with an innate ability to recognize 'precognitive' events through 'conscious, sub-conscious,' and 'unconscious' dream states that exceeded many of the presumed 'psychic faculties' the Indigo Child was thought to possess. Abilities that surpassed any 'déjà rêvé' faculties the rest of man may have experienced at one time or another.

We all now know that Indigo's have the innate ability to draw information from an unseen 'consciousness' that encompasses the entire universe, space, time or dimension. For them, it's often an 'instantaneous awareness' to 'knowledge that is amazingly accurate and irrespective of the linear timeline we as humans expect, regarding time, space, or dimension.

Everyone's 'dreams' are a derivative extrapolated from the most 'subjective' source a person possesses—their own personal point-of-view; whether or not a person chooses to 'actualize' any new 'reality layers' offered them through a 'precognitive dream state,' is entirely up to them. It is after all, a difficult choice to subject ourselves to, considering we are after all, we are creatures of habit who nearly always choose to remain within our own comfort zone. However, it's not because we don't want change, it's because as humans we fear change.

Our 'reality layer' is a by-product of our life cycle that originates within our thoughts and subliminal desires. It is therefore logical to assume that since our dreams are also by-products of our thoughts and desires, they may in fact also be the catalyst responsible for internalizing a 'reality programing.' One that translates itself into the way we experience and actualize the other lives by the 'reality' we create to become our life. It's as real as it gets.

A Conclusion to the Paradox

As we analyze the 'precognitive dream paradox' process, we should also realize that other 'physical realities' have most likely had also appeared to us. Although not all dreams offer up alternate layers of reality, as a 'precognitive premonition' may do, it is obvious that we have been offered many other dimensional alternatives throughout our lifetime, some that may have even violated our 'normal comfort zones,' only to be rejected. However, once our choice the 'alternate offering' was subconsciously made – through 'precognitive premonition' – the one chosen, will be translated into an 'actualized reality layer' and are now 'realizing.'

Whew! So now, ask yourself, "Are your own thoughts keeping you back from your potential?" The implications of change stemming from a 'precognitive dream' can change everything about the way we think, how we act, and what direction we choose to take our lives. Simply be creating the 'reality layer' we choose the life we live. 'We attract what we think about' is indeed a profound implication that is not only mind boggling, it has staggering implications…and we ourselves are solely responsible by whatever thoughts entertain for creating our current 'layer of reality' Indigo or not!

LE CLAIR INDIGO CAPACITÉ

"Hear your fate, O dwellers in Sparta of the wide spaces; either your famed, great town must be sacked by Perseus' sons, or, if that be not, the whole land of Lacedaemon, shall mourn the death of a king of the house of Heracles. For not the strength of lions or of bulls shall hold him, strength against strength; for he has the power of Zeus, and will not, is checked until one of these two he has consumed." [87]

The Oracle of Delphi

There are seven very similar, yet distinct 'Le Clair Capacité' (the clear capacities) that many of the Indigo generations demonstrate when receiving 'precognitive' information, and why it extends far beyond being merely a 'premonition.' Their innate ability to span a vast consciousness that transcends space, time, and dimensions is what provides an 'instantaneous awareness' to information and knowledge that translates their 'knowing' abilities into a detailed, clear, and concise recollection of data. To better define the Indigo 'perspective of awareness,' of what they experience we must first understand what had for eons, been attributed to 'mystics, oracles,' and 'psychics.'

In French, the word 'clair' translates as a prefix to mean 'clearly' preceding our current understanding of the five senses as elements that will also comprises five distinct 'faculties.' The common being; clairvoyance (clearly see), clairaudience (clearly hear), clairsentience (clearly sense – empathy), clairtangence (clearly touch – psychometry), claircognizance (clearly know), and the two least common faculties clairgustance (clearly taste), and clairalience (clearly smell).

Clairvoyance

Of all the 'claire' faculties, this is by far the most common Indigo's trait; and rightly so because it translates as having the ability of being 'clear sighted.' All Indigo's display the capacity to see people, events, and locations regardless of our linear understanding of time, space, and dimensions.

All of which include 'precognition, premonition,' and 'perception.' Indigo's can distinguish information at such a high level of 'consciousness' that they have an intrinsic ability to expand on the information received from the 'universal consciousness;' one that extends far beyond the 'psychics' perception 'premonition.' It is for this reason the Indigo can offer up a clear and concise 'reading' that contains intrinsic value of the individual being read, which is not full of befuddled, discombobulated, and confusing information designed by many 'charlatans' to bewilder and confuse an unsuspecting 'mark (target).'

'Clairvoyance' translates as a 'clear vision,' which is definitely describes how an Indigo can expand on the definition of clear and concise. For Indigos possess an uncanny and innate intuitive knowledge that can only be described as an acute keenness of mental perception, understanding, discernment and judgment.

Throughout the centuries, anyone who demonstrated 'clairvoyance' was revered either as wither an 'oracle, medium,' and at times, a 'witch' because of their uncanny ability to communicate with the spirit world and pass messages back-and-forth between the living and the dead and could foresee far into the future to predict outcomes. One of the many reasons I have such profound reservations about people professing to be 'clairvoyant or psychic,' or claim to be 'Indigo;' is because the world is full of 'charlatans' preying on the ignorant. Many of whom resort to theatrics as a means to confuse their targets with fabrications and ambiguity in a foolhardy attempt to portray themselves as an 'experienced medium, oracle, or even a psychic;' incompetence hidden behind 'smoke and mirrors.'

What charlatans don't realize is that an Indigo is able to 'see through people' and can easily identify a fraud, angering the Indigo by dishonesty and deceit with an instantaneous dislike, distrust, and distain. I know whenever I have encountered charlatans I cannot, and will not tolerate them, especially when I sense their blatantly obvious 'ulterior motive.' I find them reprehensible and most Indigo Children takes great joy in revealing them for the 'narcissistic charlatan liars' they are and will 'rake them publically over the coals' for it, with no holds barred.

The Consciousness of the Other Side

When I was a young boy, I recall reading a story written in 1895 by science fiction writer H.G. Wells (one of my favorite authors today) entitled, "The Door in the Wall." It's about a lonely boy missing his deceased mother who discovers while walking the streets of London a small green door set into a white wall. Fascinated by the door, he decides to open it. When he entered, he met a young girl in a whimsical garden who eventually becomes his 'soul mate.'

We have already established Indigos demonstrate an uncanny 'intuitive awareness' of people that exceeds mankind's limited understanding of other dimensions. This ability allows Indigo's the innate capacity to instantaneously experience all viable 'realities.' 'Precognition' also allows them to sense resonant signatures' that allows them the uncanny ability to access information from a source in which every soul's 'consciousness' seems to exists within the universe; most likely the very same 'universal consciousness.' For the most important memories, experiences, and knowledge are stored there, according to the 'quantum theory,' is the most like place where the 'consciousness' of those who have passed most likely exists, and the Indigo can also feel the souls of others within this dimensional realm.

'For all that we know, every quantum object; a particle of light, a particle of matter like that of an atom, or any other small molecule – can simultaneously exist in different places at the same time.' said Vlatko Vedral, professor of physics at the University of Oxford. "How such properties might translate into the reality we perceive within our human senses remains yet a mystery."

I believe as many others do, that our soul is a form of energy that exists in abundance throughout the vast universe, including other dimensions, perhaps a place where all souls may very well migrate after death. We all know religion since the dawn of humankind, has tried to determine a specific place where our souls may travel after death; we have even given them the names. Modern religion references them only descriptively as 'heaven, hell,' and for some religions, it also includes 'purgatory.' Surprisingly, the numbers of those that don't believed we possess a 'soul' are increasing, for them death simply means we cease to exist at all and death is nothing more than a switch being turned off.
Does our soul actually exist? Of that, I have no doubt, for I and have seen a lot of evidence to the fact that our 'consciousness' or 'soul' if you will, it <u>does not</u> perish after death. In fact, many quantum physicists will agree, and have proven that the 'universe' does in fact, have a 'consciousness.'

Compared to the human brain it is also the perfect quantum computer where our mind stores our 'consciousness (soul);' information written at the quantum level directly—memories and information not stored within our brain. Thus, after death, it has always been, and continues to exist as part of the 'universal consciousness.' When our physical body dies, our 'conscious souls,' and continues to reside on a quantum level, as part of the 'universal consciousness;' the very same source that Indigos tap into 'intuitively.' So yes, we continue to exist therein indefinitely as a whole, while retaining our 'individuality,' connected to this vast source of knowledge.

Dr. Robert Lanza, a physician and scientist at Wake Forest University in North Carolina, has no doubt at all that 'life' does not end when our physical body dies; but continues to exist forever beyond our limited concept of time and space. As an expert in regenerative medicine, Dr. Lanza is well-known for his extensive stem cell research, and as a respected scientist he has recently became involved with quantum mechanics and astrophysics which gave birth to a controversial new type of physics called 'biocentrism;' causing quite a stir in the scientific community.[61]

His theory is simple; death does not exist, but is in fact nothing more than an illusion in everyone's mind, and the reason many believe that when our physical body dies, so does our consciousness; the soul. Now if you believed that, I don't believe you would have read this far into this book, because there are many others who also believe our 'consciousness (soul)' continues to exist without any constraint to time, space, or dimension.

So the question remains; where does the 'consciousness' we call a 'soul' go" His answer; anywhere it wants. The answer is a based on a theory that postulates quite well within the science of quantum mechanics in that certain particles (energy) can be present and exist anywhere within the universe, or countless other universes, simultaneously. Now don't worry, I'm not going to confuse you with this, so please bear with me…within each universe, or in a number of other multiple universes and other scenarios, we continue to exist. [62]

Interestingly enough, a 'heightened sense of awareness' was noted in a person's brain activity just prior to clinical brain death by a study completed at the University Of Michigan School Of Medicine, conducted by a team of neuroscientists. The study suggested, that the level of activity observed during a person's final 'active death' sequence (what they tag as the CAS3 stage) not only mimics the same stage of a person's waking state, it in fact may also reflect a heightened 'state of conscious awareness' during death. Quite similarly, an Indigo's 'highly lucid' state is not only a more 'real-than-real' mental experience, people having survived a 'near-death experience (NDE) also have reported pretty-bold claims worthy of consideration that quantifies 'consciousness' as a critical part to their claim. Their argument being, that there exists evidence demonstrating that during the final stages, just before death, the brain is actually much more 'conscious' and 'aware' when the graphs get compared to graphs of during brain's normal 'actively waking state' to the 'consciousness' after an eight-hour sleep. But the big question is 'consciousness-related' and the activity quantified?'

Unfortunately to date, there is still no handy-dandy "Index of Consciousness" in existence today that can easily identify, be used, or even come close to inferring a subject's true 'state of awareness.' However, if such an "Index of Consciousness" existed for humans, it would be dependent on how it index had been derived. After all, the scientific team conducted their experiments by euthanizing rodents to graph their findings Quite a quagmire when you consider how controversial animal research already is today, but it would be helpful if we could someday get a hint of what activity a human brain actually experience during the process of dying; including near-death-experiences. [63]

All this means, is that when our body dies, our souls can choose to continue existing with in this universe, or move on into another universe by absorbing what I have been calling a soul's 'consciousness' and from there, migrate into the other universe. This implies ('quantumly' speaking) that when a person whose physical body had died, their souls do not travel through the some strange tunnel to end up in heaven, hell, or purgatory, they can move on to another similar world, or even another universe; perhaps one that we may be inhabited by beings similar to us. Regardless of what choices our soul has, we remain very much 'consciously aware' and 'alive' without the limitations of a physical body...that is able to travel through an infinite number of dimensions, dimension by dimension indefinitely.

Nonetheless, I feel it is important to point out that although I believe this research demonstrates the reason many people experience through the dying process a period of 'active cognitive processing' that allows them to see the 'souls' of others who had passed before them, and waiting on the 'other side' to receive them into the 'collective.' This study at least suggests a 'neural' explanation that is at least plausible. In my opinion, for this team of scientists to have identified what 'neural activity' the brain experiences during the process of dying and near-death experiences is remarkable, but what yet remains to be verified is whether or not their finding are 'subjective' experiences used to qualify the study with 'objective' results. Mind you, it's not that I'm skeptical because I did after all include the study in this book; it's that I'm being cautious

Why Indigo's Appear Clairvoyant

We are all familiar with what computer encryption keys are and how they limit access to computer networks or data storage devices to protect secret information from prying eyes. If we compare these 'encryption keys' to the way an Indigo Child maintains connectivity to the 'universal consciousness,' we associate the concept to a network 'encryption key' of highly secure government network.

The combination of specific 'frequencies' in the Indigo's brain, allows them to not only transmit data into the 'quantum' consciousness but also 'access' and 'retrieve' the data as well. The specific 'frequencies' required to connect to this consciousness, are created in specific areas of the Indigo brain. It's when neurons fire in a specific sequence, an Indigo can connect to the vast pool of 'consciousness' to either communicate with a specific soul (whether they have a 'physical human body' or not), or simply gather knowledge from the collective knowledge, without the limitations of linear time, space, or dimensions. These account for the innate accuracy of what appears to be a 'clairvoyant' reading to other, but is what the Indigo Child normally does. It is simply their 'instantaneous awareness' to knowledge that transcends space and time to give the Indigo what seems to be an 'all knowing' ability that mistakes them for a 'clairvoyant medium, a fortune teller,' or a 'psychic.'

Yes, Indigos are capable of seeing what has occurred in the past, what the future has in store, and what messages a soul from another realm or dimension has to share. However, I rarely know what answers a client seeks, and thus focus on what information I had derived during what I call 'a reading.' It is important to note however, of the important information provided to the client, they will extrapolate what they deem valuable, regardless of what other witnesses may believe to be important. All I provide is hopefully enough 'viable, accurate' and 'informative' data from which they can draw their own 'educated conclusions' to make any decision they believe is necessary—a choice I refuse to make for them. Nor have I ever charged anyone do so.

Clairaudience

"When I was thirteen, I had a voice from God to help me to govern myself. The first time, I was terrified. The voice came to me about noon, it was summer, and I was in my father's garden. I saw it many times before and knew it was Saint Michael. He was not alone, but duly attended by heavenly angels; he told me Saint Catherine and Saint Margaret would come to me, and I must follow their counsel. That they were appointed to guide and counsel me in what I had to do, and that I must believe what they would tell me, for it was at our Lord's command."

- Joan of Arc, "In Her Own Words," May 1431

Many historic figures throughout history have been linked to 'hearing voices' and 'sounds' by which they have professed an ability to hear what they believed to be physical sounds, words, voices and even ideas that extended far beyond what would be considered a 'normal' reality and go straight into what was considered to be supernatural.

The ability to hear or sense a voice(s) or sound(s) by anyone demonstrating this 'faculty' will most likely earn them the title of being 'clairaudient.'

It's a 'gimme' that everyone can hear their own thoughts within their own head as if they were speak to, or at times arguing with, themselves. However, a quick reality check will normally identify that it is nothing more than our own perception of hearing that 'tiny little voice' in our head. Often, we appear to hear spoken words from the pages of a book when we're reading, as if actually been verbalized. Hearing our own thoughts within our head may at times appear as if we are indeed talking to ourselves, when in all actuality we are merely in a 'clairaudience' session with ourselves. Not much different from someone who is 'clairvoyant' using their inner eye 'to clearly see,' we are using our brain's inner ear 'to clearly hear' our very own thoughts.

'Clairaudience' is another ' faculty' Indigo's take to a new level, in that they may not only hear the other voices speaking aloud to them, they can also perceive an actual 'auditory sound' speaking to them within their head in the form of a thought.

This 'faculty' goes far beyond just hearing though, nor is the name descriptively accurate for what best describes 'clairaudience,' because 'clairaudient' implies listening with ones ears. Clairaudience can also be a projected thought from within a person's mind; as if a soul (known or unknown) were talking to the Indigo from deep within the 'universal consciousness.' Liken it to a voice that defies any constraints imposed by the limitations of space and time, and just as Joan of Arc's 'consciousness' was hearing these three souls speak to her, she truly believed they were indeed divine spirits and confidants to guide her.

'Clairaudient experiences' can range from hearing odd sounds and voices to full-fledged conversations that are considered to be 'subjective experiences,' internally heard within the Indigo mind, or an 'objective experience' heard externally as a spoken voice; although I still consider the phenomenon to be entirely 'subjective.

These three voices not only guiding her in her mission, they protected her. Joan of Arc was said to have professed her counsel of voices to be; Saint Michael the Archangel, Saint Catherine of Alexandria, and Saint Margaret (to whom at times she referred to as Marina). Then on occasion, although not frequently mentioned, Joan reported several visitations of Archangel, Saint Gabriel.

Archangel Michael was the first voice to manifest to a young Joan when she was only thirteen. It was recorded Joan had been foretold that Saint Catherine and Saint Margaret would follow as well, to relay strict instructions she was to obey. Her description of the Archangel Michael, painted him as brilliant and bold personage. While her descriptions of Catherine and Margaret were more of two gentle comforters that guided her through childhood to prime her with valuable information; from governing herself to the virtues she would require to fulfill God's mission; which at the time, she did not yet fully comprehend.
It wasn't until Joan turned seventeen, and the demeanor of the voices in her head changed as they laid out the plan to define her involvement to liberate France from the British forces for God and country. However, the question remains, did Joan attempt to make sense of what she received before she responding?

"And I answered the Voice that I was a poor girl who knows nothing of riding and warfare. How can this be? I know I am not a man…but since God had commanded me to go, I must. And because God had commanded it, had I had a hundred fathers and a hundred mothers, or had I been a king's daughter, I still would have gone." From the book, "In Her Own Words"

Joan of Arc felt she had won the devotion of the three individually distinct personalities of Saint Michael, Saint Catherine, and Saint Margaret by placing her entire destiny in the confidence of their voices. It was Joan's unwavering faith in her trusted 'clairvoyant guardians,' who explicitly provided her counsel, regardless of the warnings they had foretold of battles to be won and lost, mishaps, betrayals, personal injury that eventually ended in her capture by the crown and her death. [64]

A Mistaken Psychosis

Today, when people report hearing voices in their head, they are nearly always diagnosed as some type of psychosis. Although the concept being called upon by some unseen entity or an unearthly spirit offering advice and direction may be accepted in some cultures, modern science takes a very grim view any explanation that includes the word 'supernatural, 'paranormal' and even 'psychic' within a sentence.

It is a belief that scientists need to make up all the rules when it comes to providing possible solutions to unexplained. However, proving the existence of any of the 'clair facilities,' especially when dealing with 'hearing' voices like Joan of Arc, is not high on their list, and thus still treated as psychosis.

When a child begins to tell tales of talking to an 'imaginary friend' they are more often than not, thought to have quite an active imagination. However, if a highly creative adult expresses hearing voices in their head to explain their inspiration, they are would most likely be labeled as being a bit 'schizophrenic, off their rocker,' or just plain 'crazy;' regardless of their creative genius; and another reason why most Indigos will usually keep it to themselves.

Although I haven't a clue as to how many 'creative' and 'crazy' genius' there are, I have to say that over the last fifty years of conducting my research all over the world, the one thing I am absolutely sure of, is that today there are definitely a disproportionate number of 'crazy' cases reported to outright cases of 'pure genius.'

The reason of course being—and one of which I am totally convinced—lies with the exceptional number of television 'Looney Toon' reality shows that have made their way into people's living rooms; an attempt by television programmers to redefined the meaning of the words 'weird' or 'stupid' for the sake of entertainment. This includes all premium 'cable television' channels that once 'used to' provide high-quality educational programming: 'The History Channel, Discovery Channel, the Learning Channel,' and the 'National Geographic Channel.' All of which have introduced a barrage of lame programming that seem to have done nothing but 'dumb-down' America. Where in the world they find such a disproportionate number of 'stupid, uneducated,' and 'emotionally disturbed' or 'psychotic people' to put television during 'prime time programming' is beyond me! When all it has done, is widen the gap between 'normal, crazy' and just plain 'stupid.' What's even worse is that it has been done under the guise of an 'educational' program!' When will it end?

Sorry, it angers me, but I'll get off my soapbox now before I regress. To really understand the far-reaching implications, an attempt must be made to separate a 'lie' from 'truth' and 'fact' from 'fiction.' In order do so, the best place to begin would be with 'the present' and work backwards in time through history; my objective – to search for any obvious patterns that may shed light on the blatant madness that seems to have emerged.

Many of pundits are themselves troubled individuals who entered this genre of scientific study with the hope of resolving their own personal and emotional demons. 'Physician, heal they self;' an appropriate biblical proverb that simply means people should take care to examine their own defects before attempted to correct the faults of others. Science should instead seek a greater truth that may define our very presence and understanding of 'reality.' Which may be why many try to find legitimacy by entering the field of PSI as a 'scientific study' simply because it requires absolutely no formal processes and very little education to link the mind and how it is explored to another legitimate science discipline. All because 'supposition' is all the proof, they will every need and they do it ALL in the name of science.

Schizophrenia or Psychosis

Historically speaking, all psychiatrists, psychologists, and other mental health professionals are educated to believe that people, who report seeing ghosts or hearing voices, are often 'delusional' and/or 'psychotic schizophrenics.' To prove my point, do a Google search for 'clairvoyance' or even 'psychic' on your computer and you'll most likely get all kinds of 'fringe' information that is…well for the lack of a better descriptor…really, really 'weird' and to be brutally honest, written by a lot of strange and misguided people.

Now for chuckles-and-giggles search for the key words 'clairvoyant delusional psychotic' and your search will populate with information from various Mental Health organizations all over the world…all with varying opinions offered up as a bonafide 'psychiatric diagnosis' that ranges from being a simple 'phobia, psychosis to a severe case paranoid schizophrenia.' Including explanations that claim 'clairvoyance' or any other of the 'clair-faculties' are 'abnormal conditions' they often blame on genetic conditions that plague many a family's histories; especially those demonstrating these Indigo traits.

In 1841, the word 'psychosis' was coined and introduced in a psychiatric study conducted by Karl Friedrich Canstatt, a German physician at the University of Vienna. His published work in the "Handbuch der Medizinischen Klinik (The Handbook of the Medical Clinic)," Canstatt uses the term 'psychotic neurosis' as a shorthand notation where 'neurosis' simply refers to 'any disease of the nervous system;' more specifically referring to what he considered were psychological manifestations of a 'diseased' brain. [65]

Later a condition that expands on the condition called 'neurosis' was identified by Dr. Emile Kraepelin in 1887, and discretely referred to it as a mental illness by describing the symptoms of what we now call 'schizophrenia.' Dr. Kraepelin believed this illness is evident as far back as the Pharaohs of Ancient Egypt during the second millennium just before Christ. Recent studies into the ancient Greek and Roman literature, also shows that although the general population probably had an awareness of psychotic disorders, there was no condition that would meet the 'modern diagnostic criteria' of schizophrenia within those ancient societies. [66]

Up to this point, people throughout history who were considered to be 'off their rocker (abnormal);' regardless of whether it was caused by a mental illness, mental birth defect (such as retardation), or physical deformities, all were treated roughly in the same manner; put in locked cells and the key thrown away. Incarcerations were common for many of those 'afflicted;' from 'mental disorders' to 'evil possession of the body;' and whose treatment included torture as a means to exorcise demons, frontal lobotomies to release evil spirits, and various other less innocuous treatments.

Depending on a patient's financial ability to pay for services (institutionalization) to the Holy Church for their care and treatment, was the determination to which facility they would be locked away; dark and dreary mental asylums for 'lunatics' or humanitarian asylums for the 'insane.' Mental institutional asylums of the mid-18th century, designed to keep the patients 'out of sight' and 'out of mind;' a person's life expectancy was relatively short were quickly buried and soon forgotten.

Thus, it becomes clear that we really haven't really advanced that far. Anyone today demonstrating any of 'clair faculties' – be it 'clairvoyance, clairaudience, clairalience, clairgustance,' or 'clairsentience' – are susceptible. Today, no one in their right mind would not want to be defined as having severe hallucinations or being 'psychotic' to the point that they are having profound distortions to their 'perception of reality' instead of a 'alternate sensory experience to reality.' Others simply could not understand, or even believe it exists for that matter, and a reason some Indigos are rendered 'psychotic!'

Now don't get me wrong…this is NOT to say that there are NOT people who suffer from the severe hallucinations (Indigo included). Many are truly and seriously psychotic, suffer disorders, or delusions and definitely need to be treated medically; including, but not limited to, schizophrenia, psychotic depression, severe mania, schizoaffective disorder, certain seizures caused by abnormalities in brain, and illicit substance-induced hallucinosis—because there are! Psychotic hallucinations are very real. However, more-often-than-not correctly identified by mental health professionals, of which many are successfully treated, including, dissociative anxiety disorders, or post-traumatic stress disorders.

Regardless of where you stand on this subject, you must agree that no matter how much research one does on the subject, it is nearly impossible to do serious research on the Internet any of the clair faculties' and of 'Indigo' or even 'psychic,' without first coming across a lot of information that labels all of them as a 'psychosis.'

I would be amiss if I did not also point out that lurking in the background there is a serious connection to schizophrenia, psychosis, and mental illnesses—which are far more common conditions than families with strong 'Indigo trait' histories…a very sticky topic indeed.

A Fine Line between Schizophrenia & Creative Genius

Recently, Scott Barry Kaufman PhD, a cognitive psychologist, author and popular science writer who has built a reputation for his research on 'intelligence' and 'creativity' published a paper in which he explores possible links between the clinical description of 'schizophrenia' and people who are thought of as being 'highly creative.' [65]

Kaufman acknowledges in his work – albeit indirectly – that those who demonstrate any of the 'clair faculties' are potentially 'psychic' or 'highly creative individuals,' and thus fall under the same euphemism of being 'magical thinkers' by having 'unusual perceptions,' when it comes to describing what PSI really is. In this case, PSI is used to describe the 'psychosis' known as 'schizophrenia.' I realize you may think I'm trying to weave straw into gold here, but there is data out there being used as evidence to support this argument. In fact, there are well documented instances in which 'Indigos' and 'psychics' alike have at one time or another experienced bouts with a 'psychosis' that later was diagnosed to include 'schizophrenia;' when in fact, a diagnosis of 'psychosis' is NOT the same and should NEVER be deemed synonymous 'schizophrenia.'

Dr. Darold Treffert, author of "Islands of Genius," had spent nearly 50 years studying the extraordinary minds of savants was able to provide valuable insight to better understanding the ingenious minds of these autistic children. His techniques were designed to specifically encourage the parents of these children develop their child's full potential and help them circumvent the 'savant' label by empowering them to see their offspring as the specially gifted children they truly were.

Treffert proved, what was long-labeled as 'idiot savants' (a designation meaning an 'idiot with knowledge') did indeed have a 'higher-functioning' form of intelligence not understood by this autistic label, which often encapsulated everything from being 'mentally retarded' to 'schizophrenic.' Schizophrenia (a rare condition) as being a syndrome that affects certain individuals who display a wide spectrum of developmental disorders to qualify them as being autistic. Yet, many of the children Dr. Treffert studied demonstrated one or more areas of expertise, abilities, and brilliance; he literally sensed them as 'islands of genius' that demonstrated a 'higher intelligence' exists in their mind when contrasted to their other limitations. Treffert believed these children were able to access what he labeled 'genetic memory;' instances where these individuals would somehow 'know' things they were never taught and could not possibly know, as bouts of sudden genius he believed allowed them to tap into a 'higher form of consciousness.' [61]

When a person experiences a 'psychosis' their self-control and self-awareness is lower than that of a 'schizophrenic' person, while the duration for the 'psychosis' can range from a few days to a few weeks. 'Schizophrenia' on the other hand is a lifetime occurrence that is nearly always an uphill battle. From an 'Indigos' point-of-view I think of 'schizophrenia' as a person who's ego is way out of control; in which they begin to create and live in multiple versions of their own 'alternate realities' simultaneously; whereas a 'psychosis' is the loss of the protective ego around a single perceived version of reality.[67]

In other words, Indigos do not usually suffer as schizophrenics, but they can and sometimes do become somewhat psychotic, dependent on the extenuating circumstance for the diagnosis. Not to mention that many an Indigo Child may not be able to understand all the data they realize from the 'universal consciousness' and thus shut down into their bubble of reality…a protection mechanism, called 'autism.'

Schizophrenia vs. Creative Consciousness

In a 2005 phenomenology study (of phenomena) attempted to define the structures of experience to consciousness, was conducted by Doctors Barnaby Nelson and David Rawlings both psychologists from the Department of Psychology at the University of Melbourne, in Melbourne, Australia. Their study proposed that a mild form of schizophrenia they labeled 'schizotypy' had been positively associated to a person's experience of 'creativity' and 'consciousness.' Their theory assessed that since schizophrenia is a debilitating mental illness that roughly affects about 1% of the earth's population, in that schizophrenia had been involved and verified to 'altered states of consciousness.' Including 'abnormal' perceptual experiences (mild watered-down version of schizophrenia), and it therefore became rather evident that 'schizotypy' belonged to a consistent group of personality traits evident in nearly everyone on the globe; but at varying degrees of course.

If all this sounds familiar to 'Indigo' being a genetic factor, I meant to make that relationship!

What they discovered from their study was that when individuals within a family suffered full-fledged schizophrenia other members of the family where identified to have high levels of 'schizotypy' present within their genetic code. Leading several researchers to propose that the genetic code that underlies schizophrenia may still be within the human genome because of the creative 'benefits' schizotypy affords their genetic makeup; in-other-words, those with 'schizotypy' have genes that that may contribute to their creativity without having the debilitating genes of schizophrenia that would otherwise prevent them from achieving their maximum 'creative' potential. [67]

In research conducted by Dr. Tatyana B. Glezerman, a psychiatrist that has devoted her work to identifying link between autism, and the phenomenology of 'schizotypy' and 'creative achievement,' has focused on the 'positive' schizotypal type traits of many autistic subjects when creativity is realized. The 'negative' schizotypal traits, on the other hand, such as physical and social anhedonia (an emotional emptiness) and/or introversion tended to be scientifically associated with the phenomena of their 'creativity' and 'consciousness.'

"Autism and the Brain" explains Dr. Glezerman, "is an interdisciplinary study that provides neuro-phenomenological analysis of autism. It hypothesizes the brain networks involved in autism allowing a new understanding of why symptoms of autism go together and how they are connected to one another in a complex pattern that repeats itself in each autistic child."

Her introspections of 'Highly Functioning Autistic (HFA)' individuals, all those labeled as 'autistic savants' or 'Low Functioning Autistic (LFA)' individuals are analyzed in connection with the function of various cortical and subcortical regions (and the networks they belong to) of the brain. Their creativity offers a unique and original approach that provides a panoramic view of how an autistic individual's brain functions from LFA's to HFA's including those diagnosed as 'autistic savants' or with 'Asperger's Syndrome' broadening the spectrum of autistic-disorder boundaries. [68]

What I found most fascinating about all this research was that it afforded an even bigger question. What mechanism, or set of mechanisms, accounts for the association between 'schizotypy' and 'creativity' that distinguishes the person who is 'drowning in possibilities' from any other person capable of using their reduced latent inhibitions in such a manner that it enables 'heightened levels of creativity' to become fully realized?

I hope that as a researcher I've been able to point out that 'intelligence, working memory, consciousness,' and 'awareness' are all very likely factors to a higher executive functioning within the prefrontal cortex of the human brain. Whether it be an individual with reduced latent inhibitions, who is not going 'mad' from an influx of emotions and sensations, or found to possess a combination of a high I.Q. with reduced latent inhibitions that can be associated to their creative achievement. What is crucial in understanding the 'schizotypy flow connection,' is an openness to experience related to 'reduced latent inhibitions,' suggesting that it is open to the overall experience as related to a phenotype akin to the actual processing of information of the 'clair faculties; clairvoyance, clairsentience, and clairaudience.'

The notion that high IQs factor into an 'Indigos' abilities and traits allows them to cope successfully with a diagnosis of being schizophrenic, is not a new concept. After all, the 'conscious universe,' is all around us, and I am inclined to believe that perhaps schizophrenia is a by-product of a brain that lacks the ordinary capacity to filter out unnecessary information, both at the 'physical level' and a 'pure consciousness' level.

'Schizophrenia,' as I have pointed out, is a world in which paranoid people create as an unconscious method of dealing with 'paranoia.' It is this very paranoia that can also be used as a mechanism for shutting out the world around them with extreme fears to cut-off their internal flow of 'cognitive' and 'intuitive' information altogether; be it a normal 'consciousness' or an Indigo's ability to communicate with the 'universal consciousness.'

Indigos who demonstrate the 'clair faculty' of 'clairvoyance' don't have an automatic switch to turn it <u>on</u> or <u>off</u> ad hoc; it's just something we have to learn early in life to deal with when it comes to regulating the constant flow of 'cognitive' and 'intuitive awareness.' Yet another reason why 'Indigos' rarely seem overwhelmed to the point where they need to use a 'fear response' as a shut-down mechanism like 'schizophrenia' to do so…basically because Indigo's don't have an inflated ego to bruise nor does it need protecting.

A Fine Lines to Walk – Indigos, PSI and Psychosis

Psychosis is not an addition to a person's 'version of reality;' it's a merely break from it…people who see, talk or sense the presence of soul as a ghost or spirits is entirely 'normal,' as is anyone else who has ever had what can only be perceived as a 'psychic experience.' At times, these experiences can seem quite exceptional, but demonstrating a 'clair faculty' does not a 'psychic' make, nor does it make an Indigo's life exciting or otherwise.

I don't claim to know all the reasons why Indigos are the way they are, myself included…nor did it suddenly occur to me that I displayed these traits, and for which I scared the hell out people for as long as I can remember. For many however, it is new and often confusing and can have a deep impact on anyone's life. For me it's the way it is, and always has always been!

I have spoken with numerous people over the years from various walks of life, backgrounds, and cultures, some of whom have professed some pretty amazing and sometimes interesting stories about their 'psychic faculties;' but to be brutally honest…most are totally full of bull shit I find them boring. Now, don't get me wrong here, it's not because their psychic experiences weren't real, as some were…it's that I have been living these types events all my life and nothing they said was mind-blowing, because for me, they are normal occurrences in my life.

Recently, I'd had inadvertently been doing some peer counseling with a couple who believed they were slowly going insane. When I asked them for an explanation, I realized they were merely experiencing a new heightened sense of awareness…'an awakening' if you will, regarding events that surrounded their own family and a few friends, that frankly scared the hell out of them. Nor would they go to a doctor because they feared schizophrenia would be their diagnosis.

I informed them they weren't alone because many people are not that different from themselves; people who believed they were on the verge of a 'psychotic breakdown' as their genetics began to allow a sense of 'knowing' things they could not rationally explain.

There are many incidences where 'psychosis' related to PSI phenomenon, in this case to the 'clair faculties' is of late, frequently being reported; particularly when individuals begin to realize they have been subjected to a newfound PSI experience with a 'clair faculty' for extended periods without understanding what they were experiencing, much less why. Some so intense that their psyche had a temporary loss of control on their current 'reality.'

The US Government noticed this 'psychotic phenomena' many years ago, and handpicked a number of individuals to participate within their elite group of what is called 'remote viewers;' all chosen because of their 'exceptional clair-psychic capabilities' had them visiting psychiatrists because they lost their 'perception of reality.'

This 'psychosis' can ensue when people engage in activities such as 'remote viewing' for a long period of time happens because it requires a high level of self-confidence that extends far beyond a 'normal' person's sense of self. Many describe it as if they had 'lost their soul to the devil,' possessed and trapped by the external 'consciousness' they had accessed, and it put them in a place where they could no longer discern what was real and what was not.

The realm of our inner mind where we keep our normal barriers of ego in check, along with that part of our consciousness that holds our reality in 'check,' can vanish entirely. This can leave us open to whatever else may manifest within our own 'subconscious minds,' as something 'very real' to continue to existing within our own 'consciousness of the inner mind.' That which you can imagine, you can, and may experience. Many feel a fear overwhelms them and increases in intensity over time. Their only recourse to regain 'sanity,' is to create a 'feedback loop' and along with it, the accompanying 'psychosis.'

The Search Continues

Extrasensory perception (ESP), first coined by Dr. Joseph B. Rhine at Duke

University in North Carolina in 1940, and a founder of the scientific research department of parapsychology. Later, Dr. Rhine coined yet another general term that deemed 'parapsychology' as 'PSI.' Another catch all phrase to described all types of 'paranormal phenomena;' phenomena that could not have been perceived by the normal five human senses; and investigated the use of the 'clair faculties.'

The theory being that these perceptions (the clair faculties) manifested in certain individuals from great distances and from a time much different than our own, or from areas that were not part of our current 'physical plane (version of reality).' The Institute of Noetic Sciences as mentioned earlier concentrated its research efforts on 'intuition,' and the effects it has on 'consciousness' in our current physical world, regarding the role of 'intuition' and our conscious health and ability to heal.

Simon Hoggart and Mike Hutchinson, authors of "Bizarre Beliefs," said it best when they said, "The trouble is that the history of research into PSI is littered with failed experiments, ambiguous experiments, and experiments which are claimed as great successes but are quickly rejected by conventional scientists, and for which there has also been some pretty spectacular cheating." [70]

It is for this very reason that as I have searched my entire life seeking answers as to "Why it is I know things that I could have not possibly known," or "Why I hear voices that aren't physically spoken or had seen things that did not exist on his physical plane?" Over the years, I have read countless books by hundreds of authors, in search of answers hoping to find a glimmer of truth to what they were trying to say… and to be honest nearly all of them left me flat, as they tried to sell me one a cart of bovine manure.

I never understood "Why some people wanted to hear voices or see things that aren't really there? Were any of these books helpful at all or even remotely accurate?" Yes, a few I guess, as some did touch on concepts that began get me thinking and made some sense, but their logic and explanations fell quite short of my expectations. For the only thing offered, was nothing more than supposition, conjecture, and subjective evidence in support of their theories. I didn't want people to think I was crazy or suffered of 'psychosis.' or worse delusions; remember, Indigos were relatively unheard of, nor was the yet label coined, when I was a child. I was a man on a mission, a quest to find answers to questions for which I knew I was not alone, preferably with a reasonable, logical, and substantially sound explanations. Many other people throughout history have also actively pursued an explanation as well, by engaging in activities to provide some glimmer of insight from intuitive minds. Some chose to concentrate on ancient religions, join recluse monasteries, meditate in ashrams, or take long pilgrimages to both natural and manmade 'sacred sites' like Stonehenge, the Pyramids of Egypt, or tromp through the jungles of Yucatan in search of a Mayan shaman.

All fueled by such an intense desire to connect with 'who' they were, 'where' they came from, and 'where' they were going. All I wanted to know was nothing more than to understand the meaning of all of it – the how if it if you will – how and perhaps why the 'knowledge' that seemed to flow through me suddenly appeared in my head with an instantaneous 'intuitive awareness.' and I needed to discover this source for myself.

Usually when one embarks on any journey, they join forces with others who have already experienced a self-realization to the 'wonders' in their life. What I discovered, many instead had religious undertones quoting scriptures as answers; when they had really questioned nothing at all but succumbed and accepted what they are 'told to believe,' because 'God commanded it.'' Well I just could not accept the ambiguity nor could I ever in my right mind buy into it…but instead chose to set out into the world to discover if for myself.

I must admit that I was very lucky to have had grandmother guide me with all she had learned throughout her life, yet she too believed her abilities were a 'gift from God,' because that was all she knew how she believed. A deeply religious Roman Catholic Italian immigrant, her faith in God gave her a deeper sense of what she referred to as 'God's love;' by filling her destiny with 'special gifts' to help others as part of his greater plan. Her 'intuitive faculties' were believed (at the time) to be those of a 'psychic,' phenomena unparalleled to anything else I had ever encountered my entire life. Perhaps there was something to her belief system; and knowing what I know now…I believe she too was clearly an early Indigo Child herself on the same journey of 'self-discovery,' only her search was limited to the Roman Catholic Church for answers.

Okay, at this point you're undoubtedly wondering why I have included all this information on 'psychosis,' but more specifically on 'schizophrenia.' The answer is simply really, it's because you too are seeking the very same answers I've been writing about; especially if you've read this far.

You or someone close to you has at one-time-or-another, demonstrated what you believe to be one or more of the Indigo traits contained within these pages, and perhaps by now, even recognized it all pertained to their accurate 'precognitive' abilities; or perhaps yours…

You may even believe you're a 'psychic' or have some of the psychic faculties. However, you are not sure what it all means, or you are might be unsure whether you yourself may be an Indigo Child. Yet you're wanting answers that have a better clarification about the subject and want to understand it all yourself. Perhaps you or someone close had been diagnosed as 'psychotic' or 'schizophrenic,' or just plain 'crazy' or 'insane.' You are desperately seeking guidance for 'what-the-hell' has been going on and 'what-the-hell' to expect when you find out!

Then of course, there are those that would like to considered themselves 'Indigo,' or even 'psychic,' and want to read-up on whether or not they can develop an 'intuition' or an 'awareness;' basically expanding on what abilities they perceive themselves to have. If this is the case and to be brutally honest…if you must, you are most likely are neither.

Can 'Indigo Traits' be learned? What do you think? For those that are 'awakening' they can be tuned, but you first must be genetically predisposed, and have the necessary dormant DNA sequencing that would allow you eventually to access to the vast 'universal consciousness;' but to what extent is still unclear as a fledgling Indigo Child only now awakening. What is clear however, is that if you're feeling this way you are most probably not an Indigo Child; because all Indigo Children intuitively 'know' they are, but may be seeking a better understanding as I have of just what-the-hell is going on; especially when it regards their 'precognitive faculties.' The danger however, comes when a person claims to have 'precognitive abilities' or an acute sense 'intuition' when they don't; especially when it has been 'imagined' or merely 'desired.'

There are three groups of the four that an Indigo Child will fit into, with the Indigo traits covered by one, two, and three. However, it's the fourth that is the most dangerous and can do the most harm, those who wish to, or claim to be Indigo.

The Four Groups of Indigo Awareness

1. THEY KNOW THAT THEY KNOW – hands-down and without question Indigo Children seem to 'know' things instinctively, and do so without broadcasting their knowledge or making themselves known to others. This is the group most likely to display strong Indigo Traits. In addition to knowing things intuitively, their accuracy of knowledge is truly uncanny— if not 'spot on,' it's pretty bloody close to an accuracy of 100%. When asked to reveal what they know, an Indigo Child will be brutally honest in their reveal. Which is why, I've always told people, "Don't ask me unless you REALLY want to know the answer!"

2. THEY DON'T KNOW THAT THEY KNOW – for example, many psychics claim to experience 'déjà vu' so frequently, it makes me wonder just how deep their psychic ability really is, and at times their 'déjà vu' experiences can be quite accurate. However, an Indigo Child may have received data from the 'universal consciousness' that was at the time inconsequential information, and put to the back of their mind. Not realizing they 'don't know that they know,' when they really do, and will reveal that they know when the time is right. (I hope that wasn't too confusing.)

3. KNOW THEY DON'T KNOW – this group is the most cautious, mostly comprised by 'psychics,' and not Indigos. They go through life listening to that 'little voice' in their head without giving it much thought, however, still guided them throughout their lifetime in making all the right decisions. At times they can be, but are not often, 'intuitive' when it comes to an accurate 'premonition,' redirecting events or determining an outcome; either for

themselves or for others. Yet they are unsure most of the time of whether it's a 'psychic moment' or just a whim.

4. DON'T KNOW THAT THEY DON'T KNOW – a group who is by far, the most dangerous of them all. Comprised mostly by 'self-proclaimed psychics' or 'charlatan wanna-be psychics' or 'shysters;' and worse yet are 'perceived psychics' simply wanting attention, notoriety, and/or wealth. Those who often publish dozens of books proclaiming just how good they are, with some even becoming acclaimed 'psychics' (we all know the type); the type that charge a small fortune for their 'fictional' and 'whimsical psychic readings,' doing what a traveling carnival 'medicine man/fortune-teller' did with a roaming group of Gypsies. Their success rate is, well…non-existent and their lies often hurt people. The successes they claim are more-often-than-not fictitious and often unverifiable, or substantiated. At best very vague, with meanings can mean something anybody or everybody, and announce they realized an even well AFTER it had occurred or 'realized.' In short, all are liars, cheats, and criminals.

My hope is that whatever you have discovered about yourself or those you love from what you've read and learned within these pages will help you better understand that in order to experience 'intuition, precognition,' and 'intuitive awareness' will vary from person to person depending on where they are on their road of self-discovery. As for the Indigo Child, their 'intuitive awareness' will eventually manifest to the point that they will be able to identify and use their skills with prudence and discretion.

The skills I have learned tend to lean toward, but are not limited to, being a 'clairsentient (often called a sensitive-empath);' in that I sense the 'emotional energy' that emanates from people who openly 'transmit' their 'resonant energy.' I instinctively 'know that I know' and trust my instinct when I get that 'gut feeling' to 'beware' or 'leery' of events, people, or situations. I have an uncanny ability to instantly sense and know a person's 'intent, character,' and 'intention,' long before they make them known to me, which makes me highly 'precognitive' or 'clairvoyant; a very useful ability indeed which has 'saved my bacon' many times throughout my long life and successful career.

'Clairvoyance' is nothing more than an 'intuitive awareness' that has allowed me to sense messages (as if spoken) in my mind at times may include visions, symbols, or images in my head. I can often communicated and sense souls who have passed on or entities from unknown dimensions or realms. For those who have never experienced a true 'clairaudient' communication, it's more often than not like receiving a telepathic communication from the other side; which is why many Indigos can often be mistaken experiencing a 'hallucinatory, delusional' or 'psychotic' breakdown.

Joan of Arc was in my opinion, an experienced 'clairaudient.' Her conversation with the three souls she called 'saints' when she prayed were telepathic communications in which she received guidance, an experience that was totally normal for her, for they were very distinct voices she hear and all with their own distinct personality.

Although she heard the voices in her mind, the tone, pitch, and cadence of each voice was entirely recognizable. She knew they weren't' her own voice, thus they real souls communicating with her. From their tones of their voices, she could immediately discern which of her three guides had approached her and followed their direction for battle; no different, from the direct orders she received from any of her other commanders on the field of battle.

When Joan spoke to these 'outer voices,' she had no visual clues to reference intent, such as body language or facial expressions as she could identify the intent of her commanders. Yet she accurately understood the seriousness, and the emotional impact of their directives. Joan often demonstrated shock and fear at the tone of their conversation; as documented and witnessed by several of her commanders who testified in her defense at her trial for heresy…"Her facial expressions were of grave concern to us, as she argued with her saints." Also noted in their testimony, "The commander knew whatever action she took would determine whether the battle was won or lost; and Joan would sometimes panic, her heart rate would quicken, and the pitch of her voice would rise during her emotional and highly charged conversations." [64]

Now if you ask yourself, "Was Joan of Arc really 'psychotic, paranoid,' or 'schizophrenic' as many people have contended?" Your answer would most likely be "Probably not." For I don't believe she was 'crazy' but in fact an Indigo Child that expressed acute abilities for which I believe her to have most likely been a 'clairsentient, clairaudient,' Indigo. Her 'psychic faculties' were most likely responsible for the dramatic and historical turn her life had taken during the 14th century; a direction she associated with what she knew most…serving God in the name of Holy Catholic Church…sound familiar?

Clairsentience

This is one Indigo faculty for which I must say I am the most experienced; the innate ability to perceive 'harmonic energy signatures' that emanate from many people as they go about their daily lives; unknowingly broadcasting their emotions, feelings, intentions, and fears (the most disturbing of all); to which I can often sense their destiny, 'past, present,' or 'future.' I don't see auras, as often reported by other 'Indigos' who possess this faculty, I instead sense them.

I attribute this in conjunction with several of the 'clair faculties' that are dominated mostly by the faculty of 'clairvoyance.' I don't however attribute them to anything like a 'spirit guide, a lost soul,' or 'vibrations;' including the 'the devil, angels,' or 'elemental spirits' and other such 'entities.' Whenever I meet someone, I can usually read the person like an open book, however there are times I sense absolutely nothing at all, no matter how hard I try, and I usually don't have to try, because it's second nature, and just happens.

Since 'Clairsentience' is referred to as being the 'sensitive' or 'empathic' faculty, and should be understood as the faculty responsible for giving me and other Indigos that 'gut wrenching feeling' about certain individuals, events, or people; 'precognitions' of who they are, and what type of person they are. Perhaps it is nothing more than making a personal connection to certain souls through the 'universal consciousness,' which usually allows me to 'intuitively understand' a person's intent, including when to 'beware.' I liken it my 'intuitive early warning' system, a filter of 'precognition' that gives notice of when to stay clear of certain individuals, or face a potentially disastrous event. Think of it no different than, a beacon of light on a foggy night from a distant lighthouse warning sailors to stay clear of the rocks or warning of an impending disaster of crashing their vessel onto rocks.

'Clairsentience' is much more than just a 'feeling,' it encompasses 'experiencing' a wide set of people's 'emotional psyche;' both on a 'physical level' and a in a 'spiritual world.' It's an innate ability to 'feel' someone else on a much higher level; their health, their concerns, their desires, and their disappointments as if they were your own. In that sense, I don't just 'sense' another person…I 'feel' them. Unfortunately, many unexperienced or 'awakening sensitive-empaths' who are Indigo, will often adopt those emotions and feel them as their own, until they learn how to discern the difference!

A 'clairsentient Indigo' can unwittingly pick up another person's emotional state unintentionally. It doesn't matter whether or not that person is in close proximity or not; as clairsentient sensitivity is not limited to space, time, or dimension. In other words, Indigo's can detect another person's 'resonant frequency,' regardless of where that person may be located on the planet; because they of their innate ability to be 'intuitively connected' to the 'universal consciousness' and all encompassing..

An Indigo's Disdain for Crowds

Plain and simple, we hate being in a room with more than a few people, regardless of whether or not we know any of them; all for obvious reasons. For a moment just try to imagine how much rampant emotional energy an Indigo would be sensing in a crowded room, a stadium full of avid football fans, a political or religious convention, and even worse…an amusement park.

Now put yourself at an amusement park early morning when the facility is first opening; everyone is joyful, full of excitement, and anxious about having a good day on a family outing anticipating a great day. Now imagine that same park as the day wears on; as thousands of children begin to tire and become cranky, not taking a break for the fear of missing out on something fun. Now compound that assessment by the flaring temperament of parents emotions as they try to deal with their offspring; getting short and angry with them…now multiply all that emotion by 10,000 and I think you'll begin to get the picture. Indigo's feel it all!

As a 'sensitive-empath' teenager, I began to find I would get easily annoyed by all the emotions I sensed emanating from everyone in close proximity, eventually having to learn how to block them (it was far easier than I thought). However, I soon realized it took a lot of energy out of me, and it wasn't so simple after all. Smaller the groups are easier to block out, but nearly impossible to do with large crowds, especially for an extended period, as the energy and concentration it takes drains and exhausts me faster that the batteries of a child's toy. The main reason I have avoided crowds since I was teenager, unless it was positively and absolutely necessary! Even today, I would rather watch an event on television, than actually go to the event.

Notwithstanding, 'Indigo sensitive-empaths' may eventually find that it's not very difficult to block out small groups of people for extended periods of time—and even large groups for a short period, but it's nearly impossible to continuously block any large congregation of people all the time. Think of all the emotional 'resonant frequencies' an Indigo would be sensing as a 'clairsentient' at the 'World Series' or 'Super Bowl,' and you will understand that attempt to block them out would be a futile exercise, not to mention exhausting for the 'clairsentient' Indigo.

Even though the most experienced 'sensitive empaths,' including Indigos with lots of years of practice, will tell you that blocking unsolicited emotions is not easy and even though we try to ignore them, we can't, and thus we will NOT put ourselves into those situations if at all possible.

Recognizing a Clairsentient

All my life, and more specifically throughout my career, 'clairsentience' has provided me the uncanny faculty of sensing the intent of the people around me; regardless of whether they in close proximity or not – distance being irrelevant – especially when it involves those I love. Sometimes it's a simple case of 'Indigo awareness,' knowing and sensing their concerns without ever having spoken to them. When this occurs…which is frequent, it's usually realized as a sense of 'concern' or 'foreboding' for a particular person to the point where I find it necessary to make contact with them; and why my friends and family often call me 'witch.'

'Empathy' is makes us human, but when does 'empathy' become extremely 'sensitive?' At some point in an Indigo's life, they realize that they have somehow become 'extremely sensitive' and 'receptive' at sensing the emotions of those they love most; often able to receive that 'funny feeling' something's 'just not right,' and needs attention. Recognizing it as 'clairsentience' is as simple as knowing that when the phone rings, they'll find it's the person they were thinking of.

Having managed large computer projects and people throughout my career as a business intelligence architect, the people under my charged often learned quickly that I never asked a question of them for to I didn't already know the answer. What confused and haunted them the most was, "How the hell did he know?"

'Clairsentience' in and of itself can be a very 'emotional experience' (pun definitely intended), yet at times traumatic for the person experiencing it; it all depends on how receptive the 'clairsentient' is. The more receptive, the faster their 'ability' to detect, and with time, their 'sensitivity' will increase exponentially. Remember Indigos are 'intuitively connected' and 'aware' to the 'universal consciousness' at all times, and everyone's soul is connected to the same 'consciousness.' Thus when tragedy or disasters strikes anywhere on the planet it has a ripple effect on tens of thousands of people around the world; 9/11 is a prime example, but so was the Columbine High School shooting, the Tsunami in Indonesia, and the Japanese earthquake, flood, and ultimately the nuclear disaster. It's events like these affect the 'consciousness' because 'empathy' is our common 'human connection.' Humanity has had its share of devastation and sadness throughout the centuries, and we have learned to heal as one, all because of one basic human instinct, 'empathy.'

When a person could care less about a global disaster, it's most likely because they are somewhat 'sociopathic,' in that they lack of social moral conscious; whereas an Indigo will have an entirely different effect; they become severely despondent. Their instinct for 'empathy,' another key trait they will have all their lives, is not foreign to most of them. As sensitives, the Indigo will feel an emotion so intense one would think they had just experienced the trauma first hand for themselves. The 'depression,' that ensues may force to retreat into their own little shell, and should come as no surprise to everyone around them. Exposure to major disasters of any magnitude can create such an intense ripple in the 'universal consciousness' it is nearly impossible to ignore, especially for the heightened sense of 'empathic-sensitivity' the 'Indigo clairvoyant' goes through; a sensitivity which they (the Indigo) cannot simply bury their head deep in the sand.

Indigo Self-Preservation

There are advantages for the 'Indigo' displaying the propensity of 'clairsentience;' it provides them with an innate ability to not only recognize when someone is scanning their psyche – perhaps another Indigo – and it allows them to do the same. An experienced 'Indigo sensitive' will sense the scan, and will instinctively identify who is scoping them out and their 'intent' and will return the favor by 'scanning' them also. There are many times, I myself have been able to protect myself from becoming the unsuspecting 'target.'

Indigo's use two types of 'clairsentient' skills; 'sensory projection' and 'sensory extension.' However, at this point I feel it is important to emphasize that most Indigo's have scruples that usually incorporate a high set of morals and therefore they will not normally use this 'clair ability' superfluously.

Clairsentient Projection

'Clairsentient projection,' is an Indigo trait that allows an Indigo to read the 'harmonic transmissions' people 'emit;' first by discerning whose signal they received, and second identify the source as being a viable 'target if interest' within the group; whether they are familiar with each other or not. They are able to—and for the lack of a better descriptive—'probe' their 'target of interest,' to 'sense (read)' as well as 'project (transmit)' information to and from this unsuspecting target. When you really think about it, it can be quite scary, especially when the targets have no idea they have been detected much less by 'whom, how' or 'why;' unless of course, they too are 'clairsentient Indigos' themselves.

Clairsentient Extension

This descriptive allows a more experienced Indigo to expand their 'sensing' capabilities to a great distance and transcend their influence to go beyond the normal barriers of time and space. The extended distance of the 'sense extension' is easier when there is a personal connection to their subject. The Indigo that has developed this ability does so by using the faculties of 'clairsentience' and 'clairvoyance' in combination; allowing the Indigo to not only 'sense' the emotions of their subject, however, 'know' their location.

There have been occasions when I have suddenly became overcome by a sudden sense of discomfort, yet it wasn't mine; and usually within a few seconds I can determine the person responsible, regardless of whether or not they are in a large group or not; identify intent and quickly determine if there is anything to worry about. Everyone at one time or experiences a 'premonition' that something is just not right. Unfortunately, whenever they've become 'uneasy,' and not recognized as a 'clairsentient' warning, they ignore it and the 'warning' goes unheeded.

As an Indigo Child I've always had bells and sirens (figuratively speaking) constantly going off in my head that I could not ignore…I eventually realized them to be 'warnings' intended to keep me from danger. If you think about how many people, ignore those little bells and sirens in their head, and end raped, mugged, or murdered. If people would only paid attention to that 'little voice in their head' perhaps it would have never happened. When an Indigo, who is 'tuned-in' to their 'clairsentient faculty,' receives a 'precognition,' they usually respond to it appropriately, and get themselves out of harm's way as quickly as possible.

A 'clairsentient Indigo's' ability to scan each-and-every individual in the room does not end with an 'intuitive awareness' to the 'universal consciousness;' it's a skill that spans space, time and dimension. The Indigo can ascertain every person's intent' simply by making eye contact and instantly know everything they need to know about them; past, present, even their future from information gathered from the 'consciousness;' even before you can blink twice. Their 'knowing' allows them to that the necessary and most appropriate action necessary to circumvent any uncomfortable, undesirable, or difficult situation before it even occurs; another prime example of 'clairsentient extension.'

Indigos are also quite capable of focusing their 'clairsentient energy' as a means of transmitting their own interest or intent to a specific person in the room, and will garnish them a fleeting glance to go undetected by another Indigo's scan who may have noticed them.

As you can see, the 'clairsentient faculty' is not a cut-and-dried faculty that can be easily explained nor is everything about it strictly black or white. What I have attempted to discern herein are some basic examples from a personal experience to keep it simple. There are certainly many other points I have not covered regarding 'clairaudience.' However, I do believe I have provided you the most important points. This 'faculty' goes far beyond any of the other 'clair faculties;' and is actually the 'root cause' for everyone, including the non-Indigo, who has ever experienced a serious case of 'déjà vu.'

Clairtangence

Understanding what the 'clair-senses' can at times be quite difficult to understand. It is therefore important to note that the 'clair faculties' regarding the 'what of, what to and wherefores,' varies widely between 'Indigo Children' as well as the 'Indigo Generation.' So when it comes to just becoming familiar with 'clairaudience, clairvoyance, and clairsentience' (or any of the other 'clair faculties'), it is imperative to know that experience, skill ,and manner in which an Indigo will use them all boils down to experience.

As mentioned earlier, the recent generations have accepted these faculties as an entirely normal orientation they were born with, whereas the generations may vary. Some of the older generations are just like the newest (myself included, as I was born assuming everyone could do what I could do), but for those who are only now 'awakening' to their newfound skills it can be a confusing and difficult road not much different than puberty was growing up. Take karate, for example, there are those who have absolutely no inclination what-so-ever to remembering all the moves, while others use them well and display a wide-range of effective skillsets; from 'green-belt' to 'black-belt.'

'Clairtangence' is by far equally powerful and often referred to as the 'psychometric faculty;' an innate ability pick up an object, shake a person's hand, or simply touch the wall to automatically trigger a 'download' of data; information that includes everything that has occurred with that object, a person, or a thing simply through a 'tactile connection;' like shaking hands. When combined with any combination of the other 'clair faculties' (clairaudience, clairvoyance, or clairsentience) the 'clairtangent' information garnered by an Indigo is exponential to the combination of their other 'clair' skill-sets. For a few Indigo, it can often feel like an overwhelming phenomenon when it first occurs, with the potential of leaving them despondent to the point they shut themselves down; not unlike autism.

Case in point; recently I had attended a training conference in Southern New Mexico. As everyone arrived, the sponsor of the course began to introduce the trainer to all the attendees as they entered the conference facility. The trainer appeared to be a confident young man in his early twenty's and appeared very professional and quite confident with himself; I'll call Matthew (not his real name of course to maintain his confidentiality).

I had stepped outside to enjoy my morning coffee in the warm New Mexico winter sun, when our sponsor and Matthew came out to greet several of the attendees on the patio just outside the conference room. As the young man smiled at me and extended his open hand for me to take, I gazed into his eyes as I put my palm into his. (Believe me when I say, a person's eyes are indeed the windows to their soul.) Immediately, I saw right through the lad's outward smile and appearance; for here stood before me a young man suffering a deep, deep, sadness. However, it wasn't until I took his hand in mind that I was broadsided by a battery of information from the 'consciousness' to provided me a lot of 'insight' as to who Matthew was; as his life basically flashed through my mind as images. Although overwhelmed by the sudden data download, I kept my composure.

During lunch, Matthew approached me again on the patio and asked me what I thought of the training. So after a few moments of chitchat he turned to leave and against everything my grandmother had ever taught me, I called him back.

"Matt (as he chose to be called) I don't want you to think I'm crazy or some loony wacko that just stepped off fruit wagon because we only just met. But do you believe in precognition?" To which he countered with a questions. "What do you mean? Are you one of 'those' psychics?" he responded, making invisible quote marks with both hands in the air.

"Not at all, I'm a' sensitive.'" I responded with dignity, as his right eyebrow rose in a telltale sign of total disbelief. "I sense your skepticism and that's good, but I detect an intense all-consuming sadness in you; one that has plagued your every thought and dream for over a couple of years. I sense that you were involved in an automobile accident in which you hit a young girl early in the morning as you both were on the way to your respective schools. As a consequence of the accident, she died a couple days later in hospital."

I now had his attention.

"Now you're scaring me; how could you have possibly known that? We just met?"

"I also see you driving a small fairly new gold or bronze colored car; perhaps a 'Kia' or 'Honda;' and that the accident was not deemed to have been your fault, nor was it attributed to drugs or alcohol for which you were tested. However, you still blame yourself for the accident. However, for now, it's not the time, nor the place to discuss this. If you wish me to continue let's do it after the training course ends on Sunday (three days later), and you your mind is clear. Would that be okay with you?" His response was immediate and stated definitively, "I do want to know more…but I don't know if I can wait that long." He replied.

That night I choose not go out with other attendees after dinner to a local cowboy bar (I don't drink), and went back to my room to go to bed. As I began to doze off, I was downloaded additional information of the event by the young girl he had hit in a detailed lucid dream.

The following morning, Matt came to me and said, "I could not help but think about what you had told me," he began, "would you mind if were just you and I went to lunch to discuss this." His curiosity was peeked and wanted to know everything I knew…I agreed.

When it was time for lunch, we walked several hundred yards to a small café by the highway, placed our order, and began our chat. "I was briefed last night by a young girl that wouldn't quit hounding me until I relayed something important to you."

"The young soul preferred I called Anna, although her name was actually Anastasia; her last name was either 'Nichols' or 'Nikolai;' I believe the latter. Although I tried to ignore her presence, she insisted that I let you know what had happened, was not your fault. It was hers; and she doesn't want you to be sad anymore. She explained to me that she had been talking to her friends who went to a different school, and completely lost track of time. When she realized she was late for school, she turned and darted onto the street toward the school without looking and that was when you hit her. She was thrown about thirty feet and ended up dying in the hospital two days later."

Matt's face went white and his expression solemn as he listened to continue. "The police ascertained by witness statements you were going the speed proper limit when Anna darted out in front of your car. It all happened so quickly, there was no he could have avoided me." She told me. "And I know he's blaming himself for what happened."

"She went on to tell me that she cannot move on until she knows you're okay and stop blaming yourself." After a short pause, I asked him if he had any questions, to which he merely stated, "All I have left to say, is that you have thrown me into a complete loop because what you have just told me was never published by the press, and some weren't even in the police report. How in the hell could you have possibly known of these things? I never believed it possible."

"I really can't explain how, Matthew" I answered, "but when you shook my hand yesterday I had all these images flash through my head about you and your life; which doesn't happen with just anybody. There was a reason I was given this information from a higher consciousness that superseded my not wanting to get involved."

Sensing some doubt I began, "Remember when we shook hands yesterday morning?" He confirmed with an affirmative, "I was hit by a barrage of information from which I learned a simple gesture downloaded, but still a shitload of data about you; including that you grew up in marina close to Boca Raton. Your family's home was on street that had 'lamp' or 'gaslight' on it. You lived on either 'Lighthouse Lane' or 'Lamplighter Drive' and the house was close to the Beach. There is a waterway or a canal I believe behind the house and at the end of a short pier a boathouse, where you used to go hide when you were angry as a boy or got upset. The driveway of the house inlaid brick of pattern consisting of three different colors in a diamond and herringbone pattern. In the middle of you front yard stood several tall palm trees with several large boulders and lots of ferns and plants...." His face went white, and he began to tear up. I sensing his emotion building, I paused to ask him, "Do you wish me to continue?"

His response was soft but immediate, "No, I've heard enough and you scare the hell out of me!" To which he added, "The only point you missed, was our house was not on the beach, it was around the corner from Beach Boulevard' leading to the beach.

After a few weeks, I followed up with Matt – who had now become a believer – how things were going and he responded with the information I had given him. "I have finally let go of my grief, had a good cry over Anastasia, and I believe I've finally let go." He added,

"That night I felt so much better and relieved by knowing it really wasn't my fault and Anastasia for hounding you. But most of all, I want to thank you for telling me what you did."

"I know you are, and Anna thanked me as well just before she moved on."

People often believe that 'clairtangence' relates only objects when held or touched, for which you can now see, that is not the case and is the furthest thing from the truth.

'Psychometric projection' can relate to any object; be it houses, cars, buildings and as you have just read, people. However, more importantly the Indigo, or skilled psychic, is merely a conduit! Although many people who are not necessarily Indigo unwittingly possess this 'clair faculty,' they usually don't talk about it because they really don't understand exactly what it is, much less, how it works or what the hell just happened, nor do they wish. All because it scares the hell out them, and therefore choose instead to ignore it altogether. Therefore, the next time you see someone in an antique shop with their hands in their pockets or refusing to take anything offered them to hold for examination, you'll know why.

Psychometric Impressions

There are two very specific and very important types of 'clairtangence' to recognize:

Insentient psychometry – when items examined are objects of a personal nature owned previously, perhaps by a specific individual or family.

Intimate psychometry – a method by which 'psychometric' is automatically downloaded data from the 'universal consciousness' that transfers intimate information about a subject (person), almost as if physical contact was being made with them; not unlike a simple hand-shake.

The intensity at which an Indigo who displays this particular 'clairtangent faculty;' can be compounded when combined with any other of the 'clair faculties;' the combination causing the Indigo to experience a wider range of extreme emotions; from total euphoria to instantaneous despair. Both extremes traumatic in their own right and brought on by the Indigo's 'innate awareness;' not only 'who, what,' or 'why' the 'psychometric connections' to exist in an object, but all critical details that surround the object, location, or person; good, bad, and indifferent.

Indigos possessing this faculty – much more prevalent than one would think – are often far more capable of providing detailed information regarding the people, places, and events behind the object; although at times the details revealed may at times remain a bit sketchy. The reason being, Indigo's are much more acute to specifics; they prefer to be decidedly confident that their level of 'awareness' does not lack sufficient detail to 'intuitively define' the experience as well; in detail and confidence, although their 'best guess' is actually profoundly accurate. A simple rule of thumb to remember at time there may be a weak 'resonant energy signature' to the object, and although it's fain, the Indigo can more often than not sense what exists, with much more detail than can most experienced 'psychics.'

Many Indigo's also tend to block or ignore the 'clairtangent faculty' instead of acknowledging it. They fear the intensity of the 'energy' behind the 'transference' (what may be revealed) itself worse, than how they will feel 'emotionally' by it. Say the object is located in a 'cancer hospice thrift shop;' a store containing hundreds of objects previously owned and donated by people cancer patients; some who died, and other who recovered. Yet knowing who left their worldly possessions to the shop so they can help others is difficult at best. An object may have 'positive' impression to the 'clairtangent' touching it, or a very 'traumatic' experience. Although this is an extreme example, imagine the pain and emotional trauma a 'clairtangent' Indigo would experience from what lies therein, and from that extrapolate why most the hide their ability from others, and even stay away from these types of shops altogether.

An Insentient Psychometric Experience

Many 'Indigos' who demonstrate an 'insentient clairtangence' have at the very top of their list an acute aversion of getting anywhere near anything previously 'owned 'or 'used' by someone else; especially clothing, furniture, jewelry, and antiques. It's not that they are not useful, beautiful, or even valuable, it's that these types of objects may very well have multiple 'resonant energy signatures' from a number of previous owner, none of whom would be specifically identifiable to the 'clairtangent Indigo;' liken them to the signatures to everyone at Disneyland, as this 'energy' be easily cleansed. Especially because refinishing or restoring any old item to a nearly new condition would destroy the value of the antique itself.

What I find extremely humorous, in an odd sort of way, is that I am ether drawn into or steered away from specific areas and people because of the type of 'energy,' or 'energies,' that emanate from them. Remember, 'resonant energy signatures' are either positive or negative

For example, when I joined various projects throughout my career either, as a consultant, a project manager, or an architect, I could immediately sense everyone's 'resonant signatures' I entered the assigned work area. 'Negative resonances' (residual or not) had the office space feeling heavy, stressful, and uninviting, which for me, established the tone a project headed for failure. On the other hand, when the work area emanated a 'positive resonant signature,' the room had an inviting feeling, which immediately signaled that a successful project was in the offing: everyone was happy, on schedule, and in budget; the team's success always reflected the 'energy signatures' therein or left behind.

One other thing I failed to mention that drives me or any Indigo for that matter, batty is 'clutter;' be it a room, a house, or an office. I tend to get overwhelmed and anxious by it, a 'scattering' of energy if you will, and feel trapped by it. Don't confuse of what I speak as an occasional mess, everyone's can get messy on occasion, especially when focused. However, a mess is a mess when a person has to work around towers of clutter that has accumulated over the life of the project; becoming nothing more than very high pile of 'insentient chaos!'

An Intimate Psychometric Transference

Explaining the 'resonant energy' of 'intimate psychometry' is a bit more daunting. It works very similar to the way a radio signal emanates away from its tower (the source); much like the wave created by a pebble tossed on a still pond; the ripple creates a type of wave known as 'resonant.' This principal does not vary and is valid with electronic circuitry and our human brain: both of which generates a 'unique energetic oscillation' at varying amplitudes (in hertz - Hz). In the human brain, 'thought,' – much as a radio tower transmits broadcast signals on a specific frequency (101.5 FM for example) – a person transmits their thought as a 'resonant signature' (a wave similar, but much weaker than say 101.5 FM), to another person.

'Intimate psychometry' is the another aspect of the 'clairtangent faculty' in that it can produce a number of 'resonant frequencies' to create a series of harmonic frequencies (Hz) capable of not only transmitting energy signals from the brain, but receive them as well; a process referred to as 'telepathic transference.' The waves generated in all directions unwittingly by most people, however a few people can either target the signal to a specific individual or to a large group of people, often 'intentionally' to establish an 'intimate psychometric connection' between two (or more) minds 'telepathically.'

PSI researchers are convinced that a select few 'Indigo Children' are capable of 'intimate psychometry,' which may explain how a 'clairsentient' is able to accomplish, and experience other 'psychometric' phenomena. Skill that have even caught the attention of 'Black Op' organization in many governments, including the United States; remote viewing, out-of-body experience (OBE), and 'psychic attacks' at the top of the list. Our human brain is a marvelous took, whether in a conscious state, a subconscious state, and an 'unconscious state.' Knowing this, one can only wonder what am Indigo consciousness may one day in the not too distant future, be able to accomplish.

Remote Viewing

Basically, 'remote viewing' is a form of 'astral projection' often associated with an 'out-of-body experience–OBE,' where one's consciousness is able to travel to any location they choose and is very much a 'conscious lucid dream.'

'Remote viewing' has been around for a very long time; an ability, said to have been practiced by 'oracles.' In fact, evidence demonstrates it goes as far back as our earliest ancestors thousands of years ago. The concept, was later adopted as far back as the 1930's, and labeled 'remote viewing' when two conscientious scientists, Joseph B. Rhine (considered to be the 'Father of Modern Parapsychology)' and Dr. Louisa E. Rhine, his wife, began studying the 'Clair Faculties' of 'clairvoyance, clairsentience, clairtangence,' and 'claircognizance. '

Their ultimate goal regarding 'telepathic' and 'psychometric thought transference;' was to better understand the various 'states of consciousness' required to experience an 'out-of-body' journey (a 'lucid dream'). Their studies eventually led to an understanding of what our ancient Noetic ancestors about the skills of an 'oracle,' all to develop and produce a better 'remote viewer.'

By the end of World War II, the allied forces became quite desperate for information that would assist them to end the war with favorable results. Thus, the allied forces command turned to the Rhine studies to enlist the assistance of scientists familiar with the 'remote viewing procedures' and developed programs they had established and then enlisted the 'psychics' required. From that point on, laboratories supporting the study of 'remote viewing' were funded by the American and British military, along with all their respective intelligence channels in the use of 'remote viewing' for the sole purpose of conducting reconnaissance espionage operations.[71]

The military later defined a 'remote viewer' in 'Black Operation Program' to include only subjects with any of the 'Clare Faculties'; 'clairvoyance, clairsentience, clairtangence, claircognizance, telepathy' and 'psychometric thought transference.' Which made it clear, the government was not looking for a mere 'psychics' by definition, they required to enlist 'Indigo Children' (a term not yet coined), specifically because these 'subjects of interest' had an 'inherent ability' that displayed an 'instantaneous awareness' that redefined our human understanding of 'time, space,' and 'dimension.'

Even then, the Rhine Institute and their military cohorts understood that 'Indigo Children' were far more suited than any 'psychic' ever could be because their innate capabilities not only exceeded that of any 'psychic,' the 'Indigo Child' possessed a combined number of abilities that allowed them (the military) to gather better detailed descriptive data of any 'target' they chose. In addition, they (the Indigo Children) were able to assess, the perfect time and location for the operation nearly 'instantaneously', as well as which outcome from all the possibilities considered would yield the best results for a successful campaign. [72]

The most successful 'remote viewers' were never provided prior intelligence of any intended target, including surveillance reports prior to their sessions, which were always conducted under a 'blind condition.' Each 'remote viewer' also underwent a series of extensive training sessions at regular intervals and for varied durations in order to make what information they do provide much more proficient. This process became the standard methodology of government and military intelligence services, giving them control of the 'Indigo Children' engaged by shifting their innate ability of 'intuitive awareness.' All in an effort to maintain their normal 'awake state of consciousness' so it could be better utilized, which did not involve hypnosis or channeling; nor was the 'remote viewer' allowed to engage in any 'out-of-body experiences' that could possibly alter their normal 'state of consciousness' if at all possible. The objective was to be sure that any information gathered by the 'remote viewer' during the session could be 'verified' by comparing it to surveillance data gathered to compare it for accuracy against what little known facts were contained within the target's intelligence portfolio.

Later, during the late 1960s and early 1970s, the American Society for Psychical Research conducted a series of experiments developed by Ingo Swann, an artist and student of the PSI phenomenon from Colorado, in New York City. His research protocols suggested a wide range of changes needed to be made as improvements that could verify a successful 'remote viewing' session. Using himself as the test subject, he attempted to describe the current weather in a number of cities around the United States, after which Ingo's descriptions of what weather he perceived in those cities were verified against the national weather stations in those areas and verified by other authorities. The experiment suggested (to the PSI community) that something unusual to their current understanding of 'remote viewing' had been involved by an Indigo 'remote viewer' that would have otherwise been inaccessible through direct human perception. His results were not only provocative; they underscored the value of conducting any further detailed scientific research than his.

Several 'remote viewers' within covert operations of the United States and Soviet governments have reported that during their 'trance states,' they often felt like a fly on the wall watching the events unfold before them, which was beneficial for 'black operations.' For the military 'remote viewing' sessions would allow them to focus where and how they should conduct their 'espionage' campaign, and who in the government would be involved; another good reason the government would never admit such programs even existed; then or now.

'Clairtangent' and 'Claircognizant' Indigos have, for a very long time, been used for 'remote viewing' to provide valuable information regarding people, activities, and locations. All because, Indigo Children are 'intuitively aware' and can not only provide detailed information about a person's whereabouts, they can often reveal relevant, valuable, and detailed information regarding events that have not yet occurred; including their most likely outcome (of any actions taken). It's for this reason 'Black Ops' programs have long developed as discrete programs under the guise of protecting 'national security' interests; and the big reason Indigo Children have been exploited since the early 1950s and still continues; even I had been targeted for their clandestine operations, but refused.

Remote Viewing in the Military, Government, & Private Enterprise

By the 1970's the US Government embraced 'remote viewing' within many programs within the US Department of Defense (DOD), the Central Intelligence Agency (CIA), the National Security Administration (NSA), and its other branches of the US military; all attempting to exploit, explore, and improve on how 'remote reviewing' could improve the quality and consistency of their intelligence gathering repertoire.

The US Army by 1978 had even created a "remote viewing' collective to gather intelligence against their communist adversaries in Vietnam, China, and the Soviet Union; programs that utilized exceptional teams of Indigo 'remote viewers.' A practice that has continued to this day since the late 1980s when it was placed under the command of United States Defense Intelligence Agency (DIA); later renamed project 'Star Gate.'

I have include this information herein only as a matter of historical record. 'Remote viewing' has usurped by many operational entities – and with great success I might add – that includes all of the US Government's 'Black Op' espionage initiatives, and for quite some time now. Although, the current level of governmental involvement is quite evident, Homeland Security Administration (HSA) has operations that considered to be 'highly classified' and their involvement with 'remote viewing' and not been made public. However, one can only assumed that covert efforts to fight terrorist attack within the United States and all its interests, in fact utilize highly skilled Indigo Children as 'remote viewers;' spying and gathering intelligence on both foreign and domestic targets, nor should it be assumed that Homeland Security 'Black Op' programs only exist within the borders of the United States.

Concurrently, there are government and civilian researchers (major corporations, pharmaceutical laboratories, and financial institutions) who continue to explore and exploit this phenomenon (especially since a 1995 act of Congress transferred not only the responsibility for the 'Star Gate' program from the DIA to the CIA), with all funding from government programs diverted away from its clandestine research facilities. By the fall of 1995, declassified portions of the CIA program was released and in their report, so were all contents of their controversial research the purportedly argued 'remote viewing' was not useful as an intelligence gathering tool and therefore terminated by the CIA. Was it propaganda to confuse the population with disinformation and misdirection? My spidey sense tells me that it was, as I was approached in the fall of 2012 for a 'top secret' program as what was hinted to be 'remote viewing' under the guise of 'national security' and now that 'whistle blowers' such as Edward Snowden are now coming forward, all programs have gone deeper into woodwork. [73]

Indigo Telepathic Communications

What researchers don't realize is that everyone born has a propensity to display this inherent ability, but to what extent varies dramatically from 'person to person;' even between 'Indigo Children.' After all, how often have you known when someone was in distress or your sensed a close friend or relative needed your help?

People, who demonstrate such an inclination toward any of the 'intimate psychometric' traits like 'telepathy,' should best keep what they know to themselves; otherwise, they will quickly discover it's more a curse than a blessing; by this I mean, know what people are thinking, should rarely be acted upon. Most people with this ability receive nothing more than scattered random thoughts that are more-often-than nothing but transmitted random bits of gibberish.

While my children were growing up, and now my grandchildren, were constantly awestruck by the fact that I always knew what they were doing, where they were at, whom they were with, and what trouble they were getting into.

I was able to utilize this propensity in my work as a global business intelligence architect with IBM, managing colleague and client teams. Often my teams were left bewildered by the fact that I always seemed to know what was happening within their teams and how I knew what was going on with every aspect their project assignment; be they schedules, manpower, or complications that affected their deliverable schedules. Mind you, I didn't know these things because I had intentionally eavesdropped on their intimate thoughts, but because they were emphatically transmitting a panic when I approached.

I ignore unintentional 'personal telepathic communication (worry);' simply I knew when they had inadvertently panicked for help without wanting to appear incompetent. 'Psychometric transference of thought' is not eavesdropping when its being broadcast louder than a rock concert. It takes a lot of effort for an Indigo Child to disconnect from certainly people 'telepathically;' especially colleagues, family, friends; and on a few occasions even strangers.

I liken 'telepathy' as having a really, really large antenna array mounted on top of head that could essentially receive 'resonant signals' from Alpha Centauri four light-years away. Most of the time, it's the people important in my life that affect my consciousness and why I'll stand up to take notice.

For years, PSI investigators have debated over the various types of 'transcendental experiences' reported; most of which they believe are nothing more than hallucinatory. They often point out that these people as 'mentally ill' and 'delusional;' another reason I had kept my mouth shut as a boy hell bent on living my life out without their intervention. Recently I became fascinated by several PSI studies that all concluded 'telepathic communication' – once assumed to be hallucinatory – actually does exists and is a 'normal' experience of certain exceptional men and women they believed to be 'Indigo.'

A 'psychical' researcher from the 18th century, Edmund Gurney (1847-1888) was the first to claim he had 'empirical evidence' to the existence of 'telepathic empathy' after his study group had somehow contributed to their hallucinations when put in a 'hypnotic state.' His widely accepted work, later marginalized and discredited had been rejected by many controversial and unanswered questions to his research, only to end up nullifying his findings as being filled with nothing but conjecture and supposition.[79]

Telepathy has long been considered as an 'extra-sensory perception (or ESP),' as are the abilities of 'clairvoyance, precognition,' and 'intuition.' Today 'clairtangence' is beginning to gain wider acceptance because more and more people are demonstrating and inherent ability to this 'intimate psychometric' skill inherent to 'clairtangence.'

The Sciences of the Cold War

During the height of the 'cold war' as tensions mounted between the Soviets, Americans, and Chinese governments, there was a desperate attempt by all three governments to gather 'knowledge through consciousness,' and by any means necessary to determine the 'hidden' political agendas of their rivals. Shortly after World War II, and nearly simultaneously, all three world-power governments opted create covert operations to facilitate what we now know as 'black Ops (for black-operations) programs;' top-secret project operations usually comprised from teams of scientists familiar with the ancient sciences called 'Noetics.' These scientists desperately needed funding to further the study of 'Noetic Human Consciousness,' and at the time, they had absolutely no idea what they were getting themselves into; they were selling their souls to the devil to fund the projects but under the guise of 'Black Ops.'

So, what exactly were main objectives of these three world power governments? Simple really, to use the secrets of 'Noetic consciousness' as a secret tool to gain insight through a new 'consciousness;' psychics, oracles, remote viewers, and telepaths to help with conducting their clandestine espionage operations on potential threats; and thus, PSYOP's (Psychological Operations) came into existence in the post war modern world.

Today, 'Black Ops' is not just limited to the clandestine government agencies such as MI6, the KGB, the CIA, Mossad, or the NSA, it includes every branch in the United States, British, and Chinese military, global corporations (including private companies), major financial institutions, and secret think tank underground organizations. The 'key word' here is 'clandestine,' a word that carries a well-deserved 'negative overtone' that involves a significant amount of deception and disinformation to conceal who all the players are behind any of the 'operations.' All in an effort to make it appear as if it's nothing more than a 'false-flag' operation; and provides fodder for many 'conspiracy theories,' enough so, they provide the 'plausible deniability' governments or and other entities require to deflect and avoid culpability, if and when they get caught in the act.

Psychometric Attacks

History has riddled antiquity with mythological folklore. The oldest being from Ancient Greece that told of 'psychometric attacks' by psychotic gods, mythical creatures, and paranoid kings; all seeking out assistance from the 'black arts,' witchcraft, voodoo, magic, and necromancy. However, their favorite form of attack was that of a Noetic art known as 'psychic vampirism;' an art known only a few, that could drain the energy force from an enemy force by what we now call a 'psychometric attack.'

Be aware that a 'psychometric attack' is the most deviant form of 'intimate psychometry;' whether it is committed 'consciously' or 'unconsciously,' it can inflict great personal harm to an individual, and has been known to incapacitate entire armies and great nations.

This type of a 'telepathic attack' is usually launched as a direct spiritual or mental attack with strong emotional ramifications; transmission of negative energies that can specifically target another person, or group of people, through a concentrated 'consciousness.' Not unlike a magnifying glass can focus the sun as an intense beam of light so hot, to start a fire. The most common concentrated 'transmission of negative thought' for example would be that of a 'jealous rage' focused on a 'scorned lover.'

'Psychometric assaults' are usually influenced by narcissistic and often psychotic individuals within a person's circle of trust intimately known by the target. Although the attack is not always intentional it is, more-often-that-not, instituted by an attacker hell-bent on revenge by a conscious, unconscious, or subconscious desire to inflict harm. Although this may not always be the case, most 'unconscious telepathic psychic attacks' are often transmitted by personal thoughts so profound by a sender who is totally unaware of their attack. Actions spawned by everything from a jealousy, rage, envy, or hatred, can consume a person with such a burning anger, it consumes every waking moment of their conscious life.

Women are the ones most likely to spawn a 'psychometric attack.' Giving credence to a quote by writer William Congreve, 1670-1729, "Heaven hath no rage like love to hatred turned, nor hell a fury, like that of a woman scorned..." as women have the tendency to easily perceive their target has progressed without them and at their expense, thus leaving them behind to stagnate in their own sorrow. For example, they may believe their target's unfaithfulness was responsible for their misery and therefore they should pay their own quiescence.

There are two basic types of 'psychometric attacks:'

A *'conscious telepathic psychometric assault;'* where a person deliberately launches an attack; perhaps even using a means that many would call 'black magic' or 'witchcraft;' whether it actually involved casting a spell or not.

A *'subconscious telepathic psychometric attack;'* usually occurring to the attackers deep REM (Rapid Eye Movement) sleep state, in which the subject dreams of revenge so intently that it is inadvertently perpetuated as an indirect 'subconscious psychic attack;' and not that different from a deliberate 'conscious telepathic psychometric assault.'

Remember, everyone has the genetic potential of having one or two of the 'clair faculties;' and to varying degrees of competency, and the Indigo multiple abilities. Especially since encoded in everyone's DNA are the necessary building blocks to transmit and receive resonant energy (frequencies) from other people and/or entities; especially the Indigo Child. Keep in mind thought that a 'telepathic' or 'intimate psychometric attack' is less about you than it is about the attacker's inherent weaknesses; weaknesses that can be used against them when employing any 'protective counter measures.'

"Give someone enough rope and eventually they'll hang themselves with it..." has long been a rule of thumb that has taught me a lot of patience in my life. I learned a long time ago, that when a person consciously transmits negative energy with the intention of inflicting harm to specific individuals or an entire group, they can, and will attract the same energy back unto themselves. In other words, the 'Universal Law of Karma' will end up biting them on the ass, for 'what goes around comes around,' but often forgotten is that it can often be multiplied exponentially!

Because the symptoms that point to a 'telepathic assault' or an 'intimate psychometric attack' are not that easy to detect much less identify – especially when a person's 'clair abilities' are limited or non-existent – here are a few pointers that may help ward off an assault on your 'psyche' until you can enlist help from those who can.

However, before I continue I would like to state that you now know what an 'intimate psychometric attack' is, and you have some idea that covert 'black operations' initiated by clandestine government organization, major corporations, private companies, financial institutions, think tanks, and secret underground organizations can launch an attack on the masses. The trick is being aware of their tactics used, and hopefully be able to fend off 'telepathic assaults' or 'intimate psychometric attacks' in the future.

Defining an Intimate Psychometric Assault

You do not have to be an Indigo Child to recognize some of the biggest clues to an 'intimate psychometric attack.' For which most telltale sign is to awaken from a deep sleep by a reoccurring nightmare in which the attacker plays a pivotal role, usually as a malevolent figure. They may even manifest during a 'conscious dream state' when the mind is in a 'lucid dream;' often referred to as a 'day dream' during deep meditative thought…either way the nightmare is a good indicator of a 'telepathic psychic attack.'

What ensues is 'sleep homeostasis' – psycho-babble for 'sleep deprivation' – basically a person's biological tendency to fall sleep at random intervals because of exhaustion. The human body determines just how exhausted you are and is responsible for your body constantly feeling fatigued. Eventually, your performance becomes impaired – whether realized or not – and your body will automatically and without warning shut itself down and usually at the most inopportune time; like driving home from work.

Take notice of these 'performance-inhibiting' signs as being a consequence of your body combating extreme fatigue. It could be that your body is warning you of a 'psychometric attack.' Symptoms can include such warnings as a decreased alertness, an inability to maintain focus, severe mood swings, decreased motivation, depression, coordination, body cramps, and dizziness; even severe or migraine headaches. A sobering note to all this, is that an ultimate consequence of sleep deprivation can yield to dangerous results that are undeniably real.

Human psyche can seriously affect a person's exhaustion level, particularly their ability to concentrate. It's when people begin to question and doubt the direction their life has taken, they can begin to feel worthless and depressed – regardless of how successful they may be – they contemplate suicide.

Should this happen, take inventory on yourself, and if you find your 'normal level of energy' is impaired for no apparent reason, it's imperative you make yourself aware to the telltale signs of a 'psychic attack;' migraine headaches, dizziness, dehydration, and vomiting, which are often accompanied by visions of the attacker as 'they' choose to be seen, causing paranoia.

Case-in-Point

Recently I had an international team assisting me with a very large event planned in 2013. After securing the funding from various investors, our secretary treasurer covertly contacted an investor by email to voice her concern regarding one of our guest speakers; her unsolicited communiqué caused that investor to, unexpectedly withdraw all funding from the event.

When I contacted the investor as to why, he obliged me with an answer by sending me a copy of all her emails. I was aghast by her allegations. A person had never met, nor had she spoken to, was accused of being a fraud in her accusatory emails. The damage done, leaving me with no recourse. I therefore asked for her immediate resignation.

Her sabotage, completely destroyed months of planning, hundreds of hours of work, and many large expenses still owed for services rendered. In an effort to regroup, I organized an international meeting with the remainder of the team, and during our Skype meeting, I became suddenly dazed, nauseous, and overcome with an intense feeling of claustrophobia. With the room seemingly caving in on me, my head began to buzz with a pain I had never felt before; my eyesight blurred and my speech quivered. Although I continued with the meeting, I said nothing to my colleagues, but the newest member in our group; Matt (a shaman practitioner with Zuni heritage) immediately took notice and warned everyone, "Listen to me closely to me Jari…you're being psychically attacked by a very powerful group of people."

Another team member, who had never experienced an 'intimate psychometric attack' before agreed something just wasn't right—as did two other people on our team. Immediately I recognized who it was by the images in my head, and from where the attack came. I shouted out to Matt, "I'm too weak to block her alone Matt…I need your help!"

Together we were able to fend off her group's 'psychometric attack' by redirecting the 'negative resonant energies' she and several other people had directed at me. With the help from my team, we successfully deflected the attack back to its source – very much like a mirror reflects an image. The 'attack' lasted approximately twenty minutes and ceased as quickly as it had begun; after which all of us felt drained and exhausted.

Could I have fought off the attack by myself? To be perfectly honest, I'm not entirely sure, because it was a gang of 'bullies;' but with the assistance of the team we were able as group to engage a counter measure to deflect the 'psychometric attack' back to its source; not to mention with much more powerful 'resonance' than we had received.

Mind you, it was not in our character to launch a 'counter-attack,' for which we could have inflicted great harm, we merely reflecting the energy directed at us, back to its source.

One of my colleagues, later contacted by her, told him I had 'telepathically' attacked her. Apparently, as she related it, some of her friends became frightened of very dark and sinister energy attacking them in her house (when it was nothing more the very same energy she had directed at me; reflected back to its source), and she accused me of launching the attack. Never again has she attempted another 'psychometric attack' on me. If you remember nothing else from this story, never allow others to know your worst fears (even close friends), in so doing you could very well reveal your Achilles heel.

Claircognizance

In the book, "The Noetic Universe, The Scientific Evidence for Psychic Phenomena" by Dr. Dean Radin, senior scientist at the Institute of Noetic Science, in which Dr. Radin provides astonishing answers to many universal questions by unveiling persuasive empirical evidence to the existence of 'psychic phenomena.' In his book, he attempts to shatter many of the myths that surround PSI studies, and the governments, corporations, and academia who have embraced Noetics as an alternative science. [74]

This comes as no surprise, especially since most of the world already believes in the existence of 'psychic' phenomena. Over the last few decades, give or take a few years, something very profound has propelled mankind to look beyond our old personal belief systems when it comes to understanding the reality of what 'psychic phenomena' really is; especially now that we know about Indigo Children.

Just how do Indigo Children fit into the overall picture, now that Noetic Science has begun reemerge as a widely accepted scientific explanation to 'claircognizance,' and not even considered as 'psychic' at all. Many believe there are newer ways of evaluating and understanding the massive amounts of evidence collected by hundreds, if not thousands of researchers around the world.

The point I'm trying to make here is that most, if not all Indigo Children are 'claircognizant' in that they can access information from the 'universal consciousness in such a way, that instinctively they always seem to 'know that they know' accurate information they could have even possibly known, nor can they really explain why, much less how they do.
Claircognizance provides the 'Indigo' an extraordinary ability to realize information about a person, object, place, or event with an 'intrinsic knowledge' that is natural and effortless to the Indigo; an inherent primal modality, that takes 'precognition'

far beyond the 'awareness' our ancient ancestors used as a survival mechanism, it's 'instantaneous.'

'Claircognizance' is by far different the most different of all the 'clair modalities;' clairvoyance, clairaudience, and clairsentience, as it does not rely on any of our other five 'senses;' particularly sight, sound, and touch. Yet it is just as mysterious as it is accurate, in it is more difficult to recognize, and just another factor that sets the Indigo Child apart from a 'psychic,' that takes 'precognition' to a 'whole new level.'

Why is that?" one may ask. The answer is simple, it's the 'proof in the pudding' when it relates to an 'accurate precognitive experience.' Understand however, intuition is one thing, it's 'knowing' without a doubt that sets Indigo 'warnings' apart and should not be taken with a grain of salt…as many do come to pass.

During my childhood I often astonished people…okay, I scared the hell out of them, especially when I would suddenly blurt out an 'unsolicited precognition' as quickly as it entered my mind. Today, I just don't do that, as those who really get to know me, I still do. I just can help myself and guilt sets in thinking about Grandma's warnings, but when I do, it's usually for a damn good reason. Does everyone heed my advice? No, of course not, however, there have been many times when my warnings went unheeded, only to be regretted later.

It was my first year at university and after a hard day of classes, I headed to the dining room at my dorm room for supper. One of my dorm brothers putting a load of clothes into the washing machine as I made my way around him and his dirty laundry; without stopping, I said stated aloud as I passed, "Don't use that machine it's going to catch fire." and continued on my merry way. He just chuckled and replied, "Yea right Ms. Dixon;" a reference to a famous psychic by the name of Jean Dixon in case you didn't catch that…and who was nearly always wrong.

As I sat down with a healthy serving of meatballs, guess who came running through the dining room searching in panic for a fire extinguisher. Finding one in the kitchen, he darted through the double doors, and was heard yelling at the top of his voice, "Jari is a bloody witch!" As it turned out the circuit box had shorted out caught flame; and by the looks of things, a rather big flame.

So how did I knew this was going happen and why did I say anything at all? I don't really remember, other than I was presented with an image in my mind of a fire raging behind the machine as walked past…and opened my mouth just as fast as it had entered my mind.

Warding Off Eminent Danger

Many years ago, a colleague on one of my assignments happened to lived close by and asked me for a lift to the office; her car being serviced. Since we both worked on the same project but in separate buildings in the complex, we agreed to meet up after work at a small bakery shop for a cup of coffee before heading out on the long ride home.

The shop, in an older section of downtown Los Angeles, was a long and narrow edifice. The baked goods counter was at the far rear and the shop, with two rows of padded booths on each side of the building. By the time I arrived, the only available booth when I arrived was directly behind the cash register counter at the front entrance.

After having been served coffee I interrupted her in mid-sentence and adamantly blurted, "We have to leave NOW!"

"But I just sat down." She argued.

"I know, but trust me on this. We have to go!" I stood up, threw some money on the table, and pushed her out of the building. Quiet and confused she said nothing until we got on the highway. Very softly, she asked, "When do you plan on telling me WHAT THE HELL just happened?"

"You wouldn't believe me if I did. But it was imperative we got out of there." To which she retorted, "Try me. You'll be surprised."

Mockingly she asked, "Are you psychic or something? Because you need to know I don't believe in that crap." For which, I said nothing, and quietly drove on.

As we approached our exit, I quietly informed her, "Your husband is going to be chasing your two dogs (a greyhound and a Great Dane) down Garden Grove Boulevard when we get off the freeway."

Smug and condescending, her response was, "Impossible, it'll never happen. You know damn well they're both chained up in the back yard to a brick wall."

As we reached the first traffic light at the intersection of Beach and Garden Grove, we sat quietly waiting for the light to change. Suddenly, dog number one emerged from our right running past our car and across six lanes of traffic on Beach, with dog number two and her husband, giving chase. Out of breath and leash in hand, we could see the look of terror on his face as he darted past us, with a look of terror on his face and in hot pursuit.

Quite for what appeared to be an eternity, she turned to me and very softly whispered, "Now, I'm scared! How long did you say you've been a witch?"
The following morning we returned to the coffee shop for coffee expecting a Danish, only to discover the cafe sealed with the all-to-familiar yellow police tape. Out of curiosity we crossed the street to a corner market and asked the owners if knew they what had happened at the coffee shop.

"Yea, some guy held up the place about six fifteen yesterday with a gun, and apparently after she gave him the money in the drawer he fired off a few shots…we even heard them all the way over here. He killed two people; the cashier at counter and the guy that had just sat down at the table behind the cashier."

At the time, I really didn't understand that the modality of 'claircognizance' much less explain it; I just knew what I knew; and it was a definitive 'precognitive warning' I paid attention to. I didn't know what was going to transpire, I just knew we had to leave.

'Claircognizance' doesn't usually provide rhyme, reason, or logic to the 'precognition,' in this case was it was a warning, from what I have come to learn was through the 'universal consciousness.' It was 'instantaneous,' did not need interpretation, explanation, or debate, and left no room for a misunderstanding. The message was clear, "Get out now."

So how does one always recognize 'claircognizance?' Not as often as we people should, and to be brutally honest, not even Indigo Children. I didn't know myself until I was much older, and definitely not one anyone can develop at will. People are either 'intuitive' or they're not.

What I find a bit humorous is when an older Indigo child is becoming more aware of 'claircognizance;' it's nearly always in hindsight. However, it's only when you realize what it is, while it's happening that most people (including Indigo) understand what 'awareness' and 'precognition' really are when experienced together…a 'claircognizant moment!' It is learning to recognize it, trust it, and believe it, without question that takes practice.

INTELLIGENCE DOES NOT AN INDIGO MAKE

"The highest form of intelligence is to be able to observe yourself without passing judgment, and then make all the necessary corrections yourself."

Author Unknown

When a person has mastered any of the 'clair faculties,' it discloses absolutely nothing of an individual's intelligence. Nor does one have to be intelligent to have any of the 'clair faculties.' However, the fact remains, 'Indigo Children' tend to have both an intelligence that is unparalleled to many of their peers and the dexterity of accentuated many of the 'clair faculties.'

Does that mean that a 'highly intelligence' person doesn't demonstrate any of the 'clair faculties?' Clearly NO, nor was it meant to insinuates this (before I start getting any emails). What I am attempting to point out is that the 'Indigo Child' not only demonstrates a propensity to having a super 'intelligence,' but when it's combined with an innate ability to connect to the 'universal consciousness' it provides them an 'intuitive awareness' that can utilize the 'clair faculties' to an advantage.

I recently discovered a Kentucky newspaper article regarding IQ testing, which led me to a 1912 matriculation examination that 8th grade students had to pass before allowed entry to high school. Which by the way, reminded me of an off-beat 2006 sci-fi comedy entitled, "Idiocracy," in which several scientific studies around the same period pointed out that mankind on average has been in the process of being 'dumbed down' for a long time now. The pretense of the film was that a young soldier of 'average intelligence' was chosen for a 'top secret' military experiment that would put him into an induced 'coma' with the intent of simulating a one-year hibernation. Forgotten after the 'top secret' project is shut down he was not discovered until the year 2505. Awakened from his stasis, he soon realizes he is now living within a society where intelligence has taken a colossal plunge, making him the most intelligent man on the planet.

A very accurate metaphor of what appears to be happening today; for this phenomena is evident not only in the United States, but in many other cultures and societies all around the world. So much so that over the last 100 years, cultures have become so 'complacent' with public education, IQ levels around the world have 'plummeted' considerably. Considering this has happened in only a century, what appears ever so gradual was actually like fighter jet nose-diving on a target, and we are only now beginning to realize it!

Recently, an eighth grade matriculation exam of a 1912 matriculation test – donated by the Bullitt County Kentucky's Historical Museum, in Bullitt County, Kentucky – to include as a baseline for the study. After reviewing the century old newspaper clipping of the exam, I was surprised to discover just how difficult the questions were (see Appendix A), although it strained my memory I was unable to answer them all, but overall I did quite well. My first thought was, "Could high school students (not 8th graders) today pass the very same exam?" I can't really say for sure, but it seems to me the most likely answer to this question would be a resounding 'NO;' at least not based on what I read regarding a national sampling of IQ statistics of American high school graduates in the class of 2012; the numbers speak for themselves and are shocking to say the least! [75]

Although not tested on this 1912 exam, I really doubt many 8th grade students today would have passed it…and for that matter, many adults. But when you think about it, the abundance of evident, and only confirms the fact that 'America' is 'dumbing down,' and this is based on a various number of sources that included the U.S. Department of Education and a 2002 research study conducted by National Geographic that offered quite-a-bit of empirical evidence to confirm this trend.

National Geographic revealed many startling statistics regarding their results in their study entitled; "U.S. Young Adults Are Lagging," of which they state, "Despite the daily bombardment of news from the Middle East, Central Asia, and other world trouble spots, roughly 85% of young Americans could not even find Afghanistan, Iraq, Iran or Israel on a map, according our study."

They discovered that many Americans between the ages 18 to 24 came in "next to last" among nine other countries included in another study by NatGeo; "Roper's 2002 Global Geographic Literacy Survey," which tested over 3,000 young adults of the same age group in Canada, France, Germany, Great Britain, Italy, Japan, Mexico, Sweden, and the United States; Sweden, Germany. Italy took top honors topping the list.

The same 56 questions in the 1912 matriculation test were asked to a sampling of students from all across the United States; of the young American graduates surveyed in the study, it was revealed that the average number of students that of those students that actually answered the questions, only 23% of them were correct. Similar tests given outside the United States, and most notably by young adults educated in Mexico, seemed to have had a great difficulty with basic geography questions. Nor was it surprising to discover that young Canadians and young British students throughout Great Britain (Ireland, Wales, Scotland, and England) did not fare much better.

The poor results of the American sampling discovered that only 30% of the American students could identify the Pacific Ocean (the world's largest body ocean), on a map. 56% of them could not even locate India; home to nearly 17% of people on the planet; and only 19% of the students could name four countries that have officially acknowledged the possession of nuclear weapons.

Americans students were terribly deficient in geography. When NatGeo showed Americans a blank world map and asked them to identify a very limited number of countries, most 'could not.' In fact, only 37% of all Americans between the ages of 18 and 24 could even find Iraq on a map, although the United States was at the time, actively involved in the Gulf War with Iraq.

Young Americans scored horribly deficient when it came to mathematics and science; 15-year-old American students didn't even rank in the 'top half' of all the world's industrialized nations in mathematical or scientific literacy. Even more shocking was that only 28% of the graduating students surveyed knew what the Supreme Court of USA even did; and only 10% knew how many supreme justices are serving on the Supreme Court bench.

Only 26% knew the Bill of Rights were the first Ten Amendments to the Constitution of the United States, yet fell short on what they protected. Not surprising since, only 27% knew there are two governing legislative branches of the United States government. Moreover, and what was totally surprising, was that only14% of the students could tell National Geographic who wrote the Declaration of Independence, and far fewer whose signature was the most prominent at the bottom. Yet, I found to be really, really, scary was that only 23% of these graduates knew the year the Declaration of Independence when it signed!

Of the seniors surveyed, 43% could identify the two major political parties of the United States, but only 11% could tell NatGeo without guessing how many years a United States Senator was eligible to serve. Astoundingly, only 23% knew the President of the United States served a four-year term and without conviction how many terms the president can legally serve. Yet, 29% knew that fact that his charge to be the Executive Branch of the United States!

Let's face it, facts are facts, and although fact's can be manipulated to paint any picture by whoever is presenting the statistics; the fact remains that 'educated' Americans are not nearly as mentally sharp as they once were. What is even more depressing about this revelation is that with each generation that passes, the numbers have only gotten progressively worse and by all indicators, the downhill trend will only continue to spiral.

Granted, the education system was a lot different in 1912 than it is today; and some may even argue there was a lot less history to remember. But it is important to note that 'most children' in 1912, did not, and could not attend school because they weren't allowed to; and of those that did, most dropped out of school before even completing the sixth grade. Add to that an equation that factors in segregation, ethnic ghettos, and inner city crime, you'll only discover that the minority groups with the inner cities of America, were not well educated at all; with most unable to read at all, sign their name, much less speak English at all. As immigrants in 1912, children were obliged to work in sweatshops from a very early age and had no time for school. By the end of the decade, WWI began and ended, and shortly followed by a 'great depression' that crippled most American households. All these events definitely had a severe impact on what few educational systems existed, and what often gets them categorized as having no 'intelligence,' when in fact it was only 'ignorance,' and being ignorant taught.

Ignorance is NOWHERE near stupid, because regardless of how much education a person may have 'stupid is still stupid.' It can't be taught and there is no class or teacher in the world good enough to teach 'common sense;' because either have it or not. Moreover, intelligence of the general population cannot be measured entirely on how much education a person has been exposed to or for that matter by an IQ test alone, for that only measures a person's ability to recall 'learned knowledge.'

Children today, regardless of race, origin, ethnicity, or socio-economic status now have educational systems in place that were unavailable and unheard of in 1912. Although some may not be perfect, they are not even, remotely as they were in 1912. Take from this what you will…but when you really think about it; what really matters is what it all means to you and what you think can be done about it.

A Reserved Approach

It is necessary to use caution when labeling or classifying anyone as 'super intelligent, Indigo,' or 'otherwise.' It cannot, and should not, be ascertained with merely an IQ measurement, which is only designed to determine a person's 'Intelligence Quotient (IQ);' merely a number to put scale to an 'academic' aptitude. It is nothing more than an ability to retrieve engraved information from memory vs. their real 'intellectual potential.' In short, I have worked with people who have had multiple PhDs throughout my career, but they were still 'stupid.'

Just having an 'intellectual ability' falls far short in the science of measuring intelligence, mainly because no one seemed to take into account a person's 'potential' to demonstrate 'creative intelligence!' In my opinion, how one thinks is far more important, especially when one considers all the many other social factors that would need consideration, including opportunity, upbringing, personal values, socio-economic factors, mental state, and background, to even come close to measuring their 'ability;' IQ tests fall far short.

Even IQ test scores themselves vary widely from test to test; often quite dramatically. Not everyone feels 100% all the time, and debilitating factors and circumstances can and do have an effect on the results of any test.

Nor should we forget 'stupid is what stupid does,' regardless of how many degrees a person may have accumulated in their lifetime, or how much knowledge they can quote verbatim from memory; it just can't fix stupid!

Today, we still don't have a test to measure 'intelligence' and 'aptitude' together. Yet, when you consider what an Indigo Child can do that is not only 'innate,' it's an 'instantaneous awareness' to a previously unidentified 'consciousness' that when combined with 'intelligence' and 'aptitude' that boggles the mind; and reason you've nearly read the entire book.

Indigo Children are not at all that mysterious, nor are they all that 'wonderful,' for they, like myself are torn between being treated 'normally' while still maintaining the nuance of being 'different.' Tools are designed to label people, are far overrated, and do absolutely nothing for measuring a person's potential. Because every test out there, can (in my opinion) do more harm than good, simply because 'classifications' and 'labels' will never allow the 'Indigo' or the 'mentally challenged' to 'adequately demonstrate their full potential because on an inadequate 'intelligence' test, or worse, when they get misclassified by an IQ score because they had an 'off' day.

Case-in-Point

Over my lifetime, I like many other kids in America were required to take diverse number of IQ tests from K through 12, but rarely were any of the aptitude tests that I took make any bloody sense. Remember, I grew up 'intelligent' enough to figure out what they were looking for, and really loved giving them answers that often surprised them! Take for example the one test that most schools are required by law to take; the 'Minnesota Multiphasic Personality Inventory (MMPI for short)' test, definitely a poor excuse for an 'aptitude test.' The MMPI is nothing more than a screening that determines personality and psychosocial disorders in adolescent children between 14 to 18, and young adults 18 and over. It is explained as being nothing more than a frequently administered clinical assessment test of well over 350 questions designed as a neuropsychological battery of questions (which are scored as tick boxes for multiple choice and true and false statements) to evaluate a child's cognitive functioning.

First introduced by the University of Minnesota in 1942 as the MMPI, it was later in 1998 revised as the MMPI-2, and again in 1992 as the MMPI-A for adolescents between 14 and 18. This test should be administered, scored, and assessed by skilled professionals trained interpreting the overall results displayed on a graph. Yet most school districts allow the teachers themselves to perform the testing in their classrooms. Therefore, misdiagnoses from the test results that can include everything from "Post Traumatic Stress Disorder (PTSD)' to 'depression' and 'alcoholism (on the MacAndrew Alcoholism Scale (MACR).'

All because of data input problems, incorrect analysis of K-Corrected or non-K-Corrected T Scores used for clinical psychological assessments of the children being tested and the young adults. Add to that, control of demographics differences between groups, all of which could contribute to placement of certain scores because of a child's and young adult's environment; or misunderstanding or error reading they code types while making an assessment that could put the child back a grade in school, or have them seeing the school psychologist on a regular basis.

There are 10 clinical scales and 3 validity scales for the MMPI, not to mention the hose of other supplementary scales. These clinical T-scales originally intended to characterize 'pure' groups of adolescents with those psychologically compromised with psychiatric disorders. Therefore, the actual names of the scales proclaiming resolute, often audacious, and very exotic psychiatric labels for those tested. As an example; 'scale 1' refers to the hypochondriasis scale, 'scale 8' to the schizophrenic scale, 'scale 9' is the hypomania (irritability) scale, 'scale 4' is the psychopathic deviants scale, and 'scale 7' is for those with psych-asthenia (obsessive compulsive, excessive anxiety, and compulsions) scale. Other scales are far easier to understand that includes simple symptoms, 'scale 2' for depression; 'scale 3' for hysteria; 'scale 5' for masculinity-femininity issues; 'scale 6' for paranoia; and 'scale 0' is a social introvert.

Ironically, every time I took this test I screwed with the teacher's mind and all those reading my scores… I had to take the test every year, and pretty much, ended up with nearly every possible scale classification. It wasn't until the fourth or fifth attempt to mess with their minds, caught, I was forced to confess of my deviant behavior by finagling the answers to trigger a different result.

With my cover blown the school district classified all my tests as null, and never gave them to me again. As far as my IQ, I often scored quite high, and the school labeled me 'super intelligent.' However, I didn't tell them that I was holding back, because I just wanted to be normal like all the other kids in class, and in so doing my grades only reflected slightly 'above average.'

My cover was blown one day while napping during algebra class, as the teacher's monotone voice caused me to doze off. It was either sleep quietly in class or leave for the boy's bathroom to hang myself. Abruptly, I was awakened by a sharp sting across my back by the instructor's pointer, looking up she immediately posed the question, "Am I keeping you awake Jari?" to which I could not resist replying with sarcastic wit, "Not at all..." and laid my head back down on the desk. Needless-to-say I ended up going to the headmaster's office for my insubordination.

Once seated in his office we just quietly stared at each other for about five minutes before he finally spoke up, "I'm really quite surprised at you young man, especially after looking at your IQ tests, and your aptitude tests (referring to the MMPI's I had taken) were all inconclusive. I wonder why that is...however, you grades do not come close to reflecting your potential. What, if I may ask, do you think the problem is here?"

Okay, he opened the door and I ended up waltzing right through it, "Do you want an honest answer or just the answer you want to hear?" I asked knowing full well, I may just end up in detention yet again, in his office filing papers. My sarcasm however, ended up being wasted by his sincerity, "I wouldn't have it any other way, please, the truth."

"Frankly, I am bored out of my (transitive verb that begins with F) mind. Plain and simple," I replied, "I only took this particular class because I was forced to for I had not yet taken Algebra. Yet, I have taken and passed advanced calculus, physics, chemistry, and trigonometry from the school from which I transferred. The teacher would mark my answers marked wrong when they were correct, simply because I did not get my answer as the teacher had 'taught the class,' and in 'less steps' I might add!"

To my surprise, he asked, "That doesn't sound right, explain."

"I solved all her algebra problems differently than how she was teaching them and got the answer quicker than she had and using less steps than she had to derive the very same answer!" I pulled several tests from my book bag and showed him.

He was not only aghast, he was furious it had even happened and immediately recognized the problem lay with the teacher, who was so fixated on teaching everyone else in the class a specific set of instruction. She never even considered us 'intelligent' individual's with different and perhaps advanced 'aptitudes' and 'skills,' nor did she even consider learning from her students. So instead of giving me a perfect score for all the correct answers, or even asking me what technique I had used, she had just assumed I had cheated and marked the answer wrong because all she did was notice that the number of steps I used, did not jive with hers.

So how often does this scenario happen today, more frequently than you might think?

School districts are slowly starting to learn that 'highly intelligent' or 'Indigo Children' students are bored crazy by complacent teachers, yet fail to realize that these are the children being 'left behind' in a process that caters only to the slower students. Many of whom will never really understand the lesson, nor really want to. Therefore, the school is denying others a proper education or from ever allowing these 'intelligent' children from ever achieving their 'full potential' much less from ever building upon it…and that is simply not right, nor is it fair!

What is Entitlement to an Education Really Mean?

The American Congress and Senate passed the "No Child Left Behind" Act and it became law when signed by President George W. Bush in 2001. The law, designed to reauthorize the Elementary and Secondary Education Act of 1965, attempts to bring about significant changes for educators as a means to enhance reading programs and mandate 'public' schoolchildren become proficient in reading by the third grade.

Since the 'No Child Left Behind (NCLB)' law took effect in 2002, many believe it has had a sweeping impact on the way U.S. public schools teach, affecting what students are taught, the tests they take, the way teachers are trained, and how federal money is spent on education or withheld for non-compliance.

Debates continue to rage on however as to whether the law has effectively improved academic achievement across the country. When the law, scheduled to be renewed by Congress in 2007, instead stalled all efforts to do so amid criticism by partisan politics on both sides of the fence; Democrats and Republicans and in both houses, which only ended in very vocal disagreements over how to improve the law. According to U.S. Deputy Secretary of Education at the time, Ray Simon, believed the NCLB law would most likely, not be reauthorized until 2010.

In August of 2013, the debate on how to fix the law, with most states requesting waivers from certain provisions of the federal education law expired at the end of the 2013-2014 school years.

"America's most sweeping education law – the Elementary and Secondary Education Act (ESEA), also known as No Child Left Behind – is outmoded and constrains state and district efforts for innovation and reform dwindled. The smartest way to fix that is through a reauthorized ESEA law, but Congress has not agreed on a responsible bill, therefore the federal government has worked with states to develop waiver agreements that unleash local leaders' energy for change and ensure equity, protect the most vulnerable students, and encourage standards that keep America competitive. The waiver renewal process announced today will support states in continuing positive change and ensuring all children receive a high-quality education – but I look forward to a day when we can announce a new ESEA law that supports every state."

U.S. Education Secretary Arne Duncan (2013)

Thirty-four states applied for and received waivers for the 2012-2013 school year, including Arizona, Arkansas, Colorado, Connecticut, Delaware, Florida, Georgia, Idaho, Indiana, Kansas, Kentucky, Louisiana, Maryland, Massachusetts, Michigan, Minnesota, Mississippi, Missouri, Nevada, New Jersey, New Mexico, New York, North Carolina, Ohio, Oklahoma, Oregon, Rhode Island, South Carolina, South Dakota, Tennessee, Utah, Virginia, Washington, Wisconsin, and the District of Columbia.

However, will the 'hypothetical' reforms that failed ever address the needs of the 'highly intelligent' students? They hadn't before, and I certainly don't believe they ever will! The law was originally written to only address students performing below acceptable proficiency levels, based on age, and who fall below the minimum 'average' intelligence scale established by the US government for their grade (class). Because of this, 'highly intelligent students' have to deal with the unintended 'negative consequences' of the law, for in the 2001 act, it did not include special courses of study for any of the 'highly' intelligent students and most likely, never will.

The act itself, as written, forced many school districts across the country to reassign teaching staff from working with 'specially gifted' education programs to redirect focus instead on students needing 'special attention' and 'repetitive testing preparation.' The law stipulated they must concentrate efforts on students who are lagging within the nation's classrooms; the fallout of course, are the nations 'intelligent children' who will be forced to stay where they are; in 'repetitive, special attention classes' bored out of their minds. In particular, the 'highly intelligent' and 'Indigo Children' must continue to endure being bored day-after-day. To date, they are still being ignored the majority of our nation's school curriculums who simply keep saying, "We can't afford it!" without the federal funds. Personally, I believe it's a travesty, in and of itself, a violation of the concept to "Leave No Child Behind." As of 2015, no bill still has written and nor has the old act been renewed, shelved by both houses and both parties, they have ceased the debates for pursuing different agendas like keeping the war machine rolling in foreign lands and preparations for the new elections.

AN INDIGO AWARENESS

"My brain is only a receiver, in the Universe there is a core from which we obtain knowledge, strength, and inspiration. I have not penetrated into the secrets of this, core, but I know that it exists"

Nickola Tesla

During my life, I just seemed to know things I should have had no way of knowing and was inspired to seek out why. It's been a long journey of self-discovery I shared with a few close friends, and one of those friends told me to 'Trust your instincts, and yourself…you will then find the answers you seek.

That friend was the writer of the book, "The Lonely Sense," Robert Cracknell. As I read his book, suggested by a close friend, I could swear Robert was speaking to me with is every word. Here was a man who throughout his 35 plus year career had solved dozens of high profile cases as a 'private investigator' and who also happened to be 'psychic.' This concept intrigued me, for I never considered myself to be a psychic per se, but at times an 'empath' as I seem to sense emotions of those around me. What I discovered about Robert in his writing was that throughout his career working privately and with police authorities throughout the United Kingdom after their cases their trails ran cold, he trusted his instinct. Eventually he was dubbed "UK's Number One Psychic Detective" for which he attributed his success to his innate prowess as a 'psychic,' and like me, he never once charged a penny for his help; thus earning him a notoriety that can stand up to any form of scrutiny.

In a later conversation with Bob (as he prefers to be called), we sat at his table in Cyprus to discuss my research, and what I perceived my abilities were. He listened and on occasion would nod while rattled on. I told him I believed my 'innate' senses were due to an 'intuitive awareness' like his, other than I have not used mine for solving crimes as he had. It was when he shared with me that his ability was due to a 'consciousness' he could access intuitively and to what he attributed to his skills. At that moment, I reveal to Bob that I had finally found what I had been searching for these many years. It had just made itself known to me for the first time in my life and I now understood what this previously unseen force was.

After I explained to Bob about the revelation of a 'universal consciousness' from which my 'intuitive awareness' seemed to emanate from, he sat silently for a few moments pondering my hypothesis. After what seemed hours, Bob eventually began to speak. "I now feel that if my generation was the forerunner…as you said earlier the 'dawning of Aquarius,' … is responsible for you finding this new and totally unexpected 'awakening' of 'intuitive awareness' and 'consciousness;' then you have granted this 'old timer' an epiphany if you will. For I too am only now gaining a much better understanding by your words and to everything I have gone through my entire life, and for that reason I find this concept is not at all difficult to understand and to embrace."

As Bob continued, I hung on every word, "I do not deny an influence beyond my own 'awareness' and 'intelligence,' but accept the fact that I had been denied its existence for so many years. For there has always been an exterior force in my life that seems to be demanding we use it and embrace our 'awareness' as a normal faculty we possess. As of today, I believe that this 'intuitive awareness' is of a 'universal consciousness' to which we are all connected and very much what the concept of God as a divinity may well in fact represent. As I have always maintained 'God' is indeed a universal power that has always been impotent, and only he has allowed us to realize the reason for that impotence. He needed is us (our souls) and he is truly omnipotent; because we exist on the same plain that comprises all the souls within this 'universal consciousness' you so eloquently described. We now need this 'intuitive awareness' of that 'consciousness' more than we ever have before…and it also needs us…because with all the chaos the world in, and the entire world now in utter 'crisis' spawned by mankind's ignorance, arrogance, ego, and greed, what better time than now to become aware."

I don't believe Bob was ever really a 'psychic,' but the word fit to identify him. He was like me, just another 'Indigo Child' form an older generation seeking out answers no different than I, and like myself Bob too had been seeking out an answer his entire life. I am also sure we are not alone in this search…perhaps even you have hopes in attaining a logical explanation. After all, we are all connected through the 'universal consciousness' and that gives meaning to all our lives, and hopefully one day we will finally have an answer to the biggest question of all, "What is my place in the greater scheme of life here on Earth?"

Over many years, I have read, studied, and analyzed many different scriptures, including dozens of translations that tried to explain away many stories in the "Holy Bible;" both philosophical and spiritual works, by Greek, Latin and Hebrew scholars; I've read the Koran, the Torah, Buddhist doctrines, and yes many 'spiritualist movement' writings. My mother and grandmother were devout Catholics; and every Italian family would love to have their first-born son to become a priest in the Holy Roman Catholic Church, and mine was no different, which is why I enrolled myself to a Jesuit seminary before finishing high school. I sought asked answers not only from the Church in Rome, but from the Baptists, the Presbyterians, the Lutherans, and the Jews, and even the Mormons. To date, I have found nothing profound and therefore I believed my search to be in vain.

I've read countless books and followed countless movements; and being the 'free thinker' always daring to think 'outside the box,' and precisely why I chose to become an 'outsider' looking in; just as Robert Cracknell described himself in his book "The Lonely Sense." Yet, despite it all, it wasn't until I realized that I needed to stop searching for answers or listening to what others believed they had discovered, and come to the profound realization that I needed to start 'thinking' for myself; and once I did, many answers began to slowly reveal themselves; but not until I was ready to hear them.

Surprisingly, the answers I received came from the very source I had sought. Imagine that. I had been 'intuitively aware' and accessing that source my entire life without ever realizing it. It turned out to be the very same source that finally allowed me to discover that it was comprised of a countless souls and spanned the universe, without regard to time, space, or dimension; there for countless millennia acting in unison as an omnipotent being comprised of every living soul in the universe; indeed, a 'universal consciousness.'

Dr. Stephen Hawking in his book, "The Grand Design," he attempts to answer the 'burning question' of whether or not the 'grand design' of the universe was created by an omnipotent; the creator we call 'God.' He goes on to provide several scientific analogies in an effort to provide an appropriate answer as to when and how the universe began; as well as why we are here.

Later his book became a featured television series, entitled, "Into the Universe," where he attempted to answer an even BIGGER question, "Is there a God?"

"So when people ask me if a God created the universe, I tell them that the question itself makes no sense. Time didn't exist before the 'Big Bang,' so there is no 'time' for God to make the universe in. It's like asking for directions to the edge of the Earth. The Earth is a sphere; it doesn't have an edge, so looking for it is a futile exercise.

We are each free to believe what we want, and it's my view that the simplest explanation is, there is no God. No one created the universe, and no one directs our fate. This leads me to a profound realization, there is probably no heaven, and no afterlife either. We have this one life to appreciate the grand design of the universe, and for that, I am extremely grateful." [79]

-- **Dr. Stephen Hawking**

Of course, his statement only led to ire thousands upon thousands of people around the world who believe in the existence of a single supreme and omnipotent being, their voices rose in protest…not that there's anything wrong with people believing as they do. Still Creationists took their argument to an entirely different level by stating Hawking's scientific explanation actually verifies God is so much more intelligent than Stephen Hawking could ever possibly comprehend or imagine, and therefore because HE cannot comprehend it, God must therefore be a divine power greater than the sum of us.

ONE FINAL THOUGHT

"Being aware is paying attention. Once you have done that, everything will begin to make sense. The trick is listening to what you already know and begin thinking for yourself."

Jari A. Mikkola

Although I consider myself a well-educated and intelligent man, my journey in life has been a long, arduous, and prosperous journey. Yet I continue to study, research and learn well into my 'golden' years. I am not a physician, though I have studied medical sciences, I am not a physicist, yet I demonstrate an above-average understanding of the physics and the mathematics that drives it. I am not an expert of anything, although I am a well-educated man. I believe it is when a person believes they are an expert that they instead find failure.

We are after all, what our thoughts define us to be. Therefore, we should all take great care not to let our alligator mouths override our canary brains, reminding me of an old proverb, "It is far better to thought of as a fool, than to open your mouth to remove all doubt."

Learning to Think for Yourself

We have learned that an IQ test demonstrates only a person's ability to retain 'knowledge' but does nothing to determine their 'aptitude.' The first is useless and means nothing until people begin to 'think for themselves.' I don't always see things 'as they are,' I wonder what's possible, what is plausible or logical, and go off to discovery if it's probable. We all create a version of reality that suits us and within the reality layer that defines who we are and just what our comfort zone is within this vast universe we live.

Robert T. Carol said it best when he described William of Ockham's well known conclusion theory known as 'Ockham's Razor' when he said, "In analyzing simplicity (referencing Ockham's Razor), it can be difficult to keep its two facets apart – elegance and parsimony. Principles such as Occam's razor are frequently stated in a way which is ambiguity between two similar notions ... While these two facets of simplicity are frequently conflated it is important to treat them as distinct. One reason for doing so is that considerations of parsimony and of elegance typically pull us in different directions." [80]

Although this principle has been a useful ideology for many scientists for quite some time as a pretense that states, "when two or more competing theories attempt to make the exact same prediction or reach the same conclusion, the simplest one is the one most likely to be better of the two."

What I have presented herein is nothing more than what I consider to have ascertained from my own personal logical thought processes; in other words, I have share with you, what I have been 'thinking' about myself for many years. I simply stopped trying to discover what others had learned and tried to teach me as truth, I instead reached my own conclusions – regardless of whether others believe them to be either 'on' or 'off' the mark; I thought for myself. I believe the analysis I have presented here to you is sound, and I have provided you a very large amount of data from both sides of the fence to absorb. I have reviewed, analyzed, and reviewed again a very large mountain of material, but in the end, the conclusions are mine; which may very well contradict what Ockham believed in, 'taking the easiest way out.'

Be Not Deceived

Apotheosis; from the Greek word 'apotheoun' – means 'to deify, or exalt as a God.' A subject who has been elevated to the point of 'exaltation,' in many cultures since the dawn of man to create and worship unseen 'divine beings.' Theologically, 'apotheosis' references the concept of presenting an 'idea' to the masses that eventually creates the concept of a 'divinity' being 'like-God.'

Although there are many other writers, researchers, and educators who presented other theories regarding a 'universal consciousness' – some making sense only to the author, most fall short, while others only offer tidbits of valuable ideology. Yet many made absolutely no sense to me at all and left me in the cold with theories that were, for most part loaded with more 'supposition' than 'objective' substance, and failed in their attempt to formulate any logical conclusion. A 'conclusion' that was merely a 'guess' or an 'opinion' based on little or no facts or evidence at all to support, much less define the basis from which their 'logic' had been derived.

The world is undeniably going through a new phase unlike anything experienced every before in recorded history, and humanity is accelerating toward a 'new awakening' of 'intuition, awareness' and 'consciousness,' that is becoming all the more evident with each and every generation since the turn of the century.

Over the years, many people have been asking Dr. Steven Hawkins a question that he had eluded for years, 'Is there a God?' On his Discovery Channel's program "Curiosity," he not only replied to their inquiries, but with great ire, he eloquently responded at the end of his program …"When people ask me if a God created the universe, I tell them that the question itself makes no sense. Time didn't exist before the 'Big Bang,' so there is no time in which God could make the universe. It's like asking for directions to the edge of the earth. The earth is a sphere; it doesn't have an edge, so looking for it is a futile exercise.

We are each free to believe what we want, and it is my view that the simplest explanation is there is no God. No one created the universe and no one directs our fate. This leads me to a profound realization ... There is probably no heaven and no afterlife either. We have this one life to appreciate the grand design of the universe, and for that, I am extremely grateful."

An Eternal Self-Awareness

Long before writing this book, I have believed that my physical human body is only a host in which my soul resides on a small blue planet on the edge of galaxy in a vast universe we have all come to call 'Earth.' When my host body becomes old and frail, it will eventually fail me and I too shall die. During the process of dying my soul will separate its symbiotic connection to my body, when my brain finally shuts down; and the 'mind' that connected my soul, controlled my thought, and allowed me to store all the knowledge, memories, and loves I had been blessed with, will also disengage it's connection to the 'universal consciousness.' I will cease to exist in this world. Yet, nothing will be lost, for with that vast universe, my 'conscious soul' will continue to reside, becoming part of it once again, able to transcend space, time, and dimensions, with great ease.

Everything I have learned, all I have experienced, and everyone I have loved in this lifetime, I will take with me, while maintaining my connection to them through the very same consciousness. A consciousness that will continue on, as an individual soul totally 'self-aware' as an 'individuality' within a vast chasm of souls; then someday if I choose, perhaps I'll take everything I ever knew in this lifetime with me to another life to learn new lessons somewhere else in the universe.

An easy thought, for I already believe I have had several iterations of life on this planet over last several millennia, and have completed a full life cycle, learning what I need to in each of them. Thus, I may not choose to ever return again, perhaps instead I will move on to live another life on another planet in the far reaches of the universe, or choose an alternate dimension. Whether my consciousness travels billions of light years away from Earth, with a different but not dissimilar life-cycle host housing my soul to begin another facet of life, or I choose to explore all the knowledge and experience of others within the 'consciousness,' is a concept I can barely wrap my head around, let alone fathom.

We are all part of a greater 'consciousness,' some very old souls who have retain their individuality, knowledge and memories for eons, while for others it's a new and wonderful experience. And when one really stops to think about it, all these souls from the universe, in one consciousness, could in fact present the possibility that as a collective, with an endless 'consciousness' and empowered by an 'infinite knowledge,' could very much be considered 'omnipotent' or 'God-like' in and of itself, and 'God' has been within us all along.

SUMMATION

"Life is not about defining yourself. Life is all about creating yourself. There is a difference."

George Bernard Shaw

Mind you, this book was originally intended to be an article for my magazine, "The Journal of Anomalous Science," however, as I wrote the article, it soon became a thesis and the thesis this book. My mind was constantly spinning on what to include in the article, and exactly why it evolved to what you are currently reading. I couldn't help myself, for there was too much information that needed to be included, and article became unacceptable and I just kept on typing. This is the result.

When I began my research many years ago, very little information was available, and although I visited many libraries across the country and abroad, many boasting to possess impressive collections, few offered me any pertinent data. Sure, many had large collections on various topics that included books, thesis papers, research papers, interviews, video, and/or other pertinent data; and always categorized under the subject matter of 'metaphysical.'

One of the most common elements that I kept encountering was that the average number of 'highly intelligent' had taken a dramatic rise since World War II; an unexpected trend that seemed to have begun around the turn-of-the-century. It wasn't however, until the last few generations when studies on 'intelligence' had begun to make phenomenal appearance, and accessible via the Internet.

Amazingly, I discovered that since the WWII to the present, but more dramatically over the last twenty-five to thirty years, children born during this period seemed to possess similar 'intuitive awareness traits' with such an 'innate intelligence, heightened sense of fairness,' and a profound sense of 'precognitive' abilities, that were unsurpassed in history. Psychologists during the 50s and 60s were even calling these kids the 'children of tomorrow.' Today, we know them as 'Indigo Children.' A name used to describe the fantastic 'traits' and 'abilities' they seemed to all demonstrate.

When I began, I found no sources anywhere that did not connect an 'Indigo Child' to some very strange notions of 'metaphysical poppy-cock.' A common source I can only assume, because I really did not want to dig another rabbit hole to fall in to.

I knew, being one myself, that "Indigo Children' represented the 'sum of all consciousness,' one comprised of other souls, the perhaps included souls throughout the entire universe;' a unified single 'entity' that could even transcended 'time, space,' and yes, 'dimension.

I believed as many physicists did, energy is a constant, leading me to wonder whether human 'thought' was in fact 'pure energy' in motion. After all, many scientists who have studied our human brains to gain a better understanding of where our 'thoughts' originate believed similarly; long before we could fully understand where those thoughts originated, much less were stored.

This led me to believe our brains only acted as a physical conduit, a connection, to an unforeseen force that stores our important 'lifetime memories;' and being a business intelligence architect for IBM, I could relate 'consciousness' to an 'iCloud' technology. It made perfect sense to me and quickly became not only the most logical, possible, plausible, and probable solution of where we store data, but more importantly, what 'consciousness' really was. An answer, that made a hell of a lot more sense than all that metaphysical mumbo-jumbo crap others keep trying to pawn off as fact to an unsuspecting target.

As an iCloud technology only stores pertinent data, I do not believe the 'universal consciousness' would allow, or even accept frivolous short-term memories, nor would it demand any devotion from the living as an 'omnipotent deity' that requires total submission, prayer, and worship.

The 'universal consciousness' would not threaten, judge, or condemn souls from the collective for having been malevolent, benevolent, or benign. I believe it would be a 'cohesive collective consciousness' that reaches far beyond any of known star system or galactic clusters – and even dimensional space – scattered throughout this great universe; even in places where space and time no longer exist. A matrix unlike anything we could ever begin to understand.

Of everything I covered within these pages, the brain, frequencies, intelligence, Clair faculties, high intelligence, or gifted children – Indigo or otherwise – I believe to be clues we have all witnessed during our evolutionary process. Emerging into something wonderful, as our human DNA transcends to a higher level with changes well underway. Humans are transitioning toward an increased 'awareness,' a new form of 'consciousness' that will eventually allow mankind to fully connect to the rest of the universe… After all, didn't the same cosmic dust that litters the entire universe create us?

As mankind is only now going through a major evolutionary phase, one of a 'higher intelligence,' evident by the many advancements humanity has made over the last 50+ years when it's compared to the last 500, 5,000, or 50,000 years, but we still have a very long way to go. Humanity still fails to realize that we are still juvenile in cosmic universe when it comes to understanding everything there is to know about how the universe works, but we are now beginning to scratch the surface. Yet, it is very much, as if evolution has just strapped on a jet pack to increase the evolution of humanity at a phenomenal rate.

It may still take thousands of years and several more generations to really notice the changes, bur remember most of significant scientific and technological discoveries mankind has made throughout history, have mostly occurred within the last 50-70 years; when compared to the last 5000 years.

One final word of warning; I must point out that although 'intelligence' is on the rise, so has the 'dumbing down' of man – and which is a considerably larger percentage group. Meaning that Darwin's theory of natural selection will surely rear its face on those at the bottom of the totem pole as the 21st century ends.

ABOUT THE AUTHOR

There are many unanswered questions regarding what many refer to as the Indigo consciousness, the least of which is "What is it exactly?" With still a bigger question is, "How is it possible and why doesn't everyone have the same or similar ability?"

Jari Mikkola has published scores of articles for various publications over the last 20 years and is an accomplished researcher, investigator, and analyst, and currently working as the director of World Nexus Publications, and is the editor for the 'Journal of Anomalous Science,' the 'Dimension Zone, Occam's Enigma, DZ Nucleus,' and 'Desert Highlands Paranormal Research.' His career as a global consultant with IBM working as a Global Business Intelligence Architect has taken him all over the world to work shoulder-to-shoulder with people from various countries and cultures throughout his entire career.

In this book, he delves into the science behind consciousness, the brain, DNA, our mind and soul. Throughout these pages, he eloquently explains in ley terms just how an Indigo Child seems to be able to traverse an unseen 'universal consciousness' with an effortless awareness that disregards to time, space, or dimension.

"An Awakening; the Emergence of Indigo Consciousness," is a brilliant piece of work, that attempts to piece together the complexities of how the human brain functions and how it is responsible for an " emergence of consciousness," and how it is attributed to a newer generation of Indigos who are making a grandiose appearance today.

The book also covers the unique characteristics demonstrated by these exceptional individuals, which are far too distinct to dismiss. Beginning with the question, "Why don't they don't easily fit into a mainstream culture?"

Indigos are unusually sensitive, aware, highly insightful, articulate, and empathetic, and often excel in science, music, and the arts. They have little desire to fit into the mainstream; school, work, or social circle, have an extreme intolerance for injustice wherever they encounter it. Jari also eloquently explains why these highly functioning individuals are frequently misdiagnosed with syndromes such as ADD, ADHD, autism, and Asperger's, for which they are prescribed Ritalin or other mind altering drugs to make them function in a more "normal" manner within society. Yet, their intellectual maturity far exceeds their years putting their abilities decades beyond any previous generations of Indigo.

Jari has managed to offer clear insight into the world of Indigo Children, as his book is full of first-person, and first hand experiences as an Indigo Child himself. The emergence of an extremely large numbers of Indigo Children throughout the world, with such an advanced stage of awareness is not an accident. Their time is now and they are here at this specific time of humankind's evolution for a reason.

BIBLIOGRAPHY

1. "The Inside Story: Interdisciplinary Perspectives," Robbie Davis-Floyd, P. Sven Arvidson (Psychology Press, 1997).
2. "Intuition and Consciousness," A. D. Rosenblatt & J. T. Thickstun (Psychoanalytic Quarterly pages 63:696-714, 1994.)
3. "Jacob Boehme-The Teutonic Philosopher," by W. P. Swainson, William Rider & Son, Ltd, London, 1921.
4. "In Search of the Miraculous; the Teachings of Gurdjieff," by P.D. Ouspensky, Harvest Books, 2001.
5. "Mayan Calendar and the Transformation of Consciousness," by Carl Johan Calleman, PhD, Inner Traditions, 2004.
6. "Intuition in the Context of Discovery," by Kenneth S Bowers, Glenn Regehr, Claude Balthazard, and Kevin Parker, published in "Cognitive Psychology" Volume 22, Issue 1 - January 1990.
7. "The Intuitive Algorithm," by Abraham Thomas, East West Books, 2004.
8. "The Brain From Top To Bottom," McGill University, http://thebrain.mcgill.ca/
9. "How Does Your Memory Work," BBC Television, http://www.youtube.com/watch?v=pxVb6M8UPTQ
10. "Biology of Memory," by Karl H. Pribram and Donald E. Broadbent, Academic Press Inc; First Edition, 1970.
11. "Moheb Where Are Old Memories Stored in the Brain?" Costandi, postgraduate student, Wellcome Laboratory for Molecular Pharmacology at University College, London.
12. "Descartes's Concept of Mind," by Alanen, Lilli, Harvard University Press, 2003.
13. "The Pineal Gland," by Richard Wurtman M.D. & Julius Axelrod PhD., an article in Scientific American, 1965.
14. "Serotonin: The Crucial Substance that Turns Dreams On and Off," by B.L. Jacobs, Psychology Today, March 1976.
15. "Understanding Your Life through Color," by Nancy Ann Tappe, self-published on Lulu, 2009.
16. "The Indigo Children: The New Kids Have Arrived," by Lee Carroll and Jan Tober, Hay House, May 1999.
17. "The Brain's 'Radio Stations' Have Much to Tell Scientists," By Michael C. Purdy, February 7, 2011.
18. "Edgar Cayce's Twelve Lessons in Personal Spirituality" by Kevin J. Todeschi, Pnterest Press, 2010.
19. "Ikhwan al-Safa' A History of Muslim Philosophy," by Omar, A. Farrukh, Edited and Introduced by M.M. Sharif. Wiesabaden: Otta Harrassowitz, 1963.
20. "The Creative Mind: An Introduction to Metaphysics," by Henri Bergson, 1946, Dover Publications.
21. "The Einstein Papers: A Man of Many Parts," in a letter quoted by Walter Sullivan 1950, New `York Times, 1972.
22. "Relativity; the Special and the General Theory," by Albert Einstein, Crown Trade Paperbacks (1961).
23. "Ikhwan al-Safa' A History of Muslim Philosophy," by Omar, A. Farrukh, Edited and Introduced by M.M. Sharif. Wiesabaden: Otta Harrassowitz, 1963.
24. "The Spark of Life - Electricity in the Body," by Prof Frances Ashcroft, University of Oxford, 2013.
25. Wikipedia – http://en.wikipedia.org/wiki/Electroencephalography/
26. "National Institute of General Medical Sciences," http://www.nigms.nih.gov/.
27. Wikipedia – http://en.wikipedia.org/wiki/Electroencephalography, and http://en.wikipedia.org/wiki/Radio frequency.

28. "Solar Revolution: Why Mankind is on the Cusp of an Evolutionary Leap," by Dieter Broers, First English language edition by Scorpio Verlag GmbH & Co. KG, Berlin, Translated by Robert Nusbaum.

29. "A Review of CritAcisms of the Quantum Mechanical Theory of PSI Phenomena," by Evan Harris Walker, Journal of Parapsychology, 1984.

30. "Helping Your Highly Gifted Child," by Stephanie S. Tolan, EC Digest, 1990.

31. "Genetic Studies of Genius," by Lewis M. Terman, Stanford University Press, 1925.

32. "Children above 180 IQ Stanford-Binet: Origin and Development," by Leta S. Hollingworth, World Book, 1942).

33. "A cross-Sectional Developmental Study of the Social Relations of Students Who Enter College Early," by Paul M. Janos & Nancy M. Robinson, Gifted Child Quarterly, 1988.

34. "Brain Evolution and Uniqueness in the Human Genome," by J.P. Amadio and C.A. Walsh, Division of Genetics at Children's Hospital Boston, Harvard University Research Letter, Sept. 2006.

35. "National Institute of General Medical Sciences," National Institute of General Medical Sciences at the National Institute of Health, at http://www.nigms.nih.gov/.

36. "The Ongoing Adaptive Evolution of ASPM and Microcephalin is Not Explained by Increased Intelligence," by Nitzan Mekel-Bobrov, Danielle Posthuma, Sandra L. Gilbert, Penelope Lind, M. Florencia Gosso, Michelle Luciano, Sarah E. Harris, Timothy C. Bates, Tinca J.C. Polderman, Lawrence J. Whalley, Helen Fox, John M. Starr, Patrick D. Evans, Grant W. Montgomery, Croydon Fernandes, Peter Heutink, Nicholas G. Martin, Dorret I. Boomsma, Ian J. Deary, Margaret J. Wright, Eco J.C. de Geus, and Bruce T. Lahn, The Oxford Journal Press, 2007.

37. "Genetic Switches Play Big Role in Human Evolution," by John Carberry, Cornell University, 2006.

38. "Genetics and Intelligence: A Review," by L. Erlenmeyer-Kimling and Lissy F.Jarvik, Science Journal, 1963.

39. "Behavioural Genetic Studies of Intelligence," by Thomas J. Bouchard, Jr. and Matthew Mcgue, Psychology Department, University of Minnesota, published by Science Journal, 1981

40. "The Human Journey," a joint study by National Geographic & IBM known as "The Genome Project," https://genographic.nationalgeographic.com/.

41. "TAL Effectors: Highly Adaptable Phytobacterial Virulence Factors and Readily Engineered DNA-Targeting Proteins," by Erin L. Doyle, Barry L. Stoddard, Daniel F. Voytas, Adam J. Bogdanove, in the journal "Trends in Cell Biology," Volume 23, May 2013.

42. "Rapid 'open-Source' Engineering of Customized Zinc Finger Nucleases for Highly Efficient Gene Modification." by Maeder, ML, Thibodeau-Beganny, S, Osiak, A, Wright, DA, Anthony, RM, Eichtinger, M, Jiang, T, Foley, JE Winfrey, RJ, Townsend, JA, Unger-Wallace, E, Sander, JD, Muller-Lerch, F, Fu, F, Pearlberg, J, Gobel, C, Dassie, JP, Pruett-Miller, SM, Porteus, MH. Sgroi, DC, Lafrate, AJ, Dobbs, D, McCray, PB, Cathomen, T, Voytas, DF, Joung, JK. , Molecular Cell Biology Journal" Molecular Pathology Unit & Center for Cancer Research, Massachusetts General Hospital, Charlestown, MA, July 2008.

43. "My 3 Cents on Cancer" by Jack Andraka," TEDx video on YouTube, 2013.

44. "Children Who Remember Previous Lives: A Question of Reincarnation," by Dr. Ian Stevenson, McFarland Revised edition, 2000.

45. "Return to Life: Extraordinary Cases of Children Who Remember Past Lives," by Jim B. Tucker, St. Martin's Press, 2013.

46. "The Human Genome Project Archive," http://web.ornl.gov/sci/techresources/Human_Genome/index.shtml.

47. "The Creation of Scientific Effects - Heinrich Hertz and Electric Waves," by Jed Z. Buchwald, University of Chicago Press, 1994.

48. "Current Status of Antisense DNA Methods in Behavioral Studies," by Sonoko Ogawa and Donald W. Pfaff, Laboratory of Neurobiology & Behavior, Rockefeller University, New York, 1998.

49. "Herpes Simplex Virus," by H.R. Godfrey, N.J. Godfrey, J.C. Godfrey, and D. Riley, by resources derived from the University of Maryland Medical Center, 2001.

50. "How Radio Signals Work," by James Sinclair, McGraw Hill, 1998.

51. "Tesla Man Out Of Time," by Margaret Cheney, Dorset Press, 1989.

52. "The Psychology of Déjà Vu," by Dr. Vernon M. Neppe, Witwatersrand University Press. 1983.

53. "Lucid Dreaming - A Gateway to the Inner Self," by Robert Waggoner, Moment Point Press, 2009.

54. "Children's Past Lives," by Carol Bowman, Bantam Publishing, 1998.

55. "A Dynamical Theory of the Electromagnetic Field," by Maxwell, James Clerk, Philosophical Transactions of the Royal Society of London, of Maxwell's presentation to the Royal Society, 8 December, 1864.

56. "Zero Power and Selflessness: What Meditation and Conscious Perception Have in Common," by Sean O'Nuallain, Sean, Journal of Cognitive Sciences, May 2009.

57. "Lucid Dreaming: A State of Consciousness with Features of Both Waking and non-Lucid Dreaming," by Ursula Voss, Romain Holzmann, Inka Tuin, and J Allan. Hobson, US National Library of Medicine National Institutes of Health, 2009.

58. "Ultimate Computing," by Dr. Stuart Hameroff, Elsevier, 1987.

59. "The Emperor's New Mind," by Roger Pemrose, Oxford University Press, 1989.

60. "The Scientific Study of Dreams: Neural Networks, Cognitive Development, and Content Analysis," by William G. Domhoff, American Psychological Association (APA), 2003.

61. "Islands of Genius: The Bountiful Mind of the Autistic, Acquired, and Sudden Savant," by Darold A. Treffert, Jessica Kingsley Publishing, 2011.

62. "Biocentrism: How Life and Consciousness Are the Keys to Understanding the Nature of the Universe," by Robert Lanza and Bob Berman, Ben Bella Books, 2010.

63. "Surge of Neurophysiological Coherence and Connectivity in the Dying Brain," J. Borjigin, U.C. Lee, T. Liu,D. Pal, S. Huff, D. Klarr, J. Sloboda, J. Hernandez, N.M. Wang, and G.A. Mashour, Proceedings of the National Academy of Sciences, 2013.

64. "Joan of Arc: In Her Own Words," translated by Willard Trask, Turtle Point Press, 2004.

65. "The Complexity of Greatness - Beyond Talent or Practice," by Scott B. Kaufman, Oxford University Press, 2013.

66. "The Cambridge Handbook of Intelligence," by Scott B. Kaufman & Robert Sternberg, Cambridge University Press, 2011.

67. "Relating Schizotypy and Personality to the Phenomenology of Creativity." by Barnaby Nelson & David Rawlings, Schizophrenia Bulletin, August, 2008.

68. "The Ultimate Time Machine: A Remote Viewer's Perception of Time and Predictions for the New Millennium," by Joseph McMoneagle, Hampton Roads Publishing, 1998.

69. Springer Science, 2013.

70. "Bizarre Beliefs," by Simon Hoggart and Mike Hutchinson, Richard Cohen Books, 1995.

71. "Remote Viewers: The Secret History of America's Psychic Spies," by Jim Schnabel, Dell Publishing, 1997.

72. "The Ultimate Time Machine: A Remote Viewer's Perception of Time and Predictions for the New Millennium," by Joseph McMoneagle, Hampton Roads Publishing, 1998.

73. "The Seventh Sense: The Secrets of Remote Viewing as Told by a 'Psychic Spy' for the U.S. Military," by Lyn Buchanan, araview Pocket Books, 2003.

74. "The Noetic Universe," by Dr. Dean Radin, Trans-World Digital Publishing (Kindle), 2011."Eighth Grade Examination for Bullitt County Schools," http://www.bullittcountyhistory.com/bchistory/schoolexam1912.html, original source unknown, 1912.

75. "Straight Talk About Mental Tests", by Dr. Arthur Jensen, The Free Press (Macmillan Publishing) New York, 1981.

76. "The Intelligence Men: Makers of the IQ Controversy" by Raymond E. Fancher, Norton & Company, NY, 1985.

77. "National IQ Scores by Country Rankings," by Richard Lynn, Tatu Hanhanen, and Jelte Wicherts, Photius, 2012.

78. "Behavioural Genetic Studies of Intelligence," by Thomas J. Bouchard, Jr. and Matthew Mcgue, Psychology Department, University of Minnesota, published by Science Journal, 1981

79. "Occam's Razor: The Skeptic's Dictionary," by Robert T. Carroll, 2012

80. "Straight Talk About Mental Tests", by Dr. Arthur Jensen, The Free Press (Macmillan Publishing) New York, 1981.
81. "The Intelligence Men: Makers of the IQ Controversy" by Raymond E. Fancher, Norton & Company, NY, 1985.
82. "National IQ Scores by Country Rankings," by Richard Lynn, Tatu Hanhanen, and Jelte Wicherts, Photius, 2012.
83. "Behavioural Genetic Studies of Intelligence," by Thomas J. Bouchard, Jr. and Matthew Mcgue, Psychology Department, University of Minnesota, published by Science Journal, 1981
84. "Occam's Razor: The Skeptic's Dictionary," by Robert T. Carroll, 2012.
85. "10 Resons Being Intelligent is Difficult," an article by Kovie Biakolo, November 2013.
86. "Sample Mensa Workout," https://www.mensa.org/workout.
87. Section on Delphi and the Pythian Oracle" from the book of Herodotus by Macaulay, G. C.

APPENDIX "A" - QUESTIONS

Eighth Grade Examination for Bullitt County Schools, November 1912
(NOTE: this document is included herein as provided by its source.)

Spelling (Given by Teacher)

Exaggerate, incentive, conscious, pennyweight, chandelier, patient, potential, creature, participate, authentic, bequeath, diminish, genuine, vinegar, incident, monotony, hyphen, antecedent, autumn, hideous, relieve, conceive, control symptom, rhinoceros, adjective, partial, musician, architect, exhaust, diagram, endeavor, scissors, associate, saucepan, benefit, masculine, synopsis, circulate, eccentric.

Reading & Writing (Given By Teacher)

Reading and writing.

Arithmetic

1. Write in words the following: .5764; .000003; .123416; 653.0965; 43.37.
2. Solve: 35-7 plus 4, 5-8 plus 5-14 —59.112
3. Find cost at 12 ½ cents per sq. yd. of kalsomining the walls of a room 20 ft. long, 16 ft. wide and 9 ft. high, deducting 1 door 8 ft. by 4 ft. 6 in. and 2 windows 5 ft. by 3 ft. 6 in. each.
4. A man bought a farm for $2400 and sold it for $2700. What percent did he gain?
5. A man sold a watch for $180. And lost 16 2/3 a/c. What was the cost of the watch?
6. Find the amount of $5030 for 3 yrs. 3 mo. and 3 days, at 8 percent.
7. A school enrolled 120 pupils and the number of boys was two thirds of the number of girls. How many of boys and how many girls have enrolled for school.
8. How long a rope is required to reach from the top of a building 40 ft. high, to the ground 30 ft. from the base of the building?
9. How many steps 2 ft. 4 in. each will a man take in walking 2 ¼ miles?
10. At $1.62 ½ a chord what would be the cost of a pile of wood 24 ft. long, 4 ft. wide, and 6 ft. 3 in. high?

Grammar

1. How many parts of speech are there? Define each.
2. Define proper noun; common noun. Name the properties of a noun.
3. What is a personal pronoun? Decline I.
4. Whap properties have verbs?
5. "William struck James." Change the voice of the verb.
6. Adjectives have how many Degrees of Comparison…compare good, wise, beautiful?
7. Diagram: "The Lord loveth a cheerful giver."
8. Parse all the words in the following sentences: "John ran over the bridge" and "Helen's parents lover her."

Geography

1. Define longitude and latitude.
2. Name and give boundaries of the five zones.
3. Tell what you know of the Gulf Stream.
4. Locate Erie Canal; what waters does it connect, and why is it important?
5. Locate the following countries, and which border each other: Turkey, Greece, Servia, Montenegro, and Romania.
6. Name and give the capitals of States touching the Ohio River.

7. Locate these cities: Mobile, Quebec, Buenos Aires, Liverpool, and Honolulu.
8. Name in the order of their size the three largest States in the United States.
9. Locate the following mountains; Blue Ridge, Himalaya, Alps, and Wasatch.
10. Through what waters would a vessel pass in going from England through the Suez Canal to Manila?

Physiology

1. How does the liver compare in size with other glands in the human body? Where is it located? What does it secrete?
2. Name the organs of circulation.
3. Describe the heart.
4. Compare arteries and veins as to function. Where is the blood carried to be purified?
5. Where is the chief nervous center of the body?
6. Define cerebrum; cerebellum.
7. What are the functions (or uses) of the spinal column?
8. Why should we study physiology?
9. Give at least five rules to be observed in maintaining good health?

Civil Government

1. Define the following forms of government; Democracy, Limited Monarchy, Absolute Monarchy, and Republic. Give examples of each.
2. To what four governments are students in school subjected?
3. Name five county officers, and the principal duties of each.
4. Name and define the three branches of the government of the United States.
5. Give three duties of the President. What is meant by the veto power?
6. Name three rights given to Congress by the Constitution and two rights denied Congress.
7. In the election of a President and Vice-President, how many electoral votes in each State?
8. Give the eligibility of President, Vice-President and Governor of Kentucky.
9. What is copyright? Patent right?
10. Describe the manner in which the President and Vice-President of the United States are elected.

History

1. Who first discovered the following places: Florida, Pacific Ocean, Mississippi River, St. Lawrence River?
2. Sketch briefly Sir Walter Raleigh, Peter Stuyvesant.
3. By who were the following settled: Ga. Md. Mass. R.I., Fla.?

4. During what wars were the following battles fought: Brandywine, Great Meadows, Lundy's Lane, Antietam, and Buena Vista?
5. Describe the Battle of Quebec.
6. Give the cause of the War of 1812 and name an important battle fought during that war.
7. Name 2 presidents who have died in office: three who were assassinated?
8. Name the last battle of the Civil War; French and Indian War, and the commanders of each battle.
9. What president was impeached, and on what charge?
10. Who invented the following: Magnetic, Telegraph, Cotton Gin, Sewing Machine, Telephone, and the Phonograph?

APPENDIX "B" - ANSWERS

Eighth Grade Examination for Bullitt County Schools, November 1912
(NOTE: this document is included herein as provided by its source.)

The museum staff has put together the following answer sheet for the 1912 examination displayed of Appendix B. As noted on that page, the test focused on some things that were more relevant at that time than now, and it should not be used to compare student knowledge then and now.

Spelling, Reading, and Writing

It is unknown what was required for reading and writing.

Arithmetic

Question #1: Write in words the following:

.5764 = five thousand seven hundred sixty-four ten-thousandths; .000003 = three millionths;

.123416 = one hundred twenty-three thousand four hundred (and) sixteen millionths;

653.0965 = six hundred fifty-three and nine hundred sixty-five ten-thousandths;

43.37 = forty-three and thirty-seven one-hundredths.

Question #2: Solve: 35.7 plus 4, 5.8 plus 5.14 - 59.112.

35.7 + 4 = 39.7
5.8 + 5.14 - 59.112 = -48.172

Question #3: Find cost at 12½ cents per sq. yd. of kalsomining the walls of a room 20 ft. long, 16 ft. wide and 9 ft. high, deducting 1 door 8 ft. by 4 ft 6 in. and 2 windows 5 ft. by 3 ft. 6 in. each.

The two long walls are 20' by 9' or 180 square feet each. The other two walls are 16' by 9' or 144 square feet each. The door space to be deducted is 8' by 4.5' or 36 square feet. The two window spaces to be deducted are 5' by 3.5' or 17.5 square feet each. Thus we have (180 × 2) + (144 × 2) - 36 - (17.5 × 2) which reduces to 360 + 288 - 36 - 35 or 648 - 71 = 577 square feet. Since a square yard = 9 square feet, we divide 577 by 9 and get 64.1 square yards. At 12.5 cents per square yard, the cost will be $8.01, rounded to the nearest cent.

By the way, "kalsomining" is whitewash, a calcium-based cheaper paint. A quote: "Too rich for whitewash, too poor for paint."

Question #4: A man bought a farm for $2400 and sold it for $2700. What percent did he gain?

$2700 - $2400 = $300. Divide the increase by the original amount, or 300 ÷ 2400 = .125 or 12.5%

Question #5: A man sold a watch for $180 and lost 16%. What was the cost of the watch?

Assuming that "a/c" means percent, the solution is to divide the sale price of $180 by .833 [100% - 16.67% = 83.3% or .833]. Thus 180 ÷ .833 = 216.086 or $216.09 rounded to the nearest cent.

Alternately, if the student recognized that 16 %, then $180 is (?) of the original price; thus the original price was $180 divided by (?), which is exactly $216.00. No rounding is necessary.

Question #6: Find the amount of $50.30 for 3 yrs., 3 mo. and 3 days, at 8 percent.

Assuming that the question is asking for a total of the principal plus interest earned over the stated time, the answer will be $63.41 using principal × rate × time.) 3 years; 3 months, 3 days would equal 3.258 years. $50.30 × .08 × 3.258 = $13.11 interest.

Question #7: A school enrolled 120 pupils and the number of boys was two thirds of the number of girls. How many of each sex were enrolled?

Since the number of boys equals (?) to the number of girls, or B = (?)G [or .67G], we can write the equation as 1.67G = 120. Divide both sides of the equation by 1.67 and the equation becomes G = 120 ÷ 1.67 which equals 71.856 which rounds to the whole number of 72. Since the number of girls is 72, 120 - 72 = 48 boys.

Alternately, using just fractions, B = (?) G and B + G = 120, we get (5/3) G = 120. Staying in fractions, we can multiple both sides of the equation by 3, giving 5G = 360, or G = 72, from which we can determine that B = 48. Rounding to whole numbers thus becomes unnecessary.

Question #8: How long a rope is required to reach from the top of a building 40 ft. high, to the ground 30 ft. from the base of the building?

The answer is 50 feet. Use the Pythagorean Theorem (a2 + b2 = c2). Also, we have been reminded by Craig Siefkas of the rule for right triangles called the 3-4-5 rule. He said, *"If you have a right triangle with one side being 3 units long, one side 4 units long, then the third and longest side will be 5 units long. In this case the unit is 10 feet. The reason this is such an important rule to many is that when you are building a barn, shed, or house, you must 'square' the building. Typically a farmer or carpenter's longest tape will be 50 feet long, so you run one wall out 30 feet, the second wall out 40 feet, and the building will be square when the distance between them is 50 feet. Of course, if you wish you can use 'units' of 5 feet, or 15 feet × 20 feet × 25 feet; or units of 3 feet giving you 9 feet × 12 feet × 15 feet; or any other length 'unit' you desire. Many a building has been squared up using this rule, with no knowledge of the Pythagorean Theorem."*

Question #9: How many steps 2 ft. 4 in. each will a man take in walking 2¼ miles?

Assuming the question is saying 2¼ miles, 5280 feet (in a mile) times 2¼ miles = 11,880 feet. Divide that by the size of step (2? feet) = 5,092 steps.

Question #10: At \$1.62½ a cord, what will be the cost of a pile of wood 24 ft. long, 4 ft. wide and 6 ft. 3 in. high?

\$7.62 — It's a simple volume problem where one cord at $4 \times 4 \times 8$ feet = 128 cubic feet; $24 \times 4 \times 6¼$ = 600 cubic feet. Divide cord volume into measured volume; times \$1.62½.

Grammar

Question #1: How many parts of speech are there? Define each.

Traditionally (and almost certainly in 1912) there were eight grammatical parts of speech identified this way (taken from Wikipedia).

Noun: any abstract or concrete entity; a person (police officer, Michael), place (coastline, London), thing (necktie, television), idea (happiness), or quality (bravery)

- **Pronoun:** any substitute for a noun or noun phrase
- **Adjective**: any qualifier of a noun
- **Verb:** any action (walk), occurrence (happen), or state of being (be)
- **Adverb**: any qualifier of an adjective, verb, clause, sentence, or other adverb
- **Preposition:** any establisher of relation and syntactic context
- **Conjunction:** any syntactic connector
- ***Interjection:*** *any emotional greeting (or "exclamation")*

Other more recent sources separate the articles (a, an, the) as a part of speech, and drop the interjection.

"Most grammarians recognize eight parts of speech in classifying all the words in the language which are used in connected discourse. Some grammarians exclude the interjection from the list of parts of speech; others separate the articles (the, a, an) from the adjective division; and others classify the expletive as a full part of speech. ... School grammars generally recognize the traditional eight parts of speech."

Taken from page 16 "Descriptive English Grammar" by Homer C. House and Susan Emolyn Harmon, Second Edition; Prentice-Hall, Inc., Englewood Cliffs, N.J., 1950.

Question #2: Define proper noun; common noun. Name the properties of a noun.

A proper noun is the name of a specific person, place, or thing (such as "Tuesday").

A common noun refers to a person, place, or thing in a general sense (The "town" is not far away.)

The properties of a noun include...

    1. Gender (masculine or feminine)

    2. Number (singular, plural)

    3. Person (first, second, or third)

    4. Case (subject, object, or construct-possessive)

Question #3: What is a Personal Pronoun? Decline I.

A personal pronoun is a pronoun that refers to a particular person, group, or thing.

The following chart is copied directly from Wikipedia – The basic personal pronouns of modern English are shown in the table below. (For the distinction between the forms, see the previous section, and Case usage below.)

Personal pronouns in standard Modern English

	Singular					Plural				
	Subject	Object	Possessive determiner	Possessive pronoun	Reflexive	Subject	Object	Possessive determiner	Possessive pronoun	Reflexive
First	I	me	my	mine	myself	we	us	our	ours	ourselves

Second		you		your	yours	yourself		you		your	yours	yourselves
Third	**Masculine**	he	him		his		himself						
	Feminine	she		her	hers	herself		they	them	their	theirs	themselves
	Neuter	it			its		itself						
	Non-specific	they	them	their	theirs	themselves						

"English personal pronouns have three inflections related to the purpose they serve in a sentence or phrase: nominative, accusative (objective), and possessive. For the first person singular, these are I, me, and mine, respectively." For more details, see this site.

Question #4: What properties have verbs?

The properties of verbs are person, number, tense, voice, and mood.

Question #5: "William struck James." Change the Voice of the verb.

"William struck James." is in active voice. Passive voice would be "James was struck by William."

Question #6: Adjectives have how many Degrees of Comparison? Compare good; wise, beautiful.

Adjectives have three degrees of comparison.

positive	comparative	superlative

good	better	best
wise	wiser	wisest
beautiful	more beautiful	most beautiful

Question #7: Diagram: The Lord loveth a cheerful giver.

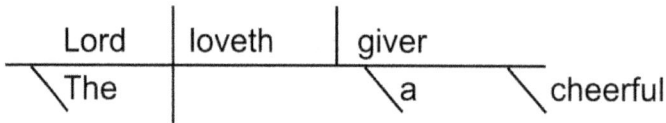

Question #8: Parse all the words in the following sentences:

"John ran over the bridge."

'John' is a proper noun used as the subject of the sentence.

'Ran' is an intransitive verb and forms the simple predicate of the sentence.

'Over the bridge' is a prepositional phrase that modifies the verb and answers the question "Where did John run?"

'Over' is the preposition; *'bridge'* is the object of the preposition, and *'the'* is an article adjective indicating which bridge.

"Helen's parents love her."

'Parents' is a common noun used as the subject of the sentence.

'Helen's' is a possessive noun used to identify the parents.

'Love' is a transitive verb and forms the simple predicate of the sentence.

'Her' is an objective pronoun used as the direct object of the verb's action.

Geography

Question #1: Define longitude and latitude.

Longitude and latitude are the imaginary lines that divide the Earth into measurable horizontal and vertical lines. Latitude lines are measured from the equator to the poles. Longitude lines extend from the north to south poles and are measured east and west from the prime meridian to the International Date Line.

Question #2: Name and give the boundaries of the five zones.

1. 'North Frigid Zone' is north of the Arctic Circle.
2. 'North Temperate Zone' is between the Arctic Circle and the Tropic of Cancer.
3. 'Torrid Zone' is between the Tropical Circles.
4. 'South Temperate Zone' is between the Tropic of Capricorn and the Antarctic Circle.
5. 'South Frigid Zone' is south of the Antarctic Circle.

Question #3: Tell what you know of the Gulf Stream.

The Gulf Stream is a warm ocean current that flows from the Gulf of Mexico parallel with the US coast toward Newfoundland, Canada, and then continues across the Atlantic Ocean toward northwestern Europe as the North Atlantic Drift.

Question #4: Locate Erie Canal; what waters does it connect, and why is it important?

The Erie Canal is a waterway in New York that runs about 363 miles from Albany, New York, on the Hudson River to Buffalo, New York, at Lake Erie, completing a navigable water route from the Atlantic Ocean to the Great Lakes. It was the first transportation system between the eastern seaboard (New York City) and the western interior (Great Lakes, Chicago) of the United States that did not require portage.

Question #5: Locate the following countries, which border each other:

Turkey [Ottoman Empire], Greece, Servia [Serbia today], Montenegro, Roumania [early spelling of Romania]. These are all in south-central Europe. See the map to the right.

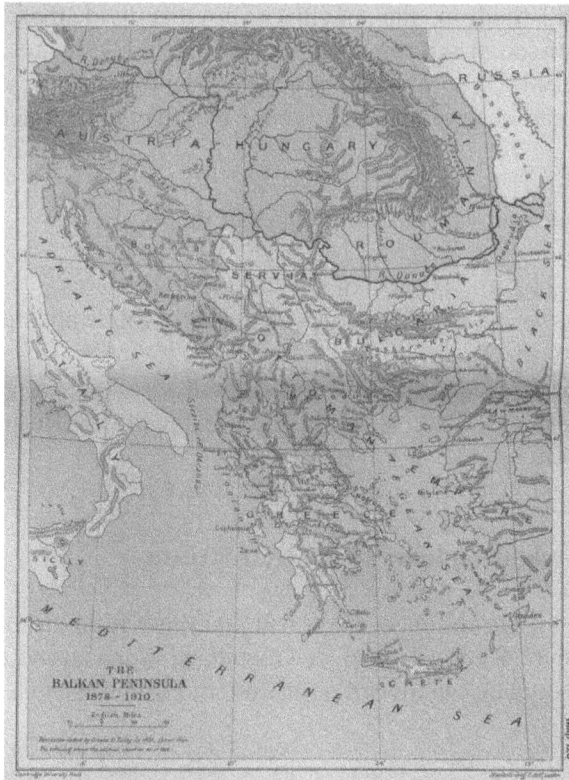

Map courtesy of the University of Texas Libraries, The University of Texas at Austin.

Question #6: Name and give the capitals of States touching the Ohio River.

Kentucky – Frankfort, Ohio – Columbus, Indiana – Indianapolis, West Virginia – Charleston, Pennsylvania – Harrisburg, Illinois – Springfield.

Question #7: Locate these cities: Mobile, Quebec, Buenos Aires, Liverpool, and Honolulu.

Mobile – Alabama, Quebec – Canada, Buenos Aires – Argentina, Liverpool – England, Honolulu – Hawaii.

Question #8: Name in order by size the three largest States in the United States.

Texas, California, Montana (Remember this is 1912, and at the time of the test; Alaska was not yet a state).

Question #9: Locate the following mountains: Blue Ridge, Himalaya, Andes, Alps, Wasatch.

Blue Ridge – eastern U.S. from Georgia to Pennsylvania; Himalaya – Asia, separating the plains of the Indian subcontinent from the Tibetan Plateau; Andes – western South America extending from north to south through Venezuela, Colombia, Ecuador, Peru, Bolivia, Chile and Argentina; Alps – alpine countries in central Europe; Wasatch – Utah.

Question #10: Through what waters would a vessel pass in going from England through the Suez Canal to Manila?

A ship going from England to Manilla by way of the Suez Canal would pass through (perhaps) the English Channel, the North Atlantic Ocean, Bay of Biscay (possibly), Strait of Gibraltar, Mediterranean Sea, Suez Canal, Red Sea, Gulf of Aden/Arabian Sea, Indian Ocean, Gulf of Thailand (may have been called Gulf of Siam at that time), South China Sea.

Physiology

Question #1: How does the liver compare in size with other glands in the human body? Where is it located? What does it secrete?

The liver is the largest gland in the body. It lies below the diaphragm in the abdominal-pelvic region of the abdomen. It secretes bile.

Question #2: Name the organs of circulation.

The likely intent of this question was to determine the elements of the human cardiovascular system, which include the heart, lungs, and blood vessels.

Question #3: Describe the heart.

The heart is the vital organ of the body that pumps the blood. It is about the size of a fist. The four sections of the human heart are the left atrium, right atrium, left ventricle, and right ventricle.

Question #4: Compare arteries and veins as to function. Where does the blood carried to be purified?

Arteries distribute oxygenated blood throughout the body, while veins carry de-oxygenated blood to the heart. The liver and kidneys purify the blood. Note: H.L. King of Lexington KY points out that *"arteries channel blood away from the heart; veins channel it toward the heart. The key is to note that the pulmonary artery channels oxygen-depleted blood from the right ventricle to the lungs. It then returns, oxygenated, to the left atrium via the pulmonary veins."*

Question #5: Where is the chief nervous center of the body?

The body's chief nervous center includes first the brain and then the spinal cord.

Question #6: Define Cerebrum; Cerebellum.

The Cerebellum is located just above the brain stem and controls balance, equilibrium and fine movement coordination. The Cerebrum is located in the front portion of the forebrain, and determines intelligence, personality, interpretation of sensory impulses and motor function. It also helps with planning and organization as well as touch sensation.

Question #7: What are the functions (or uses) of the spinal column?

The spinal column supports the body and provides protection for the spinal cord.

Question #8: Why should we study Physiology?

We should study physiology so that we may better understand our body as well as how to take care of it better, as well as understand the functioning of other creatures. A good understanding of physiology (how the body works) is the basis of all medicine. Without knowing how the body works, or its make-up and how it can go wrong, we cannot even begin to design effective treatments and interventions, including surgery or new pharmaceutical drugs.

Question #9: Give at least five rules to be observed in maintaining good health.

Eat right, exercise, get proper sleep, drink plenty of water, and maintain proper hygiene (of course, there are some other possible answers).

Civil Government

Question #1: Define the following forms of government: Democracy, Limit Monarchy, Absolute Monarchy, and Republic. Give examples of each.

While a 'pure' democracy includes all of its population making all of decisions as a group, as a practical matter this will not work except in quite small groups. Most countries that claim to be democracies normally have a representative form of government, as does our own nation, which is better defined as a republic. A modern definition of democracy, taken from the *'Democracy Building'* web site is a "form of government, where a constitution guarantees basic personal and political rights, fair and free elections, and independent courts of law." It is quite likely that the expected example in 1912 was the United States itself.

(Understand that some people may object to the selection choice being that of the United States would be the most likely answer for this question, as it is instead a republic. However, since there did not exist a single nation in 1912 that could be considered a pure democracy, and therefore the best assumption.)

> **Limited or constitutional monarchy** is a form of government in which a monarch acts as head of state within the guidelines of a constitution. *(Great Britain is the best answer for this question in1912.)*

> **In an absolute monarchy,** the monarch wields unrestricted political power over the sovereign state and its people. Until 1905 the Tsars of Russia governed as absolute monarchs. Another possible example might have been Kaiser Wilhelm II of Germany and Prussia.

> **A republic** is a government where the head of state is not a monarch, and leadership positions are; elected directly or appointed, but never inherited. *('The French Republic' would have been the best answer to this 1912 question.)*

Question #2: Which four governments are students in school subjected?

As citizens of the United States, the Commonwealth of Kentucky, the county of Bullitt, and the local school system, these students would be subject to the jurisdiction of the local school board, and the county, state, and federal governments.

Question #3: Name five county officers and list what the principal duties of each.

The students may have been required to identify the current officers by name, but we will assume they were to identify them by office.

- The county judge in 1912 served both as an executive head of county government and as a judicial judge. He was also a member of the county fiscal court, the legislative body of the county.
- Magistrates served as members of the fiscal court, and also have minor judicial duties.

- The sheriff and his deputies were responsible for enforcing the law within the county.
- The county court clerk had multiple duties including serving as the county court's clerk and clerk of the fiscal court. He was also responsible for maintaining county records including deeds, marriage records, and wills.
- The county jailer was responsible for overseeing the incarceration of prisoners.

Question #4: Name and define the three branches of the government of the United States.

The federal government is composed of three distinct branches: *legislative, executive* and *judicial.* The legislative branch includes the Congress (Senate & House of Representatives), which is responsible for the passage of all federal laws as outlined by the Constitution. The executive branch includes the president and vice president along with the various executive cabinets. The president is the head of state and commander in chief of the armed forces. He has the responsibility of negotiating treaties, and appointing cabinet members with the concurrence of the Senate. The judicial branch is responsible for interpretation of laws, and in determining the outcome of civil and criminal cases; headed by the Supreme Court.

Question # 5: Give three duties of the President. What does having the power to veto mean?

The president is constitutionally obligated to *"take care that the laws be faithfully executed."* He appoints ambassadors, member of his Cabinet, and federal judges with the advice and consent of the Senate. He directs foreign policy and is commander in chief of the armed forces. He has the power of the veto and all bills passed by Congress and presented to the office of the president for his/her signature. He may sign the bill, allowing it to become law; he may veto it and return it to Congress with his objections; or he may take no action. If he vetoes the bill, Congress may override his veto by voting two-thirds majority approval. If he takes no action for ten working days, and Congress is still in session, then the bill becomes law without his signature. However if Congress has adjourned, the bill does not become law. This right called a 'pocket veto.'

Question #6: Name three rights given Congress by the Constitution and two rights denied Congress.

Only Congress can declare war. Only Congress can impeach (House), try (Senate), and remove office holders, including the President and Supreme Court Justices from office. Only Congress can raise and lower taxes.

Congress cannot pass a law that turns an act into a crime, after the act was committed, nor accept a title of nobility, suspend a writ of habeas corpus (except under special circumstances), or pass a Bill of Attainder (which means they can't punish anyone or group without a trial), tax any goods exported from any state, and Congress cannot vote themselves a pay raise during their current term in office.

(Note: This answer may not be quite correct, as Constitutional amendments kept changing Congresses power over the years.)

Question #7: In the election of a president and vice-president, and how many electoral votes is each State allowed?

Each state receives a number of presidential electors in the Electoral College equal to the number of congressional districts in that state (which varies by state population, but is never less than one) plus the number of senators, which is always equal to two. At the time of this test, Kentucky had 13 electoral votes out of 531 electoral votes nationwide. Today Kentucky has 8 electoral votes out of 538 nationwide.

Question #8: Give the eligibility of president, vice president, and Governor of Kentucky.

The president and vice-president of the United States must be a natural born citizen of the United States, be at least thirty-five years old, and have been a permanent resident in the United States for at least fourteen years. The governor of Kentucky must be at least thirty years of age and have resided in the state for at least six years preceding the general election; and never fought a duel.

Question #9: What is a copyright? What is a Patent right?

Copyright is a legal concept, enacted by most governments, giving the creator of an original work exclusive right to it, usually for a limited time. A patent is a form of intellectual property. It consists of a set of exclusive rights granted by a sovereign state to an inventor or their assignee for a limited period, in exchange for the public disclosure of the invention.

Question #10: Describe the manner in which the president and vice-president of

the United States are elected.

The president and vice-president are selected by a group of electors known as the Electoral College. Each state is granted a number of electors equal to the number of its members of the United States Congress (Senate and House of Representatives). To be elected, the president and vice-president, running as a team, must receive a majority of the electoral votes. If no one receives a majority, then the members of the House of Representatives select the president. Each state receives one vote, with its representatives voting as a bloc.

Although there is no legal requirement to do so, a state's electors almost always cast their ballots according to how the state's citizens voted in the general election.

History

Question #1: Who first discovered the following places: Florida, Pacific Ocean, Mississippi River, and Saint Lawrence River?

Juan Ponce de León made the first European expedition to Florida, which he named. Vasco Núñez de Balboa is best known for having crossed the Isthmus of Panama to the Pacific Ocean. Spanish explorer Hernando de Soto became the first recorded European to reach the Mississippi River. Jacques Cartier was the first European to describe and map the Gulf of Saint Lawrence and the shores of the Saint Lawrence River.

(These were likely the expected answers on the 1912 test. Although Native Americans were present in these places before the arrival of the Europeans, the names of their people who first visited these sites are lost in the mists of time.)

Question #2: Sketch briefly Sir Walter Raleigh, Peter Stuyvesant.

Sir Walter Raleigh was an English aristocrat, writer, poet, soldier, courtier, spy, and explorer. He is well known for popularizing tobacco in England. In 1594, Raleigh heard of a "City of Gold" in South America and sailed to find it without success. For various reasons, he was executed in 1618.

Peter Stuyvesant served as the last Dutch Director-General of the colony of New Netherland from 1647 until it was ceded to the English in 1664, after which it was renamed New York. He was a major figure in the early history of New York City.

Question #3: By whom were the following settled: Georgia, Maryland, Massachusetts, Rhode Island, Florida?

In November 1732, the ship Anne sailed from Britain carrying 114 colonists, including General James Oglethorpe, who settled at what became Savannah, Georgia.

Maryland, was first settled by a very large group of Roman Catholic families led by the Calvert family as a place where they could freely practice their faith.

The first English settlers in Massachusetts, the Pilgrims, established their settlement at Plymouth in 1620.

In 1636, Roger Williams, after having been banished from the Massachusetts Bay Colony for his religious views settled at the tip of Narragansett Bay, on land that would become Rhode Island. A number of non-Puritan colonists as well as those that believed in religious freedom joined him.

Florida has had a long history of immigration, including French and Spanish settlement during the 16th century, as well as entry of new Native American groups migrating from elsewhere in the South. Florida was under colonial rule by Spain and Great Britain during the 18th and 19th centuries before becoming a territory in 1822 of the United States.

Question #4: During what wars were the following battles fought: Brandywine, Great Meadows, Lundy's Lane, Antietam, and Buena Vista?

The Battle of Brandywine, fought between the American army of Major General George Washington and the British army of General Sir William Howe on September 11, 1777, was during the Revolutionary War.

The Battle of Fort Necessity or the Battle of the Great Meadows took place on July 3, 1754 in Pennsylvania. The engagement was one of the first battles of the French and Indian War and George Washington's only military surrender.

The Battle of Lundy's Lane (also known as the Battle of Niagara Falls) was a battle of the War of 1812, which took place on 25 July 1814, in present-day Niagara Falls, Ontario.

The Battle of Antietam, also known as the Battle of Sharpsburg, was fought on Wednesday, September 17, 1862, near Sharpsburg, Maryland, and Antietam Creek, and was the first major battle in the American Civil War to take place on Union soil.

The Battle of Buena Vista, on February 23, 1847, saw the United States Army use artillery to repulse the much larger Mexican army in the Mexican-American War.

Question #5: Describe the battle of Quebec.

The Battle of Quebec, fought between American Continental Army forces and the British defenders of the city of Quebec occurred on December 31, 1775, early in the American Revolutionary War. The battle was the first major defeat of the war for the Americans, and it came at a high price. General Richard Montgomery, killed in action; Benedict Arnold, wounded, and Daniel Morgan along with more than 400 men were taken prisoners.

Question #6: Give the cause of the War of 1812, and name an important battle fought during that war.

The War of 1812 was a military conflict fought between the forces of the United States of America and those of the British Empire. The Americans declared war in 1812 for several reasons, including trade restrictions due to Britain's ongoing war with France, and the impressment of American merchant sailors into the Royal Navy. The Battle of Baltimore was the major battle by which Francis Scott Key penned the words to the National Anthem.

Question #7: Name 2 presidents who have died in office; three who were assassinated.

There were three assassinated Presidents (at the time of this 1912 test), they were Lincoln, McKinley, & Garfield. Presidents who died in office (but not assassinated) were William Henry Harrison, and Zachary Taylor.

Question #8: Name the last battle of the Civil War; War of 1812; French and Indian War, and the commanders in each battle.

Civil War: Battle of Columbus, Georgia on 16 Apr 1865; commanders were Union General James H. Wilson and Confederate Major General Howell Cobb. [See http://en.wikipedia.org/wiki/Battle_of_Columbus_(1865)] We are aware that a battle took place in Texas (Battle of Palmito Ranch) on May 12–13, 1865, shortly after the end of the American Civil War; but it occurred after Johnston's surrender to Sherman (April 26, 1865) and after the Confederacy dissolved on May 5.

War of 1812: By date, the last battle was in February 1815 at Fort Bowyer, Alabama in which a British force of at least 3000 attacked a smaller American force of fewer than 400 led by fort commander William Lawrence who surrendered on 11 Feb 1815. However the generally recognized last battle of the war was the Battle of New Orleans with Andrew Jackson leading the Americans and Edward Pakenham among the British.

French and Indian War: Battle of Signal Hill on 15 Sep 1762 with British forces led by William Amherst and French forces led by Guillaume de Bellecombe. [See http://en.wikipedia.org/wiki/Battle_of_Signal_Hill]

Question #9: What president was impeached, and on what charge?

Andrew Johnson (who succeeded Lincoln) for violating the "Tenure of Office Act", when he sought to remove his Secretary of War without Senate approval. Republicans were mad at him for being lenient to the South.

Question #10: Who invented the following: magneto, telegraph, cotton gin, sewing machine, telephone, and phonograph?

Magneto – Faraday; telegraph – Samuel Morse; cotton gin – Eli Whitney; sewing machine – generally, Elias Howe, though disputed; telephone – Alexander Graham Bell; phonograph – Thomas Alva Edison.

Included herein with permission by the:

Bullitt County History Museum
P.O. Box 206
Shepherdsville, Kentucky 40165